SUPER JOY

SUPER JOY

In Love with Living

PAUL PEARSALL, PH.D.

Doubleday

NEW YORK   LONDON   TORONTO   SYDNEY   AUCKLAND

Published by Doubleday, a division of
Bantam Doubleday Dell Publishing Group, Inc.,
666 Fifth Avenue, New York, New York 10103

Doubleday and the portrayal of an anchor with a dolphin
are trademarks of Doubleday, a division of
Bantam Doubleday Dell Publishing Group, Inc.

Library of Congress Cataloging-in-Publication Data
Pearsall, Paul.
Super joy: in love with living / Paul Pearsall. —1st ed.
p.   cm.
Bibliography: p.
Includes index.
1. Joy.   2. Conduct of life.   I. Title.
BF575.H27P43   1988   88-6926
152.4—dc19   CIP
ISBN 0-385-24459-2

BG

For my son Scott, for all the joy he brings me

Acknowledgments

My family wrote this book. My wife Celest, my two sons Roger and Scott, my mother Carol, and my brother Dennis have shared a celebration of living with me that was my inspiration to write about joy. My father Frank—and my memories of his constant happiness and love—has been the guiding light in my search for an understanding of joyful daily living.

My patients taught me the power of the joy response, and how and where to look for paths beyond mere survival and normalcy. Years before the researchers mentioned in the references for this book began to study such concepts as Suzanne Kobasa's "psychological hardiness" and Aaron Antonovsky's "sense of coherence," my patients were trying to tell me about a struggle for exceptional well-being, even at times of severe crisis and challenge in their own lives.

My medical students, residents, and undergraduates at Henry Ford College taught me about the joy and health of learning. My colleagues at Sinai Hospital of Detroit, including Dr. Norman Rosenzweig, Dr. Ronald Trunsky, Dr. John Flatter, and my secretary Ms. Ellen Schlafer, have endured my strange theories about super health and encouraged my testing of my hypotheses about a joy response. Even as we all struggled against the illness and disease troubling our patients, we were learning together that health is much more than the absence of symptoms.

My editor, Loretta Barrett, personally and professionally shared my commitment to writing about the idea of exceptional joy. The President and Publisher of Doubleday, Nancy Evans, has been a major force in allowing me to pursue a major joy in my life, the joy of writing.

My agent and good friend, Susan Cohen, once again helped me remember the joy and real purpose of writing; to attempt to bring joy to others. If this book brings even a little more joy to your life, all of the people who made this book possible will be joyful right along with you. Such is the gift I wish for everyone.

Contents

PART TWO
THE JOY OF WORKING, LOVING, AND BELIEVING

CHAPTER SEVEN
THE JOY OF MEANINGFUL WORK

CHAPTER EIGHT
THE JOY OF SYMPATHETIC LOVING

PART THREE
SIX SPECIAL JOY MESSAGES

SUPER
JOY

CHAPTER ONE

Beyond the Walls of Normalcy

> Certainly it seems more and more clear that what we call "normal" in psychology is really a psychopathology of the average, so undramatic and so widely spread that we don't even notice it.
>
> ABRAHAM MASLOW

From Death Marks to Birth Marks

I will never forget her. As she laughed, her hand went to her forehead to brush her hair from her eyes. Purple numbers were tattooed on her wrist. She called them her death marks but said that they had strangely protected and renewed her life during her suffering. She had been tortured, seen her own parents and almost all of her relatives killed, and had lived in the agony, squalor, and starvation of a prison camp for most of the young years of her life. She had every reason to be weak, bitter, sick, and depressed. Instead, she was one of the most joyful, hardiest women I have ever met.

Why did this woman radiate such a spiritual strength? Why did she not only survive but also flourish when so many others had their strength robbed from them? Why was this woman so extraordinary, so "super normal"? Why did she show such super joy?

1

Why were people with less stress and suffering in their lives less happy and healthy than this woman? How could this woman's joy have survived, or did she survive because of some inner joy? What made her such an extraordinary person? The search for the answers to these questions about the nature and strength of human joy, about the psychological hardiness that seems to guide some people through life, led to my writing this book.

Beyond Happiness

In my seventeen years of clinical work, the existence of a super joy of the human spirit emerged as the central answer to my questions about the thriving and celebration of certain people no matter what life had done to them. This super joy goes far beyond happiness or contentment. It is the regular and enduring celebration of the delight of daily living, the savoring of the moments of life that are all too often missed, eclipsed by our patterned numbness to the thrill of being alive and being human. This super joy is a joy that feeds rather than takes from the human spirit.

I came to call this human characteristic "super joy" because of its persistent, unalterable strength and its capacity to transcend any of life's challenges. It seemed to be an abnormal joy possessed by abnormally hardy people and the people who had it were far more than just normal or mentally healthy.

Addicted to Joy

What we call "normal" living is actually an addicted style of interacting with people and events within the self-imposed confines of an artificially limited range of emotional experience. We can, however, expand our emotional domain and know a daily joy that at first glance would seem impossible or unrealistic, but first we must learn to cure our addiction to the "normal" and take the risk of being "super normal."

We are all addicted to what seems "normal" for us. We are pulled through life like puppets passively responding to chemical configurations established for us from inside our own brains. We are hooked on our own patterns of highs and lows, stress and depression in reaction to daily living, forgetting that we can write our own prescription for a joy that is much more than busyness and a peacefulness far beyond despair.

Super joy is the natural human capacity for intense, volitional human elation brought about by an intentional addiction to health-protecting and -enhancing psychochemicals, a new pattern of living and thinking that takes glee to the fullest from our moment-to-moment experience of being alive. Super joy is a joy beyond the rare emotional response that may result from good luck, hard work that finally pays off, or the mere absence of depression or anxiety. Super joy is the ultimate human experience, the transcendence of normalcy to a high-level well-being, an intense awareness of the human experience typically reported only by junkies getting high on unnatural, deadly chemicals.

This book is intended to help you learn this super joy and replace your addiction to the stress and depression neurochemicals with the psychochemicals of delight. Modern psychology has been the unwitting support system for a stress-depression cycle of addiction in which we are drawn to the intensity of the urgency of living and then crash with the depression neurochemicals that provide a sometimes prolonged escape from our overheated life style.

This book is a guide for new ways to channel the human propensity for addiction. All animals have the capacity for addiction, and humans become physiologically and behaviorally addicted to eating, sex, working, and even doing nothing at all. Addictive behavior is easy because it is automatic and simple, a process whereby we seem to just allow things to "happen to us." Addiction is simply the surrendering of our "selves" to our brains, allowing chemical concoctions to be brewed for us by our brains' automatic interaction with people, events, or substances.

The payoff in brain-chemical highs when we are hooked on stress or depression is much stronger than any artificial drug or opiate, so it is difficult to take control of our brains and cook up a healthy addiction of our own choosing, an addiction to joy. We can use our addiction propensity for our health instead of against it by learning not to accept "normal" as healthy.

The Abnormality and Sickness of Being Normal

What we see around us, the daily behavior of people we interact with every day, is "normal" but not necessarily extraordinarily healthy. Our society considers hard work, intense recreation, vigorous exercise, rushing through the day, excessive eating, frequent anger, occasional deep depression, and sex without love as "normal," and we have become addicted to the brain chemicals that accompany these so-called normal behaviors.

As you read through this book you will learn to recognize your sometimes subtle and covert addiction to the stress and depression psychochemicals, an addiction that our society views as normal. You will learn to use your addictive nature to become addicted to joy, celebration, and rejoicing every day of your life, not just on vacations or when you allow yourself "just a little time for joy." You will learn the secrets of the super joy of the woman with the tattoo on her wrist, a vicious marking that she converted to a stimulus for survival.

Until you read further into this book, it may seem impossible to be joyful most of the time. Many people consider anyone who is too joyful to be "abnormal." This book will help you develop the courage to go beyond the norm of daily living, to celebrate the emperor's gleaming nakedness, to learn a new way of thinking and feeling about daily living.

Super joy is a human reflex, a prewired response system that is in danger of becoming extinct through our own neglect. Like a dormant volcano, super joy can erupt without warning. Just as the profoundly intense processes that result in volcanic eruption are bubbling just under the surface continually, so are natural joy chemicals circulating throughout our system. Sometimes, seemingly without warning, our joy overflows and comes to our rescue, and for a few brief moments we remember and re-experience what joy is really like. All too soon, however, we return to our stress or depression addictions, never really learning how to make joy a more regular part of our life. This book is about super joy in daily living, a super joy that transcends the pseudo-intensity of the stress and depression responses to daily living that have come to substitute for a higher experience of life.

The Brain's Own "Uppers" and "Downers"

My patients are sometimes surprised to learn that they are addicts to their own brain chemicals. They believe that what they do and how they feel are how they must feel and behave. Like the alcoholic who denies the impact of drinking, the stress/depression addict cannot see his or her own addictive pattern.

Even though anxiety and the stress response can kill you, it actually makes you feel temporarily good, aroused, and "high." Hurrying, worrying, fighting, and impatience result in brain-chemical changes that we get used to and come to feel comfortable with. We keep on rushing, even joking that we are "hurrying to an early grave," like the alcoholic who downs yet another drink while bragging that he or she can "handle" liquor. Ultimately, this denial of the real damage being done exacts a terrible price.

Crying, complaining, passivity, and chronic depression all damage our health, but they also "feel good" in the sense that we can get used to depression, suffering in a degree of comfort with the predictability of an emotional state that allows us to escape into a brain-induced "downer." We avoid making the changes that could result in feeling better, accepting the down brain chemicals that offer their unique brand of emotional anesthesia, the other side of our stress addiction. Where there is stress addiction, there is always depression waiting, and when there is depression, stress addiction has been there and threatens the person who considers leaving his or her depressed state. Feeling any other way than sad, and behaving and thinking in any other way than depressed, becomes more and more foreign, perhaps because we know inside us that we may rise from our depression only to fall back into our stress addiction.

Like stress addiction, depression addiction veils continuing damage to the body and weakens the immune system. In effect, we can become as accustomed to being down as we get used to being up. We end up terribly out of balance and eventually out of time unless we rediscover the joy response to daily living, the only effective antidote to the up or down addiction cycle.

Sick Science, Unhappy Normal People, and the New Science of Joyology

Modern psychology and psychiatry are sciences of sickness. I had trouble understanding how the courageous woman in the example above could not only survive but also thrive, because I was trained to look for pathology or the absence of it, for correlations between disease-causing factors and diseased people. I was not trained to look for what made people unusually strong. I had to look beyond normalcy and mental health, beyond the accepted assumptions of daily living, to understand super normalcy.

Psychology and psychiatry offer help to the emotionally ill but offer little in the way of direction for high-level emotional wellness, for how to be super healthy and super happy every day of our life. These two fields have models of sickness but no model for remarkable wellness. In the attempt to help people cope, survive, and function, psychology has failed to provide guidelines for celebration, thriving, and rejoicing, the real reasons for making the effort to cope at all. Psychology and psychiatry have no model of super mental health, only concepts for avoiding the abnormal and staying normal.

Throughout this book you will see examples of principles of a new science I call "joyology." Each tenet has been largely ignored by modern psychiatry and psychology, yet each rule is the basis for effective behavior change that results in learning the joy response. I will review each tenet several times throughout this book, using different examples to illustrate the central points about the super joy experience and joyology thinking.

I propose a new field of psychology, a field of joyology, the study of the extremely healthy, happy, delighted people of the world. I propose another way of looking at the human experience which focuses on the attempt to identify those human characteristics that relate to rapture rather than remorse and attempts to understand why and how some people become extraordinarily happy almost every day of their lives, even if and perhaps because they have experienced severe emotional and physical trauma in their lives.

The case examples in this book are cases from my own practice of joyology. I noticed early in my clinical work that some people who came to me, like the woman I mention here, were extremely mentally and physically healthy. They came for specific help with a transitional life problem, but even though traditional psychology and medicine would predict that these people should be sick, they were flourishing. They were strong enough to know when to seek help and joyful enough to benefit immediately from therapeutic intervention. These are the patients every therapist loves to work with, probably because they give more to us than we give to them. These are our "easy" patients, more than able to help us help them quickly and directly.

All of my patients' stories reported in this book are stories of joy. I have changed some circumstances to protect the confidentiality of these magnificent people. Even though they came to me for help with some problem in adjusting to everyday living, they were unique in that they were almost always joyful, even at times of challenge in their lives. Were there characteristics of these people that we could all learn? How did these people become so super joyful? Why were they so strongly addicted to "super joy"? Why did they seem immune to the stress/depression addiction cycle? What can we learn from these people about the promise of super joy for all of us?

A Joyology Case Example

Psychology and psychiatry typically describe the impact of stress on mental and physical health. A stressor is measured, a person damaged by that stressor is identified, the connection between stress and illness is documented, and principles of coping are gleaned from this examination of the sick for application to the well. The woman from the prison camp who showed the super joy capacity illustrates what happens when we use a different approach to understanding human behavior, when we look for what people do right rather than what they do wrong, when we attempt to account for super wellness instead of sickness.

The woman was over sixty years old, but her birth records were destroyed along with everything that was hers when she was placed in a concentration camp in Poland during World War II. She still shed tears as she described the incomprehensible torture of her experiences in that terrible place. She had lost all but two of her family members at that prison camp, and she herself was tortured. She was within days of being killed when the camp was liberated.

She came to me for help in communicating with her son and daughter-in-law, whom she saw as "moping, dreadfully distracted people too busy to visit a crazy old lady." She wondered what she might do to bring her family closer together and was frightened that her family was beginning to think she had what she called "old-timer's disease." Her family wondered why this woman continued to laugh, sing, cause mischief, tease and play with the children, and otherwise create excitement everywhere she went. She was certainly not acting her age.

Family therapy helped solve her communication problems with her children and their spouses but, more importantly, her family came to see what I saw: a strong, happy, celebrating woman who had every right to hate the world but instead loved everything about living. Her family discovered that they had much to learn from this unusual woman, and that they should be busy learning from her instead of trying to cope with her.

I asked this woman what made her so happy. She answered, "I think the question is wrong, Doctor. I keep wondering why everyone is too busy to be happy and yet seems to have plenty of time to be sad. It's just in me. I love life, and I learned to love it even more when I saw life treated with such disrespect, such disregard, when I was a prisoner. Maybe people just get used to life and living. Well, you don't get used to living when you can be killed any moment. I will never take life for granted. I will never miss a minute of it. My philosophy is 'So what's so important you can't laugh and love?' That's why my family thinks I'm nuts. I want to dance, to love, to smile, to fight and yell. They just don't have time for such silliness. Almost everything to them is a problem, not an opportunity. I just ask myself one question. What's the most important thing in the world right now? I always get the same answer. Life! Here's to life, Doctor. To LIFE!"

The woman lifted a paper cup of water and toasted her living, all living. There was a spark in her, a magic that every doctor, student, and secretary in my office sensed the moment she entered the waiting room. One day she saw me looking at the tattoo on her wrist, a constant reminder of the cruelty she experienced. "Oh, so you are looking at my sign again? It's a sign to remind me to live and to love. To me, it could be a heart instead of a number." We were both suddenly silent, and she reached out and patted my wrist. "We all have a sign. We just have to look for it. Have you found yours yet?" I now ask you this same question.

Joyology is the search for the "sign," the wonderful magic of joy that is buried too deep for most of us to lead daily lives with the energy and glee of this wonderful woman. My work with her and hundreds of other joyful "super normal" people resulted in the following list of principles for a new science of joy. You will see each of these principles repeated throughout this book, restated in tests designed to help you measure your own super joy, but take the time now to think about the possibility of a new psychology, a joyology. Your joy journey begins now.

Twelve Principles of Joyology

To understand more about super joy and why and how people are super joyful, we need new guidelines for a new psychology of hope, hardiness, and happiness. We need new guidelines for understanding human behavior. The following twelve principles are concepts for a different way of looking at how people live and develop day by day.

In many ways, these joyology principles are the reverse of more traditional psychological ideas, so you will have to practice a new way of thinking about a too often forgotten human capacity for super joy. The super joy patients I saw seemed to know these principles well.

1. The Making Moments Principle

We come to feel as we behave. Emotions follow behaviors, they do not precede them. To feel joyful, we must first learn to think and behave joyfully. In 1907, Dr. Israel Waynbaum suggested, and current research verifies, that our facial expressions take place *before* we experience an emotion, not after. Smiling and laughing are ways of voluntarily giving your brain an oxygen shower. When we smile, our facial muscles contract to increase the blood flow to our brains. Our tears of laughter at the end of a laughing spell are ways of relieving the buildup of blood supply to the brain. We smile to feel happy, we do not smile because we are happy.

If this new concept is difficult to accept, try the following experiment. Smile as hard as you can right now. Just force a long hard smile until you reach the end of this sentence. If you pay attention to how you are feeling now, you will notice a sensation of more warmth to the face and head. You just gave your brain an oxygen shower and in the process you may feel just a little more joyful even though you didn't do anything more than "act" joyful. In effect, you created your own joyful moment.

The woman in my example—I will call her Clare—described

her smiling as she walked near the barbed wire surrounding the prison camp. She would take some of her sparse food and feed one of the guard dogs. Clare talked of her "smile walk" every evening. When she was asked by other inmates why she was smiling and why she fed the guard dog, she would answer, "For life, for hope, for staying alive. The dog doesn't choose to be here either. He's a prisoner of this cruelty too. When I feed him, it's as if I send a message that we will all survive and take care of each other."

To learn super joy, we will have to learn to think and behave like Clare, behave in different, sometimes strange ways. We will have to learn to think in ways similar to those of Clare, who could see the seeds of joy everywhere. This book will provide specific suggestions for an entirely new "simple thinking for joy" process that asserts the importance of acting and thinking as we hope to feel.

2. The Joyful Teachers Principle

We learn more from studying happy, healthy people than we can learn from the exclusive study of the sick and the stressed. Almost all of our medical science is based on the study of the sick. If eighty percent of the people who eat the food at a picnic get sick, doctors will study why and how that eighty percent got sick. Little attention will be paid to the twenty percent who ate the same food as everyone else yet did not get sick. What was it about those people who stayed well in the face of the threat to their health? The new field of joyology depends upon our learning from the healthy, hearty, and the super survivors at least as much as we learn from the study of the process of illness.

Clare described her own learning of coping strategies. She said, "I watched the prisoners who lived, who could stay reasonably healthy. I could tell that they pretended at first that they were strong, then they actually became strong. We were all afraid, but we learned to change our feelings by acting. Those were the people I copied. The strong ones."

Here's one assignment I used with my patients. Name five people you know who you think do not seem very happy. Now name five people who seem almost unbelievably happy. Most people find it easier to name the unhappy list because we are used to looking at negatives more than positives. You might also notice that the happy list contains "stranger" people than the unhappy list. Joyful people usually break free from traditional limits and lead lives of more choice and freedom. Being free and being free right now is one of the major lessons joyful people have to teach us.

3. The Altered States Principle

There are an infinite number of states of human consciousness. Sigmund Freud suggested that, when it comes to our thoughts and feelings, we are either conscious (aware), unaware (unconscious), or somewhere between aware and unaware (preconscious). While this major breakthrough in our understanding of the human mind allowed us to see our behaviors in a new light, we now know that we are capable of an endless variety of consciousness experiences. We can even experience more than one level of consciousness or awareness simultaneously.

Clare said, "I could be many places inside that fence. They couldn't wall off my mind. I could drift away, I could fly. Some days, I felt freer than my guards. They were always on duty, but I was many things, many different things. I could look right in their eyes and smile, but what went on inside me could be something else."

Learning to be joyful is learning about the states of consciousness, how they influence our daily lives, and how to slide back and forth with ease between several levels of conscious experience. Those persons who are blind to the rainbow of consciousness experiences are less likely to discover the joy response.

Another of my patients reported, "It's like a trombone. I slide here, slide there, going octave to octave, but I always know the main tune. Most of my friends are Johnny One Notes, playing the same old song and never trying a different melody." Super joy people experience a range of consciousness, living life on several levels and in different ways, knowing many realities and many worlds.

4. The Humbled Brain Principle

The brain is not as important as it keeps telling us it is. The human brain is really a three-pound soggy lump consisting of many mini-brains arranged in a somewhat disorganized fashion. The brain is only a part of the magnificent human system, doing its job only in cooperation with the entire body system.

"Sometimes my brain would be yelling at me, telling me that I was crazy, telling me I should be afraid, that I was going to die. My brain wanted me to surrender, but my spirit took over," reported Clare. "If I had listened to my brain, I wouldn't be here now."

It is a mistake to think of the brain as the "center" of our humanness, just as ancient physicians were wrong in thinking that our emotions were in our hearts. The only significant difference between the thinking done by our kidneys, lungs, and hearts and the thinking done by the brain is the fact that the brain "knows" that it is thinking and therefore is capable of programming itself. With this self-programming comes a cerebral arrogance, an unnecessary limitation of our human potential through our deference to a brain that seems to want to do all of our experiencing for us. The "I," the self, is much more than the reverberation of neurons and we are much more than what we "think" we are. We are also what we believe, hope, feel, and sense. We can tell our brain not only what but how to think.

Our society is going through a phase of "cerebral-centrism," emphasizing the brain as the center of all meaning in living. This approach ignores the fact that our brains are nothing if they are not synchronized with the system, both body and world, in which our brains must live. In fact, true joy results when we become aware of our connectedness to everything. When our brains are humbled, put to work for us instead of working us out, we learn more about super joy.

5. The Pharmaceutical Brain Principle

The brain is a gland, not a computer. Our focus on the human brain has been characterized by computer analogies. We are even trying now to make a computer that can "think" like a human brain, but such a computer is impossible. The brain is not a complex set of electrical circuits. The brain is the largest secreting gland in the human body, and these secretions are the psychochemicals to which we become addicted.

We either become addicted to the stress and depression chemicals or we learn to become addicted to the joy chemicals. If we don't write the prescriptions for our brain to fill, the brain will write its own prescriptions. The true miracle is not the human brain itself but the fact that we can regulate the chemical combinations and doses from the largest secreting gland in the human body.

"I could get myself excited about the simplest things," said Clare. "One day I found a badge from one of the guards. It was rusted, so it was probably very old. I could just look at that badge and for me it became a Star of David. I felt chills run through me as though someone gave me a shot of something. When I got down, I would look at my star."

Super joy results when we do as Clare did and take our mental pens in hand and start writing our life scripts the way we want them to read. When we understand that every thought we have results in a spurt of psychochemicals, we begin to realize the power we have not only to destroy ourselves but to "en-joy" ourselves.

6. The Distracted Brain Principle

The brain is first and foremost a health maintenance system. While we might like to think that our brains are the center of our rational thinking, nothing could be further from the truth. The brain is dedicated to the survival of the body upon which it depends for its life. The brain's chief concern is keeping the body alive in the short run, even if its survival actions may result in premature death as the brain ignores the long-run consequences of its "survive at all costs" approach. Joyology is the study of techniques for teaching the brain a broader perspective to living than efficiency in survival. Our brains are for health, not for thinking, but we can teach our brains a more inclusive view of the world in which they live. We can teach our brains to be more than mere survivalists.

Clare reported, "Sometimes I would start to think that I should look out for me and my family only. Something kept telling me to forget everyone else, to take care of myself. Something else told me that I couldn't do that. We all needed each other. Selfishness would eventually kill us all more quickly."

Learning the joy response to life depends on getting one's own brain's attention away from its focus on its own selfish survival. We need our brains to show interest in our enjoyment, in the welfare of others, as much as to attend to our minute-to-minute individual health. The brain is infinitely capable of doing many jobs at once, but if we do not intercede, it will continue in the self-health maintenance business, leaving joy and relationship with others out of our lives as inefficient distractions, leaving stress and depression as the dominant part of our daily lives. Both stress and depression are the brain's means of staying alive in the short run. Stress chemicals keep us alert for harm, and the depression chemicals allow us escape from real or delusionary needs for constant vigilance and self-protection. Super joy has to do with living over the long run, and the brain's apparent preference for the stress and depression cycle is really a habituated comfort with living for now at the expense of the overall life experiences. The joy response has to do with enjoying living over a lifetime. A little stress, a little depression, and lots of joy should be our life formula, but the brain throws in an adaptive style of lots of stress and depression with a few pinches of joy for good measure. We need to change this mental recipe if we are ever to have super joy.

7. Our "Brain's Not Us" Principle

We are not our brain. Even though our brain "thinks" it is "us," the brain is only a body part. A simple experiment illustrates the presence of a "self" separate from the processes of the human brain. When the famous hypnotism researcher Ernest Hilgard hypnotized a man, he instructed him that he would now be totally deaf. When Dr. Hilgard clapped two pieces of wood together near the man's ear, the man showed no reaction at all. When asked if he heard the sound of wood pieces clapping together, the man replied, "No, I didn't hear it." Even though the man had voluntarily "turned off" the part of his brain responsible for interpreting sound, a "hidden observer" remained on duty, a "self" always aware of the outside and inside world, even if the listening center of the brain itself was temporarily distracted by that hidden observer.

One of the most important lessons for learning super joy is to be able to keep an eye on our brain to make sure it doesn't think and act as if it were us. You can try another experiment to see this point more clearly. As you read this sentence, your brain is working hard. Now, as you read this sentence, be aware of who you are. Even as you read these words, say to yourself, "I am reading this, but I know that I am more than whatever is doing the reading." You can actually watch your own brain reading. There is something much more profound, something much more sacred, about "self" than the brain can ever hope to understand, but you know who you are. The "you" is what is going to be doing the joyful learning in the chapters ahead.

Clare said, "Sometimes I would have long discussions with myself. It was as though 'I' was talking to 'me,' a gossip session between myself and I." Clare knew instinctively that she was much more than her brain told her she was.

8. The Lazy Brain Principle

The brain is too lazy for joy. The brain prefers efficiency and quick, easy solutions. The brain functions more like a microwave oven than a slow, steady stove preparing a tasty meal. Hope, happiness, and celebration are open-ended emotions based on unpredictability, vision, and a toleration for lack of closure and completeness. All three emotions are inefficient and depend on "what isn't yet" and "what might be," a deep faith that things will continue to be good or better. The brain prefers despair, surrender, and resignation, for these emotional states allow the brain to get on with what it considers to be its sole task: seeking stimulation and keeping itself (not necessarily "the self") alive for the moment. The brain does not want to wait to see what happens later; it wants answers now so it can move on.

"Don't you think for a moment all this came easy to me," said Clare. "Don't think I'm some kind of hero. Sometimes everything within me seemed to say, 'Give up.' But I guess it wasn't everything within me, because something was always arguing against surrender, something telling me to hope, to wait and see."

Learning super joy involves mental energizing and a discipline of thought and behavior requiring every bit as much dedication and stick-to-it-tiveness as any exercise program. Just as most of us would prefer to sleep in and avoid early morning aerobics, so most of us prefer to stay stressed or depressed, for the brain is comfortable with these patterns of immediate adjustment to the world.

Joyology principle number 1 stated that behaviors precede emotions. Motivation is also preceded by behavior, and just as you must force yourself to get up, get dressed, and go out for a brisk early morning walk, so must you start thinking and behaving joyfully before you really feel like it. Once you start the process rolling, the joy addiction will take over in a form of the "celebrator's high" equivalent to the jogger's high that calls so many runners out on cold, dark mornings.

9. The Joy as Immunity Booster Principle

The best immune system booster is a shot of super joy. Research in the new field of psychoneuroimmunology clearly demonstrates that our emotions are related to the functioning of our immune systems. While all of the facts are not yet in and the complexities of the immune system's interaction with the brain continue to elude us, it is a fact that how we feel affects when and how we get sick and get well. Super joy is a joy that results in immunoenhancement. Joyful people get sick less often and less seriously than unjoyful people, and when they do get sick, they more readily mobilize their own natural healing powers.

"It seemed as though there were sick people and well people in the camp," said Clare. "I don't know if the sick people had given up or if they were sick because they had given up, but I do know that the happier people stayed healthier."

It is important to remember that sickness is as natural as health. We all get sick, and to blame ourselves for not being joyful enough as the cause of our sickness is to misunderstand the intricacy of the mind and immune system relationship. To ignore the healing properties of joy, however, is to miss out on one of the most important weapons we have at our disposal in the rejection of the invasions of our body systems by disease-causing agents.

Modern medicine has seldom solved *any* of the major medical challenges confronting our civilization. Joy, hope, and accompanying social and cultural changes have been responsible for most of the reduction in infectious diseases. The best cultural vaccination against disease would be much more widespread joy.

10. The Hungry Brain Principle

All disease is brain disease. While our environment can kill us, this environment is really a creation of our own selfish brains that choose intense and varied stimulation over peace, quiet, and togetherness. The way we think about our world in effect creates our world, and if we think in selfish, isolationist ways, we will create a world that is governed by the survival of the strongest, meanest, quickest, and most efficient. If we all think "me first," none of us will last, yet our brains are dedicated to the priority of stimulating the individuals in which these brains live.

Brain stimulation may be in the form of the stress response or depression, for both responses suit the brain's hunger for input. The brain doesn't care if its stimulation is happy or sad. The brain only cares that it is stimulated, and once it receives that stimulation, it is unwilling to give it up easily. Addiction change is too inefficient, too inconvenient for a brain that is reluctant to change its "mind."

Perhaps the most contagious disease of our time is the infectious selfishness at the expense of our environment and the welfare of the total system. Such selfishness is the result of the brain's stimulus addiction. The brain will eat itself to death unless we provide it with a healthier diet of joy stimulation.

"It seemed as if my brain would go looking for trouble. I would try to sleep at night, and my brain would keep telling me that they were going to come and get me. I had to learn to shut that off." Clare's statement shows the brain's insatiable striving for stimulation, even if that stimulation is potentially health threatening.

As a test of this tenth joyology principle, think of any major disease that continues to be "incurable." Now try to think of any way that disease might eventually be cured without some increase in unity, some sacrifice and caring among all people. Even if some magic drug could be discovered to "cure" the disease you named, it is unlikely that such a drug could even be devised without selflessness and caring on the part of many people.

Only when the immune system is viewed as a world system will disease be reduced. The brain is wrong when it thinks that, if the body in which it lives is alive, then that is all that matters. Super joy means a system joy, and true joy is impossible while people around us are suffering and we do nothing to help.

Clare reported that she drew strength from those times when she was able to help others in the camp, even if such help appeared minor. "I would hold one man's hand every morning when the guards came," she said. "He would shake terribly as they stomped by. I would just sit and hold his hand. He said it gave him strength, but it seemed to give me more strength. I seemed to get some type of energy from calming him, from comforting him."

Clare's gesture of support created a "mini-system," a small pocket of protection that enhanced the well-being of both Clare and her coprisoner. Like immune cells that join to resist an invading virus, these two people joined together for a strength of unity and security. Super joy is a manifestation of this unity, of a coming together within the overall system regardless, even because of, the challenge.

11. The Safe Addiction Principle

The best drug-testing program is in the human brain. The brain has pretested hundreds of psychochemicals over five hundred million years. It has selected primarily the survival chemicals of stress to help us "win" and depression when we feel we have "lost." The stress chemicals help us keep going until we drop. The depression chemicals help us drop. We are on a neurohormonal carousel, and only joy can help us slow that carousel for a more enjoyable ride.

The super joy chemicals have also been well tested through the brain's million-year drug-testing program, but few of us are "taking" many of the joy juices. We are too busy "going" and "dropping," too busy using the survival addictions to pay attention to our capacity for a thrival addiction.

"I can still feel the way I felt in that camp," reported Clare. "There was a certain invigoration, even though it was hell. It's as though God gave me something to ease the pain." Clare is describing in this statement her own pretested psychochemicals, which protected her in this threatening situation, lifting her and energizing her even when her environment was the ultimate in stress and pain.

The joy response is prewired into the human system. Like a new home with wiring for phones that have not been installed, the joy response circuitry is going largely unused, or at least is underused.

The healing psychochemicals produced within the brain are there for us, but we must make connection with them.

The joy response is a reflex, a prewired response system available on demand. This joy response, super joy, is hidden away, far back in the brain medicine chest, behind the stress and depression bottles. This book is intended to help you reach far back to take a dose of the joy medication made and tested for you by the human brain.

12. The Health Is Not Enough Principle

Being healthy isn't enough. We can learn a super health, to move far beyond being normal, okay, just fine, happy, or "fine, thank you, how are you?" We can move beyond the absence of symptoms to the presence of joyful emotional vitality and vigor. In our pursuit of normalcy, we have lost sight of the extraordinary, the "super." This book is about the "super," a joy that sends vibrations of wellness through our very spirits and the spirits of those to whom we relate.

Clare described "the leaders." She said, "In the camp, some of the prisoners became like role models for the rest. People looked up to them. They just had something special." These were the super joy people, the thrivers.

When I first decided to write about super joy, some people resisted the idea. "I'm happy and so are most people," said one friend. "I don't get it. How is joy or super joy different than being happy?" The answer rests within your own experience.

Think now of a time when you were more than happy. Think of a time when you were ecstatic, jubilant, delighted, enraptured, exhilarated, fascinated, captivated, enthralled, and thrilled all at the same time. It may take some time to think of such an experience, but when you do, try to remember how you felt. That's super joy! It's real, but it is all too rare. Sometimes just recalling the event is accompanied by the brain's secretion of a dose of super joy chemicals.

You see the joy reflex in a dog when he greets his master, in a child when his or her mother returns, in the face of a parent at the birth of a child. It's a super experience because it goes beyond just being happy to being thrilled with being alive.

In the list above, only the dog greeting his master seems to experience super joy several times a week, even several times a day. The dog behaves as if his master has been gone for years, even if he or she has been gone only a few hours. The dog has mastered the "as if" approach to life that makes super joy possible on a more regular basis. Imagine if we all said hello and good-bye as if such times were truly special and unique. Foolish, you may say. Who could behave like that? We would all look crazy or abnormal. If being delighted much more often is abnormal, then this is a book about the joy of abnormal psychology.

One of the most limiting words in our vocabulary is the word "overjoyed." The problem in our society is really that we are underjoyed. We need a new psychology that is not afraid to speak of hardiness, happiness, and hope as a regular part of daily living, as an addiction to the celebration of life.

This new field of joyology with its twelve principles described here is not a Pollyannaish escapist approach to life. Rather, these principles represent a total immersion in living, an acknowledgment that there is much more to living than we are taking from our lives. Even in the terrible environment of that prison camp, Clare was able to create her own world, to mold it and survive it. She said, "There came a time when you had to decide not to surrender but to accept, to get involved in the experience and change it from inside. When you did that, you went outside the walls."

If you think the idea of total, super joy is silly, you may need this book more than anyone else, for your stress or depression addiction has blinded you to the light of life's brilliance. Open your eyes, open your heart, and the light of joy will draw you into a new joy of daily living.

A Map for the Joy Journey

I have divided this book into three sections. In Part One, I review the six major characteristics of the super joy experience. I present new ways of thinking about life experiences that are based on the joyology principles that are most likely to lead to super joy. I present a test of your own super joy quotient and review the psychochemical nature of super joy as it compares to other human responses. I end SECTION ONE with a "joy spiral" model for your own learning of the super joy response.

Part Two deals with the mind and super joy, and the issues of work, love, and faith as they relate to super joy. Both SECTIONS ONE and TWO contain self-tests to help you measure your own super joy in relation to several issues of daily living. You will see the same twelve joyology principles presented in this chapter reviewed throughout each chapter. This review and repetition with different examples is essential for the reprogramming process necessary to help you change your brain's mind to a more joyful view of life.

Part Three presents six joy letters to people with specific concerns or crises in their own lives. If you are such a person, you may want to read the letter or letters that deal with your problem before reading the first two sections. The letters and all of the material in this book contain several reviews of the super joy concept. This allows you either to read the book from beginning to end or to skip around as you find helpful. The joy letters also contain descriptions of the basic super joy principles so each letter stands as a complete joy message in itself. At the end of each letter are suggested additional readings and directions to parts of this book that go into more detail on the issue addressed in the letter.

Finally, I have included a glossary of new terms related to the new field of joyology and a complete set of references and a bibliography. Research in the field of joyology is just beginning and is drawn from diverse sources, so you may want to check some of the references for yourself to see how this exciting new field is beginning to grow and what new findings are supporting the idea that super joy is not just a dream, it is a real human gift.

"But what is it like?" asked one of my patients. "Tell me what makes up this super joy. What goes into it, what are the parts of it?" The next chapter describes one woman's super joy experience and illustrates the basic six components that make up a super joy experience.

Before you read on, take a few minutes alone, sit quietly, and think about the most joyful moment of your life. Think what life would be like if the characteristics of that wonderful time were much more a part of your everyday life. I hope and believe that the chapters to follow will help you make such a dream real.

PART ONE

Life,
Liberty,
and the
Pursuit
of
Super Joy

CHAPTER TWO

Curing the Captain Ahab Complex

Sometimes my life is like the story about the whale in *Moby Dick.*
I'm just like Captain Ahab. I seemed obsessed with just getting
through my day-to-day life, tied down to my life like Captain Ahab
tied himself to the whale. If I don't get myself untied, I'm going to
drown.

43-YEAR-OLD MOTHER

Testing for the Captain Ahab Complex

When Herman Melville describes Captain Ahab's obsession with
and eventual death because of the great white whale Moby Dick,
he is describing a characteristic of our modern living that robs us
of super joy. We become addicted, tied to an obligatory life style,
or worse, become bound by our fixation on some issue in our lives
that becomes our own Moby Dick.

Sometimes the symbolic whale that consumes our lives and ultimately brings us down is a job, or perhaps a problem with our
children, our health, or in parenting our own parents. The Captain
Ahab syndrome occurs when we allow one aspect of living, no
matter how difficult or demanding that problem may be, to consume us. The following questions will help you determine if you
are currently at sea with your own whale of a problem.

The Captain Ahab Syndrome Test

1. Do you find yourself thinking about the same problem day in and day out, even when you are busy doing other things?   _____

2. Do you feel that the problem or life issue you are concerned about is bigger than life, something you must solve but at the same time seems unsolvable?   _____

3. Do you feel that your "whale of a problem" is yours alone to deal with and that no one can really help you solve it?   _____

4. Do you sometimes wonder what your life would be like if you didn't have the major problem you have, almost feeling that if the problem were gone you would have nothing to live for?   _____

5. Does it seem that whenever you get close to solving your problem something always happens to block your progress?   _____

6. Do you almost always behave and think in terms of your problem, considering the problem before making plans or doing anything for yourself? This may happen with a career obsession, the pursuit of success, or any aspect of life you have made into a major problem area for yourself.   _____

7. Are your life progress and natural developmental sequence delayed or stopped entirely because, in your view, you have one major problem you must focus on?   _____

8. Does everything in your life revolve around your problem, with every experience, every song, every poem, every movie reminding you of some aspect of your problem?   _____

9. Do you dream and daydream about your problem?   _____

10. Does it seem almost impossible to explain the nature of your relationship to your problem area to anyone else? _____

The more "yes" answers you have to the above questions, the more severe your Ahab complex and the more the block to your super joy. You may even be experiencing physical problems related to your Ahab complex—your inability to let go of your focus on one agenda—and until you manage to untie yourself from this one big problem and find super joy, your life is unlikely to improve.

Ahab's Diseases

Several years ago, physicians described what they called the "psychosomatic seven." These are diseases that were viewed as "caused" or at least strongly related to the person's state of mind. Here's the list of diseases that relate to prolonged fixation and helplessness regarding one personal major life issue, the diseases that result from the prolonged addiction to a specific problem at the expense of joy.

1. Peptic ulcers or related gastric upset and pain. Continued and recurrent stomach upset.

2. Hypertension, sometimes marginal and especially an elevated systolic or "first number" elevation in blood pressure. This hypertension may be experienced as a sense of fullness in the extremities or as facial, arm, and hand warmth.

3. Hyperthyroidism, probably related to prolonged addiction to stress chemicals affecting the thyroid gland and causing agitation, moodiness, and metabolic problems.

4. Rheumatoid arthritis, or sporadic inflammation around the joints, probably related to continued negative effects on the immune system by prolonged stress or depression.

5. Ulcerative colitis or recurring ulceration of the colon accompanied by diarrhea, urgency to defecate, cramping, and sometimes rectal bleeding. Rectal bleeding is a danger sign and should always be checked immediately with your doctor.

6. Neurodermatitis or itching of the skin, sometimes accompanied by a mild rash.

7. Bronchial asthma, or wheezing, tightness in the chest, labored breathing, and frequent dry coughing and gasping (the sneeze, wheeze, and gasp syndrome).

There are several other diseases, perhaps all diseases, that relate to the mind/body health maintenance system, but the above psychosomatic seven seem particularly related to the Ahab complex. A dangerous feature of the stress addiction pattern is a stressor that is chronic and for which the person sees no effective coping strategy. The typical result is continued stress addiction, followed by a depression crash.

As happened to Captain Ahab, we sometimes are consumed with one aspect of our living at the expense of all others. We relentlessly pursue that one area, mentally and physically fixated on that aspect of our life. Ultimately, we become so tied to our problem area that we are drawn down by our own obsession.

Like Clare, in Chapter One, we can let the whale go free. Of course, we must deal with the realities of our severe problems, but we must not let these problems take the total of our spiritual energy. Super joy is not the prerogative of people who do not have problems, it is the natural capacity to mobilize our inner strength even in the face of challenge.

The woman in the next example cured her Ahab complex, and her experience teaches us about the major characteristics of super joy. Before reading on, however, pause to identify the whale, the one major problem among all the others that seems to be taking your super joy away. Don't fool yourself. We all have our own whale of a problem to deal with. Your whale may seem smaller than someone else's, but until you free yourself from it, super joy will elude you.

Retreating to Advance on Joy

The young mother was looking for a place she remembered from her childhood, and she was uncertain about this location. The burrs kept sticking to her slacks, and the hill seemed to be tilting up higher in front of her as she climbed. She could see the beginning of the blue line of water, and it took every last bit of her energy to keep pushing herself to the top. She stopped as she saw the summit and thought, "I'm home."

It was only a small hill, certainly not a challenge for a skilled climber, but it was her hill. She used to sit up here for hours alone, looking at the lake that seemed then to be the size of an ocean. She felt totally at peace in her childhood place and was revisiting this hideaway now as an assignment from her therapy with me. She was spending one week alone, away from her husband, parents, and children, just being "herself." She could have gone anywhere for this retreat, but she chose her childhood "spot."

Exactly one year ago on this day, her doctor had told her about a cancerous growth that threatened her life. He had unknowingly provided her with a death sentence instead of a diagnosis or plan for healing. He had added yet another whale for her already strong Ahab complex. She had evaluated her life, her relationships, what living really meant to her. She had identified her own style of overpressured, overobligated, super-mother behavior. She discovered that she was consumed by her pursuit of a perfect family, a perfect home, perfect children, and being the perfect daughter to her own parents. Perfection had been her white whale.

With the skills of her doctor, and the effects of a comprehensive and holistic plan of treatment she developed in partnership with her doctor, she had defeated the cancer and was now in perhaps the best health of her life. She had learned a lesson about her own self-neglect, not just of her physical health, but of her emotional and spiritual health. She had come to me for help now to learn to be healthy, not just "not sick." She did not want her fear of the recurrence of her cancer to become yet another white whale in her life.

As she sat on the hillside, she felt a wonderful glow. Later, in my office, she said, "It was joy. Plain and simple joy. I had lost it. I didn't need to be perfect anymore. I just needed to be me, to give my family me, not some image of a super mom and wife. I had gotten involved in working, mothering, healing, meditating, and eating just the perfect foods, but I forgot to enjoy me and my living. For a while I even tried to be the perfect patient. Once I saw what I was doing to myself and how I really wasn't making the people around me happy anyway, I knew a joy that you can't describe. Now, as I sat on that hill, I just felt what words can't express. As I looked out at that wonderful lake from that high hill, I was a child again. Living meant something more than trying to stay healthy. I felt wise, like I knew something almost beyond thinking. I felt like I was the lake, the hill, and I never want to forget that feeling. I want it more and more in my life, and I'm going to make the changes I need to make time for joy."

The woman looked at me through her tears, and with astonishment said, "My God, I'm feeling it again right now. Right now, as I talk to you. It's like it's going through my body. I want this feeling always. Always."

By going off by herself, by "retreating," this woman had advanced to a state of joy that would be with her and available to her forever. The steps I will present in the following chapters will teach you how to ensure the permanence of super joy in your life, but first I will take you through what I call the "In a Joy" formula for super joy, the major components of the human joy response as taught to me by my extraordinarily healthy patients over the years.

How to Get IN A JOY

Here are the six major characteristics of the super joy experience. It is as close as I can come to telling you what super joy is. All my patients discovering their own joy response experienced that response uniquely for them, but a common thread ran through all of their reports. The first letters of each of the six super joy components will help you remember each characteristic of super joy and help you get IN A JOY.

$I = Ineffability$

Tongue-tied with Joy

Intense emotions are always too much for words, and super joy so overwhelms the human brain that we become cerebrally tongue-tied. The brain speaks in the language of stress and depression, both of which are essentially turn-on and turn-off languages of immediate survival, but the brain is much less fluent in the dialect of delight.

Have you ever noticed how difficult it is for most people to express their intense positive feelings? Anger talk comes easily, but love talk usually causes us problems. Sometimes the brain has to talk baby talk to express love and joy, for the mind of the child serves the child while too often we as adults are servants to our own adult minds. Super joy is almost impossible to verbalize, and you will notice that, even though I picked my most articulate patients to use in my examples, each patient struggled to find the words to tell others what the joy experience is like.

"It was too powerful. It was just too much," said one woman. "You can't tell anyone exactly what real joy is because it seems so personal. Anger seems easier to describe for some reason." This woman finally gave up trying to describe joy and reported, "I became an artist. A sixty-five-year-old woman taking up art. I became an artist, and now you can see my joy. The brush is my tongue."

I suggest that one reason joy is so difficult to describe is that super joy is the most intimate of human experiences. We can't talk about it with someone else without becoming very, very close to that person. Anger is easier because anger implies a distance and a self-protective posture. Expressing joy is to show what's right for you, while expressing anger is to try to show what's wrong with someone else. We fear intimacy because the brain fears encroachment on its selfish domain and mission of self-enhancement, so joy talk is a difficult task. We can complain, mope, swear, demand, yell, and degrade much easier than we can share our spiritual celebration. The brain seems to hate letting its selfish defenses down by taking time to celebrate.

Overcoming our difficulty in sharing and describing our super joy is a major step in becoming more joyful. If we work on talking about joy more with others, we are more likely to experience joy more often. I saw a man walking away from his mailbox. He opened his letter as he walked and without warning yelled out, "Hot damn!" He proceeded to do a little joy jig. He looked up during one of his spins and saw me looking at him and smiling. He quickly regained his composure (the major joy restricter) and, without speaking, moved his lips as if to say to me, "I'm sorry." Too much joy done too openly, he assumed, but it is likely that he would have shown his anger with less embarrassment.

Even if you have to talk to yourself, talk more about joy. Verbalize your feelings and get the joy out. The more you speak of joy, the more the joy response becomes a new addiction. As happened to the woman in my office describing her joy retreat, the actual saying of joy words can help produce the psychochemical changes that are the healthy drugs to which we hope to be addicted.

N = Noesis
Knowing a New Way to Know

Super joy is another way of knowing about the world. Once you begin experiencing joy more regularly, everything you see and do, everyone with whom you interact, takes on new meaning and context. You come to "know" in an intuitive way, beyond everyday reasoning and logic.

"I don't know how I came to see things so much more clearly, but it was like when you rub your eyes in the morning and the world comes into focus," said one man. "I felt like I was knowing, seeing, perceiving as if I had hypnotized myself or something. I was like one of those *Star Trek* guys who was going where no man had gone before. I felt arrogant. I was seeing the world like no one else had ever seen it, like the first space traveler. I just knew things I never knew in a way that I never knew." This man was learning to accept the fact that he was using much more than his brain to relate to his world. He was relating in a "super" way, transcending the cortical knowing to which he had become addicted.

To learn super joy, you will have to make time to develop your awareness and perception at several levels of consciousness. Don't dismiss your premonitions, feelings of déjà vu, strange feelings, vibrations, sensations, or other sources of information that traditional psychology views as "paranormal." Remember that extrasensory perception is only "extra" because we don't allow ourselves to practice with it enough to make it just another important way of perceiving the world.

Almost everyone has had what he or she considers to be "extrasensory" experiences, so don't laugh them off as abnormal or signs of mental illness. The whole idea of super joy is to go beyond normal, beyond mental health. "Normal" people will never have "super" joy.

$A = Amazement$
The Reappreciation of Life

Super joy and increased appreciation, even amazement, for the smallest details of life go hand in hand. What we take for granted is typically potentially much more profound in its emotional impact than what we spend our time fixated upon day in and day out.

A father whom you will meet in the beginning of Chapter 4 said, "I could see the sparkle in my little girl's eyes. I had never looked that deeply in there before. Did you know that people's eyes send out a light? I never saw it until that day that I looked into, not at, my daughter's eyes for the first time." This father, whose daughter had been lost to him for only a few minutes in a shopping center, learned to savor every detail of her appearance. Super joy involves the complete tuning in to those elements of daily life with which we make only casual contact.

Try to appreciate the details of the simplest elements around you, and you will find a joy that has always been there for the taking. Try to rediscover some of the amazement of your child-hood. Look at the beauty of even artificial materials, such as the structure of lines and shadows on an office desk, or listen to the sound of someone's voice on the phone calling about a simple business matter. We miss out on joy when we fail to attend to the simple aspects of daily living, and too often we are frightened into such attention by a crisis which leads us to the resolve to live life more fully. Don't wait to be forced to pay attention to your living. Life and living are truly amazing; we just forget to pay attention to that fact sometimes.

$J = Joined$

A Return to Humanity

Every super joy experience reported to me was characterized by a renewed sense of connecting with the world. The same father who found the light in his daughter's eyes also said, "I wanted every-body to celebrate with me, everybody in the shopping center. I wanted everybody in the whole damn shopping center to stop what they were doing, join hands, and dance and sing. I felt closer to them somehow, closer because of my joy."

One reason super joy and super health have eluded us is that in our society we grow further and further apart even as our technol-ogy seems to bring us closer together. We can talk to almost any-one in the world, watch them on television, and send pages of typed text over wires to any country in the world. Our machines can talk to one another for us, yet we seem strangely isolated by all of these gains. Since we no longer have to be with people to communicate with them, we are beginning to cocoon ourselves, to withdraw and send electronic signals back and forth between our-selves only when necessary.

For one entire day, try not using the phone. If that seems impos-sible, try going one half day without making or receiving a phone call. You might even want to see people in person instead of call-ing them. Watch their surprise when you make a personal visit to pick up your own pizza instead of having one sent to your home.

One of my patients became so isolated that she had her phone's automatic dialer set up according to all of her needs. The keys simply said Food, Health, Education, Car Repair, Dentist, etc. Such phone addiction, like all addictions, gives us the false sense that we are making a great deal of contact, when in reality we are automating ourselves away from one another.

O = Open
Free at Last

Super joy is always associated with being open to risk taking. When my patients reported super joy, they almost always reported the desire to take more risks, to be more open to experiences, to reach out for more opportunities for new learning. One woman said, "I want to feel, do, listen, touch, smell, try things. I don't want to say later that I wished I had done something when it is too late to do it."

The number one complaint or lament from my older patients is that, if they had it all to do over again, they would have taken more risks. These joy risks are not just throwing caution to the wind and taking up sky diving. Joy risks include talking to that person you were afraid to start talking to first, calling that man or woman you had hoped would call you, and calling back after a job interview to see what they really thought of you or the real reason you did or didn't get that job.

You have already taken a major risk by buying this book. You have decided to go for it, to at least check in to this super joy idea, to the possibility of going for extraordinary well-being. Try taking a risk after you read this chapter. Visit that one person you thought you could never visit first. Instead of waiting for him or her to call you, go ahead and call and say you would like to come over. Super joy requires super courage, but the payoffs can make all the failed risks well worth the chance taking.

$Y = Youth$

Reborn for Joy

The reports of super joy all contained a soteriological element, a sense of being born again. Various patients over the years have talked about nirvana, enlightenment, liberation, or some religious renewal, but they all meant that they had found their internal fountain of youth. Whenever people seem younger than their years, the reason is less their physical appearance than the ageless joy with which they approach life.

"I see now why people say they feel like a kid again. I don't know if medical tests would show it, but I feel young all over, like I had a shot of happy hormone or something." This report from a seventy-three-year-old man illustrates the energizing nature of the super joy response.

We have always assumed that illness and old age can gradually take away our joy. Perhaps our lack of joy results in illness and accelerates the aging process. Just watch the behavior of old men or women when they greet a grandchild. Watch the years peel away. Being born again does not necessarily have to imply a religious change, but something seems to happen to revive the spirit, something miraculously fresh and invigorating.

One woman said, "Every time I think of my granddaughter making her first communion, it's as if I'm that age again myself. I feel closer to God as I watch her get closer to God. It renews my faith, and I just want to hug her and hug her, and it makes me young again." This grandmother's report illustrates the regression factor of super joy. Such regression is not infantilization but a return to the energy of new beginnings.

Joy not only makes you feel younger; behaving younger makes you more joyful. Skip rope or play jacks, or play any game, and see if you don't feel happier just by playing. Of course, you can ruin everything if you play the game like an adult, so allow yourself to regress in the service of joy.

Super joy, then, is characterized by an almost indescribable experience of understanding the world beyond the day-to-day knowing of stress and survival. It results in a deeper and broader appreciation, even amazement with all of living, particularly the interconnectedness of all of us on earth. It is accompanied by a sense of being reborn, open to all that life can offer, and the feeling that super joy is the ultimate of God's gifts.

Super joy can be a part of everyday life if we learn new ways of thinking about our living style. Chapter Three suggests some new joyful points of view and states the twelve principles of the new science of joyology in the form of new styles of daily thinking. Chapter Three calls into question many of the incorrect assumptions of modern life that block our access to a journey of joy, but if you feel that you are burdened by immediately pressing problems that block your attempts to find super joy, I suggest that, before you move on to Chapter Three, you turn to one of the special letters of joy for persons who feel overwhelmed and helpless. Each of these letters is based on joyology, and once you have read the letter pertaining to your specific problem area, return to Chapter Three to learn how to make joy a more regular part of your thinking, how to change your cognitive map so it leads you to super joy.

CHAPTER THREE

Joyful Thinking for Stressful Times

Did you ever get that empty feeling, like no matter how much you have, how many different things you do, you just don't feel content? I can sit on my new boat in my new boating clothes and look at the beautiful scenery, and somehow I'm happy but not as happy as I thought I would be in these circumstances.

37-YEAR-OLD MAN

No Joy in Paradise

The deep blue Hawaiian water reflected shadows of the dark green palm trees that leaned lazily over the golden-yellow beach. A warm breeze whispered through thousands of tropical flowers, misting their sweet fragrance everywhere. A happy cry of sea gulls echoed along the rich green cliffs in synchronized rhythm with the calmly dancing surf. A woman is sunbathing near the water's edge, her head tilted to receive the maximum warmth of the sun. She is vacationing in paradise, but something is wrong. Something is missing. Here in paradise, or at home or at work, something has been lost.

As I began to enter the ocean, the woman called out, "Dr. Pearsall, do you want a good story for one of your books?"

Before I could answer, the woman motioned me to join her.

"Wait until you hear about my husband," she said. "I've heard your lecture about joy and the problems people have being joyful, and my husband is a perfect case study for you."

"Where is he?" I asked.

"Oh, up there somewhere," she answered, pointing to the bright blue sky without lifting her eyes from mine.

"Oh, I'm sorry," I said as I prepared myself for yet another story about health problems, stress, or the failures of modern medicine.

"You're sorry?" she answered. "You ought to be married to him, then you would have something to be sorry about."

"I don't understand," I answered, wondering if this woman had been in the sun too long.

"Oh, I see," she explained, "No. He's not dead. He's still busy killing himself. I mean he's up there somewhere hang gliding. Yesterday he went parasailing and jet skiing. The day before he golfed until he had blisters and then he snorkeled for so long that he got a sunburn on the part of his back that was out of the water. He looked just like a red humpbacked whale." The woman laughed, but a tear rolled down her cheek, beaded into a single bubble by her abundant suntan lotion.

"Well, it sounds like he really enjoys these vacations," I said.

"No way," she replied angrily. "That's your story for your book. He never enjoys anything, he just keeps doing things. There's no joy in him, at least none that he shares with me. He's too busy doing, working, vacationing, achieving. That's why we're here. He's the number one salesman in his office, and this is his reward. Every year he wins, and the qualifications for winning get higher and higher. More production, bigger trips. I think he's aiming for a Mars trip someday."

Our discussion was suddenly interrupted by a shower of sand. The husband had joined us, sweating and panting. He drank lustily from his beer can before speaking.

"Hey, that was great," he said. "I haven't wasted one minute of this trip. I have done every single thing this resort offers. God, Pam, you miss out on everything. You don't know how to have fun. All you do is sit, rest, walk, and read. Get with it, kid, or you'll never enjoy anything."

The husband noticed a volley-ball game in process, dropped his half-empty beer can, and as he ran away yelled back, "See you later. Join me when you're ready to have fun." I could see the severe sunburn on his back. He was too rushed to feel it now, but he would be in for some real pain later.

This man represents the joy crisis in our society. A set of beliefs about daily living, a collection of assumptions about life, have become a daily dogma of intense survival that leaves little room for the release of the natural joy response from within. We think doing everything is the same as enjoying everything. We mistake stimulation for elation, external stimulation for spiritual intensity.

Take the following test on joyful thinking to assess the degree to which you think about daily living in a joyful way. This test will help you understand your own cognitive map, whether or not you are traveling the road to super joy.

The Joyful Thinking Test

Use the following scale to score yourself on this test:

5 = Strongly Agree

4 = Agree

3 = Mildly Agree

2 = Mildly Disagree

1 = Disagree

0 = Strongly Disagree

1. People should work and play to their full potential. _____

2. Underachievement is a waste of your natural skills and capabilities. _____

3. You should get the most out of everything you do. _____

4. Being very productive is a good personality trait. _____

5. You should work constantly to improve yourself. _____

6. Wasting time is wasting life. _____

7. Winning is not everything, it is the *only* thing. _____

8. If you are going to do something, do it right. _____

9. When you can do several things at once, you are getting the most out of every moment. _____

10. Being happy is the reward for hard work and sacrifice. _____

11. You should set your priorities clearly and work on the top priorities first. _____

12. You can't be really happy until you have solved most of your problems. _____

13. Being healthy means being free of physical symptoms, eating wisely, and exercising regularly. _____

14. Joyful people are usually lucky people who have few problems in their lives. _____

15. Enjoy life while you can. You are only young once. _____

16. Work now and enjoy the fruits of your labor later. _____

17. You can't be totally happy unless you are totally independent. _____

18. It is childish and unrealistic to think or act as if you can be happy all of the time. _____

19. You can thrive on stress.   _____

20. The world can be a very unhappy place. We have no right to be joyful when others are suffering.   _____

Now total your points. If you came out with more than 50 points on this Joyful Thinking Test, it is likely that you have learned to think in a joyless fashion and have accepted a set of assumptions about life that block your potential for super joy. Your addiction to the stress and addiction pattern is determined by your theory of life. Consider each Joyful Thinking Test question in detail and you will see how super joy depends on a completely new point of view regarding daily living.

Question 1: People Should Work And Play To Their Full Potential vs. How To Live Beneath Your "Potential."

Super Joy Thinking: There is no such thing as "human potential." When we pressure ourselves to do all that we should be able to do, we fail to fully experience and enjoy what we are doing.

The mother and father had waited for what seemed like hours to see the teacher of their kindergarten daughter. As they nervously took their seats, the teacher uttered the words the young parents had feared most on this parent/teacher conference night.

"I'm afraid Molly is not working up to her potential," said the teacher as he turned to the parents with a stack of what were in his opinion Molly's below-potential work samples to support his evaluation.

The parents were at the same time flattered and frustrated. They were happy that the teacher somehow knew of the genetic gift they had given their child, for they felt that this reflected positively on the heredity of their respective families. They also felt frustrated and guilty, for they thought that they must not be fulfilling their "potential" as parents, failing to help their daughter fulfill her genetic destiny.

As the teacher documented his case, he leaned forward and added in a soft voice so parents of children without potential could not hear, "I don't want to get your hopes up, but I don't think we even know your daughter's full potential." The mother and father felt guilty again, as if their daughter were taking up the potential of other children or as if they were missing something they should have identified in their child.

Unknowingly, this teacher was creating a white whale for these parents' evolving Ahab complex. The parents and teacher were now in agreement, and they plotted a stressful course to make Molly "live up to her potential or even her potential potential," and for her parents to live up to their parental potential. But what is this potential we all seem to be trying to work up to?

Our psychology of deficit, sickness, and the prevention of mental illness has been based on the false concept of "potential." Joyology suggests that the "potential" concept is a creation of mental health sciences, particularly the testing movement. All tests are designed to measure "potential," yet there has never been a test that could perform such a measurement.

The dominance of the testing movement in our society has seduced us into thinking that test scores "are" potential. Test scores are simply numbers used to arrange people in order from "less to more" on some arbitrary scale. Aptitude tests are not "apt to do" tests at all, but they do become "ought to do" tests. Tests are really only sets of mini-puzzles that measure something of what we have already learned and what we can do right now.

If Albert Einstein, one of the greatest geniuses of our time, were to take a test to measure his potential, it is likely we would find that he had no potential at all. Einstein failed miserably on simple tests, and simple arithmetic baffled him. He was labeled an educational failure at an early age. There is not a test that could measure the "potential" of an Einstein, and there are no tests that could measure little Molly's potential.

Intelligence testing is based on the idea of potential, a concept borrowed from physics. In physics, potential refers to the position of an object, as when a weight is suspended and in position to fall.

In this case, potential is a type of "dropability index." Tests ranging from the Army Alpha intelligence test to the Stanford-Binet and Wechsler intelligence tests are all intended to measure potential, ignoring the fact that people are not objects suspended in space. People are constantly changing, and there is no single factor that predicts brilliance of any type. If we persist in the pursuit of our potential, we only end up suspending ourselves in space, waiting for our potential to be released. We miss out on the power of the present when we focus so much on the pressure of potential.

Constant change and adaptation of educational and life plans are essential to any good teaching, parenting, living, and working, as is the providing of challenge and opportunity. Assigning potential or making decisions based on assumed potential has the countereffect of restricting rather than expanding our overall development and potential for joy.

To use the word "intelligence" as singular is to make a major mistake, for there are an infinite number of and varieties of "intelligences." By measuring one type, we automatically ignore the presence of all the other faces of intellect. Multiple personality is an extremely rare mental illness, but to have multiple intelligences is a human trait. Super joy depends on keeping all of our intelligences operating and not searching for an ever elusive human potential factor.

When we turn ourselves over to the testers, we destroy our super joy, for tests do not speak the language of happiness. Instead, tests speak the language of the left side of the brain: words and numbers in the abstract. Many of my patients complain that they were too early limited by some well-intentioned teacher or counselor who "knew their potential" through some analysis of a battery of tests. It is no coincidence that we use the phrase "battery of tests," almost in the sense of "assault and battery." There can be no joy when we chase the ghost of what we ought to be able to do.

If we must speak of potential, let us ask a different question. The key question is, "What is your dream?" Were you ever asked that question in school? I am not referring to the question, "What do you want to *be* when you grow up?" I am referring to the question, *"How* do you want to be when you grow up?"

Imagine a world where children answered "Happy" to the question, "How do you want to be when you grow up?" In preparing this book, I asked this question of fifty of the children of my patients. The children ranged in age from four to fifteen and were equally split as to gender. In response to the "How do you want to be?" question, every one of the fifty children responded with a career or activity plan of some type. Not one responded with an emotion such as "Happy" or "In love."

One further warning about the robbing of joy by the focus on human potential. What we are good at is not always what we are joyful at. A common myth of the sick psychology movement is that doing well at something must mean we enjoy doing it. Success or competence is not a measure of joy, only of effort and practice. If all we seek is success, all we will have is effort. Super joy involves the knowledge that you can fulfill your dreams, but you can never fulfill the false expectations of society's view of your potential or your own self-assigned potential, which becomes a "white whale" for you rather than an opportunity for growth.

Question 2: Underachievement Is A Waste Of Your Natural Skills And Capabilities vs. Avoiding The Burnout Of Your Emotional Brakes.

Super Joy Thinking: Underachievement can be very good for you. Sometimes doing less than we know we can do allows a pace to living that makes more room and time for joy. Not always doing what we can does not diminish what we are able to do.

The next set of parents in the line to visit the kindergarten teacher had twins in this kindergarten class. They sat down to hear the dual report. "Well," began the teacher, "I guess it's a bad-news-good-news deal. Your son David is underachieving. He just is not doing all that he can do all the time. Your son Steven is overachieving. He is working far above his potential. You can be proud of him."

The parents would return home prepared to urge little David to begin to work up to his capacity and to commend Steven for doing what theoretically he shouldn't have been able to do. The underlying thinking behind this approach to child rearing is that we all must do all that we can do all of the time. It has become a societal imperative that we must try to do at least what we can do and even more than we should be able to do.

Joyology teaches quite a different lesson than the obligatory effort theory. Just because a car can go a hundred miles an hour, driving that car for long periods at that speed will damage it and make it old before its time. We can constructively back off of the accelerator of life, coast sometimes, even gently apply the brakes.

I was asked to help a fourteen-year-old boy who had developed hypertension and ulcers. He had been rushed to the emergency room with a bleeding ulcer. His scores on all of his school tests were high, and he was exceeding the already high expectations of his parents and teachers, but he had blown his emotional engine in the process.

The treatment for this boy was more than medicine. He required a heavy dose of joy chemicals from within. I suggested he take one semester off to just "coast" in his classes, to intentionally underachieve for just a while. During this period he was to have fun, play, laugh, and even waste some time. When I presented this assignment, I asked the boy if there was anything he had always wanted to do but had been too busy to do.

"I really wanted to do some paint-by-numbers paintings," he answered, somewhat embarrassed. "My mother thinks such a thing is beneath me, but I sort of wanted to paint some of those dogs on velvet that you see in the stores."

"Do it," I urged, and I worked with this boy and his family to help them rethink their orientation to the balance between obligation and freedom, enjoyment and effort. There is great joy in doing what you can do and even extending yourself beyond your own sense of your limits, but there is only the stress and depression addiction cycle when you feel you must do all that you can do all of the time.

One year later the family came to me for a follow-up visit. With the work of his doctor and the changes in his approach to school, his physical symptoms had vanished. His grades suffered, going from an all-A average to Bs and As. "I'm going to step on the emotional accelerator again next year," said the boy. "It's my junior year in high school, so I want to get some good grades to get into a good college. Next year, I'm easy off the accelerator again."

The boy had never looked better, but his parents seemed concerned, worried that their son was, in the words of his father, "not ever going to be able to go all out for a long time." No one should go "all out" for long periods of time, but our stress addiction can make us feel that such behavior is exhilarating when in actuality it is emotionally and physically devastating.

The new field of joyology suggests that our depression addiction is often only the other side, the counterpart, of our stress addiction. Depression is a type of built-in body system brake, a way for the system to shut down just before or sometimes after total emotional and physical burnout. The stress may not have been noticeable to others and may have been a racing of the internal emotional engine, but the burnout is just as severe as if the person was behaving in more obvious and noticeable type A fashion of hurry, aggression, and impatience.

It is possible that we become so strongly addicted to stressful living because it somehow positions us for an intense aftermath of depression. Perhaps we push ourselves just a little further in part because we anticipate the total collapse that will follow, the emotional escape of a completely drained person. In a sense, stress is the foreplay of intense depression.

Question 3: You Should Get The Most Out Of Everything You Do vs. The Value of Just Playing Around.

Super Joy Thinking: Playing around is not something we do as a reward for "really hard work." Noncompetitive, time-wasting fun activities engaged in without full involvement are healthy in themselves.

The hang-gliding husband I met on the beach echoed one of the most frequent ideas of a modern society that blocks our super joy. He felt that we should live "hard," do everything intensely and with vigor. He felt that anything less than maximum effort, even while playing, was a human frailty, a cop-out, missing out on the full range of life experiences.

Our stress addiction, and the counteraddiction of depression, become so pervasive that even a game of checkers can be a life-and-death struggle. "I bid wrong playing bridge," said the husband. "For God's sake, you'd think I just lost our house. She doesn't play bridge, she uses it as a weapon, an arena to act out her need to win."

This husband was identifying a major problem with stress addiction; once we are addicted, we cannot turn the addiction off. It sneaks into everything we do, every activity from how we get up in the morning, how we wash our hair, to how we drive a car or feel while we are driving.

"I knew my stress addiction had the best of me," said one man. "I was stuck in another traffic jam. As I sat there for minutes with not a single move forward, I thought to myself, 'Somebody better be in a terrible accident up there to cause this delay. If this is just a stalled car, I'll kill somebody. I want to see a massive accident.' I couldn't believe what I was thinking, and when I finally got up near the accident, I felt guilty, almost like I had wished this on somebody. But you know what? I sort of thought, 'Well, okay, at least somebody was injured. I guess it was a justifiable delay.' Then I knew I was over the brink."

Try this test yourself. Notice today how you do the simple things, like getting a drink of water, buying a newspaper, entering and leaving a car or taxi. Notice how other people do these simple things. You will probably notice that you and most people are doing things with intensity and rush, not delight. We are chasing our respective white whales, but we are far from enjoying the hunt.

Society has constructed an entire set of stress addiction facilitators. Have most of society's inventions and modern conveniences really made things more enjoyable? Are we mistaking easy and fast for fun and happiness? Have we lost the balance between modern progress and personal joy? Look around you today and see what you think.

The wife of the man on the beach said, "He would never just

hit the tennis ball back and forth with me. He wants to play a game. When he says, 'Let's play,' it seems more like he's saying, 'Let's wrestle.' When we play golf, I beat him, so I suggest that we just forget keeping score. He suggested we just forget playing golf together. Now he fights tennis with his victims and I play golf with my friends."

This example shows just how destructive stress addiction can be to relationships. Joy involves connecting with other people, not defeating them, outracing them, or getting the best of them. Getting the most out of everything you do sometimes involves learning how to get a little less out of some things you do, or being able to "just play around."

Question 4: Being Very Productive Is A Good Personality Trait vs. Avoiding Production Seduction.

Super Joy Thinking: Process is more important than product. We must learn to pay more attention to the "how" instead of the "what" we are doing.

"Ladies and gentlemen, congratulations! You have done it again. You are the highest producers in our entire company. You, in effect, *are* our company. Remember the three Ps: produce, produce, produce!"

This was the opening part of an address by the chief operating officer of one of the largest insurance companies in the world. Such a philosophy has taken much of our joy away, for we now value producers over enjoyers, the performer over the audience, as if each of these elements is separate from the others. One of the highest compliments we feel we can pay someone is to say, "She or he produces."

Imagine a business meeting that includes expressions of appreciation and awards for employees who love doing what they do and who do it well but are not the highest producers. Most of the complaints I hear about companies today is that "you just don't get any service." One reason for the growing lack of service is that we do not see the service process as a product. The "product" has become synonymous with the "bottom line," the payoff, how much money is really made. The bottom line is really the top line, and beneath that line are thousands of people who are too often unhappy doing what they are supposed to be doing.

One of the fastest-growing aspects of computer technology is graphics. Computer screens now flash instantaneously colorful comparisons of where we were, where we are, and where we should be. These graphs show only a point in time, and they hide the real basis of any successful endeavor: happy people enjoying what they are doing.

Productivity is not a personality trait, it is a measure of output. Learning to be joyful depends upon focusing more on input, the enjoyment of how we work, play, and love. It is no coincidence that a slang term for making love is to "score," and men and women may ask if someone "produces" sexually. Love has become something we "make." We have lost the concept of process, and joy is tied to a journey, not a destination.

Question 5: You Should Work Constantly To Improve Yourself vs. Starting Your Own Self-Acceptance Program.

Super Joy Thinking: Self-acceptance is more important than self-improvement. There is no possibility of self-improvement without the prerequisite of self-acceptance.

"That's lovely, honey," said the mother to her seven-year-old daughter as the little girl held up a crayon drawing for her mother's approval. "It's really very, very nice. It's better than the last one, and I know you can do an even prettier one."

The not so subtle message in this mother's statement is that self-improvement is a goal always beyond our reach. We seem to see ourselves as projects in process, thinking that self-improvement is more moral and commendable than self-acceptance. We all share in a cultural inferiority complex that views self-acceptance as arrogance or surrender.

There are very few self-acceptance courses or books available. We are taught that there is always a better way to parent, to love, to work, to walk, or to eat than the way we do these things now. The speed focus of self-improvement gives further support to the idea that how we are now is in immediate need of correction. The two-minute workout, the one-minute manager, and other quick self-rebuilding programs result in a theory of daily living that questions the worth and judgment of anyone who is relatively pleased with how he or she is.

Write down ten of your personal characteristics, habits, or flaws that need correcting. Now write down ten of your characteristics that are not in need of improvement. If you are like most people, the correction list is easier to make than the acceptance list.

I suggest that, while improvement and learning are crucial to the enhancement of the human condition, so is self-acceptance. The largest percentage of people who go to psychotherapists go not in emotional crisis but in search of some way to be better persons, either for themselves or because they have been sent for repair by someone else. Ironically, most good therapists begin by trying to help their patients identify their strengths, not their weaknesses. Good therapists know that people are coming to them in spiritual crisis, asking more about the meaning of life than the meaning of last night's dream. People usually come to therapists in some form of joy crisis, with some sense of something missing from a life that seems fulfilled to others with whom they relate. It is joyology, in a study of where joy may be found for these people in their daily lives, that may hold the most answers. A study of the "spirit" as well as the "psyche," a "spiritology" along with a "psychology," is in order; a discussion of purpose as well as problem seems to hold the most hope.

We seem to be alienated from our own affection for ourselves. We believe that once we lose weight, make more money, or learn some new skill, we will then become more acceptable to ourselves. This sequence is backward. We must begin with a celebration of self, not a diagnosis of our flaws. If you can't say something good about yourself, maybe you shouldn't be saying anything at all until you look a little closer at just how special you really are. The joy response depends on a balance between becoming and being, between self-love and self-growth.

One of the most misunderstood aspects of the so-called "new age" movement is its glorification of the individual identity. Critics assert that such emphasis on self-love is pretentious at best and sacrilegious at worst. In fact, to love oneself is only possible by first learning to love others and by developing a tolerance, acceptance, and empathy that are necessary if we are ever going to get closer to one another than we have been until now. Saying that "we are God" means only that we are aware of the spiritual connection between all of us and the higher power that is all life. Self-improvement has meaning only if it begins with self-celebration, for if we cannot accept how we are it is very difficult to accept how anyone else may be.

Question 6: Wasting Time Is Wasting Life vs. Finding The Time Of Your Life.

Super Joy Thinking: Time is not flying, we are. Time is merely a theory of life, a perception of how things are and what is happening. Time does not exist. We give time whatever power over our lives the concept of time may have.

I walked along the beach on the island of Rangiroa. This is a small, beautiful island in the Tahitian French Polynesian chain. An old Tahitian man resting in a hammock, humming to himself, said, "Why are you walking so fast?"

"I didn't know I was," I answered. "I guess I'm just used to a faster pace."

"A shame," he said. "Time is too precious to waste by rushing it. When you do nothing, there is no time to waste, no time to rush. You are in control when you first do nothing. Then you can decide what you want to do, how you want to do it."

When I work with terminally ill patients I notice that, contrary to popular myth, many of these people choose to sit, to think, to fish, and to stroll during the last months of their lives. They do not typically choose to crowd as much into their remaining days as possible by engaging in constant hectic activity. They create more time by taking time, embracing moments, experiencing being alive rather than urgently trying to live.

To illustrate my point, I ask my patients to try the SDASU technique. This stands for "Sit Down and Shut Up." Just sit quietly for a few minutes without talking, waiting for someone or something, or meditating. Just sit down and be quiet. You will notice immediately that you control time when you stop, sit, and get settled.

Question 7: Winning Is Not Everything, It Is The Only Thing vs. Learning How To Love Losing.

Super Joy Thinking: Winning is not the only thing. In fact, winning is really not anything at all if winning means being first, best, and on top, for winning in this set of circumstances means that many people must lose.

I have never been to a sales meeting where someone has failed to quote the famous Vince Lombardi statement that "winning is not everything, it is the only thing." I recently spoke at a large sales conference where the theme emblazoned on the conference folder and banners was "Rage to Win!" The program began with the loud sound of a human heartbeat followed by the racing of a car engine.

"Gentlemen (and presumably ladies), start your engines!" came the loud announcement to begin the meeting, likening sales to the Indianapolis 500 auto race. At the end of the presentation the audience ran to the coffee break, devoured the doughnuts and coffee, and seemed ready to roll over any competitor. The family of the "competitors" was likened to a pit crew in a car race, and most of the attendees nodded in agreement with this conference theme.

If winning is so important, why does it seem so short-lived? Try to name the last five world champion baseball or football teams. At the time of the competition, everything seemed to ride on winning first place. After all of the cheering subsides, winning is little more than a quick fix, an intense and short high. If the training and practice were not the purpose, not the joy, then winning was only a cheap thrill at the expense of months of work and competition, just another fix in support of our stress addiction, the loss another fix for addiction to depression.

At another sales meeting, I managed to convince the organizers to add to their awards for golfing and tennis competition (for at these meetings even the fun must have winners). I suggested awards for the highest golf score and the most losses in tennis. This "joy of losing" award is now a regular part of many meetings, but I sense that beneath the laughter at the awards ceremony rests a general disrespect for losing. Laughter greets the "joy of losing" winners, while loud applause still greets the "real winners."

Question 8: If You Are Going To Do Something, Do It Right vs. How To Enjoy Incompetence.

Super Joy Thinking: Doing things wrong can be more fun than constantly struggling to do things right. In our eagerness to do things right, we are forgetting to have fun doing things.

The couple were playing a game of tennis. The woman was laughing and her male partner was smiling with every return of the ball. The club pro was watching and interrupted them.

"Sir, sir. Oh, miss. Excuse me. You are both running around your backhands. I have not seen either of you hit a backhand yet. Get the racket back, rotate your grip, and swing through."

"Oh, okay," said the man. The woman did not reply but assumed a tennis-ready position copied directly from the cover of *Tennis* magazine. The smile had left both of their faces, the quality of tennis markedly improved, and laughter was replaced with an occasional expletive.

Our society is committed to the orthodox. The wrong grip, the wrong stance, and you are failing to enjoy the game in the correct way. All of the fun is being taken out of failure. This focus on the orthodox is difficult to understand, because the most outstanding athletes in every sport are typically unorthodox in their approach to their skill. I call this success through unorthodoxy the "Ty Cobb syndrome" after one of the greatest baseball players of all time. Ty

Cobb held the bat incorrectly, threw incorrectly, and violated almost every guideline for being a good baseball player. He was successful because he was unorthodox and had a super joy for playing baseball.

Listen to sports commentators and you will hear some form of the joy of performing as the common denominator among the best athletes. Orthodoxy is only one way, perhaps a beginning first step, for learning to do something. Even then, the true creativity of doing anything in life comes from taking the unorthodox risk.

Our quest for and compliance with orthodoxy relate to the brain's preference for pattern. As I stated in Chapter 1, the brain is lazy and prefers the efficient, quick-stimulus mode of life. Unorthodoxy breaks from pattern, may not be efficient, but may considerably increase our enjoyment, and therefore our success, at whatever we are doing.

Question 9: Doing Several Things At Once Is Getting More Out Of Life vs. How To Cure The "Mad Juggler Syndrome."

Super Joy Thinking: Trying to do many things at once only diminishes the enjoyment of fully experiencing whatever we are doing.

"I can eat lunch, talk on the phone, and balance my checkbook all at one time," bragged the business woman. "Now that I have a car phone, I can drive, work, talk, and think all at once. I never skip a beat." This woman had the "mad juggler syndrome" and was proud of it, but she seldom enjoyed any one of the activities she was juggling in itself and for itself.

Our society values multiples of anything. Multiple orgasms, multiple jobs, and multiple incomes have become standards to emulate. Television commercials glorify the woman who works all day, cares for her family in the late afternoon, parties until dawn, and then returns to work without a trace of fatigue the next day. This mad juggling of life activities is another symptom of stress addiction or of coping with depression addiction through pseudo-busyness, a form of activity jitters that are the stress tremors of the toxic psychochemicals racing through our bodies.

The artifacts of our society give testimony to our valuing of multiples. It is difficult to buy a phone that simply makes and receives calls. Now our phones answer for us, send messages, play music, and tell time. "Multifunction" is a standard line on the cartons of electronic equipment. Imagine an advertisement that said, "This product only does one thing. It does it very well. Thank you for buying it."

Super joy depends on intense focus, on doing and experiencing one thing at a time. Think of the many times you have been distracted during an activity, never fully being able to return to your enjoyment because of the interruption. Have you ever been so distracted by your own busyness and concern for multiple activity that you completely lost a very good feeling you had while you were doing something? Have you ever forgotten what it is you were saying right in the middle of saying it? These are symptoms of the mad juggler syndrome and the brain's fixation on stimulation at the expense of meaning and enjoyment.

We have developed a pseudo-attention, a robotlike trance whereby we do many things but do not really know what we are doing. Take stock of your daily activities and see how many times a day you are doing just one thing at a time. You get more out of life by doing one thing intensely than by doing many things with the minimal emotional contact of a juggler's hands lightly touching the balls as they rotate in their redundant and senseless circle.

Question 10: Being Happy Is The Reward For Hard Work vs. Claiming Your Right To Joy.

Super Joy Thinking: Joy does not have to be earned. Joy is a natural human response, a natural human right. Our basic humanness does not have to be achieved, it must be received.

"You just don't have fun, have fun, have fun," said the wife to her husband. "You haven't done one thing to earn the right to sit there drinking lemonade and reading the paper. Work before pleasure."

Remnants of our puritanical heritage die hard. We still believe that joy is a reward, some form of payoff for work well done. Having fun without first having worked is seen as cheating. TGIF are initials known to almost everyone as meaning "Thank God it's Friday." We seldom hear "Thank God it's Tuesday," because Tuesday is too soon to be thankful, to celebrate, to "live it up," as if we haven't worked long or hard enough by Tuesday to deserve joy.

Young children start out with unbridled joy, but we soon teach them that they must be able to answer the question, "What are you smiling about?" There must come to be some explanation, something that deserves the smile. If we can't give a good explanation of why we are smiling, people think we are either strange or confused. Joyology suggests that super joy does not have to be defended or earned, but rather that joy is within you, ready to come out if you will only get out of joy's way by conquering your Ahab complex.

Check your own thinking about earned joy for a few days. See if you allow yourself to celebrate even if a job isn't finished or a goal completed. Check to see if you believe in the IOU theory of joy, feeling that, if you do enjoy yourself, you should somehow pay for the joy later.

I noticed a man frowning as he ate away at a mountain of ice cream. He looked up and said, "It's okay. I'm going to pay for this by running some extra miles. I promised myself a big dessert if I worked out, but I will work out later." Even though this man was joking, the message of a price tag for joy was clear.

One of my patients joked, "I don't even cut the tags off the pillows I buy. It says, 'Do not remove under penalty of law,' but I'd love to rip those dumb things right off. I know it's silly, but I seem to feel that if I rip them off too soon I might get caught. I always delay doing it until I feel I have earned the privilege. I just always have that accountability feeling." There are no price or warning tags on joy. Rip away!

Question 11: Setting Priorities vs. Making Difficult Choices.

Super Joy Thinking: Setting priorities is only a self-deception. For super joy to happen, we must make difficult choices, not just list our priorities.

One of the most destructive messages from traditional psychology is the concept of priority setting in our daily lives. Setting priorities is really only a system for avoiding the difficult choices we must make about what we want to do and when we want to do it.

When I studied the "priority lists" of my patients, I found that the lists seemed upside down. Those items that the patients saw as their highest priorities received the least attention in terms of personal time investment. Loving, family, spiritual development, meditation and prayer, children, and personal health care and exercise were always near the top of the priorities list and near the bottom of the time investment list. Priority lists become wish lists unless we decide to take the joy risk, to make decisions regarding what we consider to be the most important parts of our life and then act tangibly on those decisions.

One technique my patients found helpful was to list those elements of life they considered to be important to them. Beside each item they were asked to write the major block to making more of a personal investment in these items. I then ask them to insert the word "or" between the two columns. The patients were now confronted with a list of decisions that needed to be made if super joy was to be possible. Try this assignment yourself and see what joy decisions await you.

Question 12: Solving All Or Most Of Your Problems Before You Celebrate vs. Living Comfortably Without Closure.

Super Joy Thinking: If we wait for everything we want accomplished to be completed before we celebrate, we will miss the party of life.

Most symphonic works end with a major chord, the "da da" that gives us a sense of completion and finality. "As soon as the kids are finished with college and I have vested interest in my retirement plan, we are going to start to live a little ourselves," said one man. This "da da" approach to life restricts our joy as we await a major life chord that will never come. The symphony of life is forever an unfinished symphony written primarily in minor chords, and you will not enjoy the entire concert if you live in expectation of a final signal note to begin your joy.

One concept that helped my patients avoid the "da da" phenomenon was to have them schedule immediate gratification of some of their dreams. My patients were asked to make sure that every week of their lives they did something that they had thought of doing only much later in life. "We took a long trip together," said one wife. "We always thought we would travel when the kids were older. It took real effort to arrange it, but we did it. We are going to travel together more now." This couple brought more joy to their lives by playing the music of life their own way and to their own beat.

Question 13: Super Joy Is Only For The Super Healthy vs. Taking The Sickness Out Of Disease.

Super Joy Thinking: You don't have to be fit to be healthy. Even when we are sick, we can find joy.

Our cosmopolitan medicine has taught us that fitness is the same as health. Medicine assumes that the tests it uses are the measures of health, when such tests are merely arbitrary comparative measures of body system function. The dichotomy between health and disease is an artificial one; we are all somewhere on a continuum of health and disease every moment of our lives, not in one category or the other.

We have become health paranoids, and in the process we have lost much of our joy. A key concept of joyology is that it is not only how we eat, what we inherit, how we exercise, and how many vitamins we take that determine our health. There is something intangible, almost magical, that keeps some people healthy even when the body system is not "at ease." Clare, the woman surviving the prison camp, remained healthy throughout one of the most disease-producing experiences imaginable, and she credited that health to her own super joy for living.

Some of the most joyful people I have ever met are people who are struggling with disease. Somehow these people remain joyful, not "sick." They may struggle with pain, fatigue, and fear as all of us do when we are confronting disease, but they have super joy to help them in that struggle. These are the abnormal people, the people who seem strange, weird, and atypical. They have something that carries them through and, like Clare, that something seems to be super joy, the ability to take the behavioral risks that at the same time lead to and accompany a fascination with life, an amazement and youthful wonder at the interconnectedness of us all.

I am not suggesting that we stop taking good care of ourselves. I am suggesting that we care for ourselves joyfully, not out of fear of disease and death. Most people do not have cancer. Large percentages of people will not die of heart attacks or strokes, and of those persons who do, most of them will not have any of the traditional risk factors associated with heart disease. There is something more to being healthy than caring for our physical bodies. We require the nurturing of joy.

I suggest that you make a list right now of how many of your body systems are working well. Even if you are dealing with disease at this time in your life, even a very serious disease, take inventory of your body systems that are working just fine. By congratulating the systems that are working well, you have supported your natural internal healing power. There is a healthy way to be ill, and that way depends on understanding that disease is a natural part of life. Don't forget your health when you're ill, and the joy of well-being can help you get better.

Question 14: Joy Is A Form Of Luck For The Fortunate Few vs. Seeing Crisis As The Most Intense Form Of Growth.

Super Joy Thinking: All true growth comes from crisis. There is an intricate and complex reciprocity between the hideousness of life's traumas and the elation of life's joys.

The waiter at my table was from Indonesia. He had been smiling throughout his wonderfully immediate and caring service, and he was taking time now to talk with me about his own life. I asked him if he had received feedback on a letter of commendation I had sent on his behalf to the main office of the cruise line. He responded that he had never heard a thing about the letter.

"They don't tell us about the good letters. We only hear about the bad ones," he told me.

"That's terrible," I said. "That's not fair at all."

"No," he smiled, "it's not terrible or unfair. It just is."

This wonderful equanimity was characteristic of most of the Indonesian crew on this cruise. They saw life's problems as a part of life experience, not as provocation for anger or revenge.

"How do you manage to take things so calmly?" I asked the waiter.

He smiled again and answered, "We have so many problems that no one of them seems so big as one of yours. If you live with problems, you grow strong. If you live without problems, you don't grow to much at all. You expect good and are angry at the bad. We see only life and living, with the good and bad as part of the world, like storms and sunny days. How could there be happiness if there were no sadness? They are the same. If you are sad, you know someone must be very happy somewhere, because happy and sad are one."

This philosophical waiter was another super joy person. Many of the passengers found him strange, but I have stated that the super joy people always appear unusual. Joy is all around us; we just need to pay more attention to the people who are showing it.

There is a major difference between denying real problems and the avoidance of agonizing over those things we cannot change. Denial is dangerous, for it results from failure to acknowledge facts. Avoidance is healthy, because avoidance is the dismissal from our living of those implications and speculations about which we can do nothing.

Think of the major crisis in your life up to this point. To make the point clearly, write down the event or dictate the details into a tape recorder. Next, no matter how devastating that event may have been, think about or write down positive personal change that came about because of the crisis. This will take considerable thought, but the process itself promotes super joy because it teaches the lesson of the cyclical nature of life, the bad with the good, of personal growth even at times of loss and pain.

Question 15: You're Only Young Once vs. You're Only Young If You Find And Keep Super Joy In Your Life.

Super Joy Thinking: Youth does not have a monopoly on joy. The urgency to pack excitement and celebration into life's early years only interferes with the joy of a full perspective of life as a continuing, changing, unfolding process.

"Man, I'm gonna grab it while I can," said the young executive. "I'm gonna get it before I'm too old to enjoy it." This man exemplifies the ageist orientation of our society, and the fear that aging is synonymous with decreasing joy.

Traditional psychology embraces an adult development theory that suggests a "joy curve." It is hypothesized that a youthful body and mind take us joyfully if insecurely into middle age, where we all have our "crisis," followed by slow and gradual acceptance of failing faculties and the acceptance of death. Look at any chart on human adult development and you will see unhappy, morose words everywhere. Psychology and psychiatry promote the idea that we run like the wind to the top of the aging hill, stop with fear and doubt at the apex of the hill, and then resign ourselves to a slow, boring slide into aging oblivion. This approach does not take joyology into account, the fact that all phases of life have their own joy.

We sometimes mistake the stress addiction of our young people for great joy. My clinical experience indicates that young people are not our most joyful people. If you read the letter to sad young people in Section Three of this book, you will understand that all life has its pressures, and stress and depression addiction is particularly tempting to children and teenagers, who are presented more options than ever before for getting high before they can really get anything straight.

I watched two tennis games being played on parallel courts. In one game between two young women, the ball shot back and forth over the net, punctuated with grunts and the strong ping of the ball hitting the strings of each player's racket. In the other game, between four much older women, the ball seemed to take minutes to arrive at one side of the net or the other. The players talked to one another about various topics even as they played. A missed ball was allowed to roll away and was replaced with a new one from shopping bags kept in the middle of the court on each side of the net. Was one game "better" than the other?

The problem with getting older isn't "being older" but making the long transitions through the aging process in a society that thinks of aging as the last gasp before the end of life. Remember that psychology and psychiatry are fields largely designed and populated by young and middle-aged professionals. Most of the writing and research is done by this group, so their bias, fear, and lack of experience with being older predetermine the mental health movement's view of joy and aging. Self-fulfilling prophecies are as dangerous for older people as they are for children, so don't let the traditional mental health movement take the joy out of getting older.

To understand more about aging and joy, talk with some people who are much older than you are. Ask them how they feel about where they are in life. When I have done this, I have found that older people do not long to be younger. In fact, I sometimes hear just the opposite. "I wouldn't want to go back to that age if you paid me," said one eighty-five-year-old woman. "It would be nice to feel a little better, but I don't remember feeling all that good when I was young anyway. I never paid attention to how I felt. The way I see things now is so much more meaningful than when I was young." This woman represents the general satisfaction with aging that I have noticed in many of my interviews.

One older man said, "Aging wouldn't be too bad at all if our society wasn't so damned afraid of old people." It's the fear, not the facts of getting older, that can block super joy.

Question 16: I'll Enjoy Life When I Retire vs. The Joy Of Early Retirement.

Super Joy Thinking: If retirement means having and taking the time to enjoy life to the fullest, then we should consider retiring throughout life, well before age sixty-five or some arbitrary cutoff point for a societal-assigned living style.

"When I retire, I'm going to get me a small boat, find a big, quiet lake, and fish my brains out every day. No more hassles, no more work, work, work, just live, live, live." This report by a forty-year-old man illustrates the retirement myth of the traditional adult development model. We assume that we will have time "later," and the golden years myth suggests that, after working hard enough for long enough and after sacrificing enough, we will reap our reward of retirement. My interviews with people who have retired indicate quite another story.

"I don't have any more time now than when I was working," said one retired man. "I seem to be going to doctors and struggling to make ends meet. Our society isn't ready for a bunch of old people who don't work. I should be working. In fact, I wish I could have retired until I was about sixty and then started working." Although this man is partly joking, it is true that retirement is not all we are promised it will be.

Financial pressures, distance from family, health problems, the struggle to maintain and establish social contacts, and the too long delayed awareness of our own mortality can tarnish the gold of the years of our retirement. My work with patients indicates that people lead their retirement years exactly as they led their working years. No magic transition from the hard metal of youth to the glow of gold during the later years is likely to take place. You should be leading your life now just as you will when you are retired: working, loving, fishing, walking, and enjoying. Such a life style now is the best retirement plan of all.

Traditional psychology divides life into stages and passages. Joyology sees life more as spiral, with the person circling back and forth through various experiences, up and down, not by steps, but in a pulsating life rhythm of expanding and sometimes narrowing range of life experiences. If we smooth away the step approach to living and replace it with an ebbing and flowing of change and growth independent of age, all of our years can become golden.

Another issue that causes some people to misunderstand the potential of joy in older years is the fear of death. My interviews indicate that the fear of death is a middle-years phenomenon. The younger people I interview seldom consider themselves mortal, the middle-aged people are trying to defeat death by outrunning it, but the older people are typically not concerned with death and have accepted dying as a part of living.

Until our society matures enough to see death for what it is, a transition instead of an end, we will continue to fear death or to lead our lives trying to avoid it. At the very least, we must learn that death has nothing whatsoever to do with age.

Question 17: Joy Is Being Independent vs. The End Of Doing Our Own Thing.

Super Joy Thinking: Interdependence is more important than independence. We have tended to overvalue the "me" at the expense of the "us."

Traditional psychology emphasizes being your own person, pulling your own strings, doing your own thing, getting your head straight, finding yourself, getting into yourself, and a collection of other individualistic approaches to living. I mentioned earlier that self-love is a prerequisite for joy, but loving self can only take place after we are able to love others, not before.

A major myth of old psychiatry is that you must love yourself first, then you can love someone else. Joyology suggests just the opposite approach. Children must learn to love parents, relate to siblings and peers, and in so doing learn who they are as a part of a system, not just as an individual.

I have defined psychology as the study of the id by the odd. The students who select and are selected by graduate psychology and psychiatry programs are not selected for their capacity for super joy or their intact view of the world system. Most psychologists and psychiatrists select their respective fields not only to help others with their problems but to learn how to cope better themselves. Too much of psychotherapy becomes the individual therapist's theories or philosophy of self-fulfillment and self-representation instead of responsive intervention to help people toward a more joyful life in the context of both a world-system view and a model of super wellness.

Psychoanalytic therapy is a particularly selfish approach to attempting to understand life. It was designed by a man who himself was deeply unhappy most of his life and saw joy as equivalent to underlying sexual needs rather than spiritual strength and a connecting with the world. Sigmund Freud was far from a model of health for his patients to learn from.

The traditional analytic practice of talking for hours with a passive listener about one's own views of one's life reinforces the narcissism that sometimes leads the person to the therapist in the first place. Joyology suggests that individual therapy be replaced with marital and family therapy, bringing the system, not just the person, into better focus. The joyology therapist should be a person who is interested in a model of health, not a rooting out of what is incorrectly seen as the dark side of human nature. The underlying assumption of super joy and the practice of joyology is that people are innately good and that what lies deep within them is even better.

A society of selflessness in place of selfishness would be a more joyful place in which to live. If we learned to play games for fun instead of against "an opponent," if we learned to share sex rather than to do it to someone, if we learned to see ourselves in everyone else and overcame our suspicion and a psychologically oriented society's view that our basic human nature is an unhappy, selfish nature, we would be much closer to super joy.

One technique for learning how not to do your own thing is to take one day during which you attempt to see in everyone with whom you interact some feature similar to one of your own characteristics. Listen for voice, watch for gesture, sense feelings of insecurity, fear, and hope that seem similar to your feelings. See how many similarities between yourself and others you can find in one day. We are all much more alike than different, so see if you can experience the joy of finding all of those people who really are just like you.

Question 18: The Childishness Of Constant Joy vs. Changing Emotional Gears To Overjoy.

Super Joy Thinking: It is impossible to have too much joy. Joy is the healthiest, most fulfilling of all human responses. Attempting to contain your joy only results in the loss of the natural joy response. Nobody ever enjoyed himself or herself to death.

"For heaven's sake, Al, calm down. You're acting like a complete fool. Can't you contain yourself?" This wife was talking to her husband as he played in the swimming pool. He was sliding off the pool slide with the kids, screaming with delight as he went under the water, and jumping with glee out of the water, spouting water from his mouth. "Act your age, Al. Everyone is watching," continued the wife. "Do you want to get us thrown out of here?"

This wife was embarrassed by super joy, the complete letting go and regression that come with the celebration of what we are doing. Suspending self-control is not the same as being irresponsible or living dangerously. Only when our behavior interferes with the joy of others has our own joyful behavior truly gone out of control.

Anthropologist Ashley Montagu calls the study of natural childhood fun and freedom "neoteny," and he notes the natural health and immunity that accompany what we call childish self-expression. The new field of "gelontology" is the study of the salutary effect of raucous laughter. Joyology includes both fields of study. Traditional psychology calls such suspension of self-monitoring "regression in the service of the ego," meaning that we can intentionally let go, be free, and reap the benefits of total joy and abandonment of needless restrictions on the expression of our feelings.

You can change your emotional gears to overjoy by just once in a while doing something crazy, wild, and strange. "It may sound like not too much to you," said one woman, "but I walked down the busy sidewalk whistling. I just whistled out loud. Some people looked at me, maybe because I really don't know how to whistle. I just sort of let out high-pitched air through my lips. It wasn't like me to do that at all, but it felt wonderful once I got past the strangeness of the whole thing." Try something like this. Change emotional gears a few times a day, and you will be much less likely to burn out your emotional clutch.

Question 19: Getting High On Stress And Depression vs. Admitting That You Are A Stress/Depression Addict.

Super Joy Thinking: Living hard and fast and then crashing and burning out is accompanied by massive psychochemical changes in our bodies. We can mistake being high or being depressed as the only intense emotional states. Being joyful is different than being "high." Being joyful is being intensely peaceful, no matter how we are behaving externally.

"I flourish on stress." "I'm at my best when I'm under stress." "Stress motivates me." These statements are common, and they reveal the major misunderstanding about joy in our society. The human joy response is not the stress or depression response, it is a unique healing, healthy human response of profound comfort with who we are, where we are, and the satisfaction and even celebration of being human.

My own research indicates that people are capable of running very "hot" and "cold" in terms of their psychochemical porridge. Hot people are prone to what is called maladaptive hyperarousal, with the body going into hormonal overdrive at the slightest provocation. When we are running cold, we are characterized by a learned helplessness, a bathing of the body in the equally damaging cold psychochemical porridge of the brain's surrender to what it sees as a hopeless situation. We can all run hot and cold at various times of the day and for long periods of time in our lives. The joy response is a balance of these hot and cold psychochemicals, a time when the body systems are in almost perfect harmony. We can bring about this balance by thinking in less stressful or depressed ways, by not getting in joy's way.

To admit your stress and/or depression addiction, you must do three things. First, examine your daily emotional style. Are you high, low, or in transition between these two states much of the time? Are you hyperreactive to events at work or at home, with your emotional style dictated by these events or your ruminations about them? Second, acknowledge that being happy or sad can be responses to stress addiction, either happy with the stress or sad with the letdown or aftermath of the stress response. Finally, assess your overall health. Do not look just for major symptoms but also for the Ahab illnesses such as allergies, colds, headaches, fatigue, indigestion, bowel problems, minor infections, and nausea. When you learn the joy response, your general health improves significantly, and you rise refreshed in the morning and fall almost immediately into a restful sleep at night.

In curing any addiction, the most difficult step is acknowledging the existence of the addiction itself. Take that step for yourself, and you are on the way to a healthier, more joyful life.

Question 20: No Right To Joy vs. Passing Your Joy On To Others.

Super Joy Thinking: Joy is as contagious as stress and depression. Our own joy is healing and helpful to others, because it can energize us to help and share with others. Altruism is a major feature of the super joy response.

"I don't know how you can talk about joy when so many people are suffering in the world." The woman said this following one of my lectures on the joy response. "We should be in mourning, not in joy."

I explained to her that being joyful was not a means of denying the suffering of our world or blinding ourselves to the needs of others while we go selfishly on our merry way. We cannot help others, we cannot attend to the needs of the world community, until we are able to be joyful and to be energized by that joy. We cannot know super joy, however, until we are able to help others, to care deeply about the welfare of everyone, and are able to demonstrate our concerns by real helping behaviors, by actually doing for and giving to others. There is no separating self from other.

There is a real biochemical reaction in our bodies when we are altruistic. The immune system is strengthened, and we actually become healthier when we reach out to assist other people. Research has shown that even the simple act of watching someone help someone else results in immediate and measurable enhancement of the immune system.

When we elect our politicians, I wonder why we fail to ask about their joyfulness. Certainly the President of the United States should be a joyful person, someone who celebrates her or his living and is deeply concerned with the welfare of the world. Our country and our world would be better served by leaders who went beyond the plastic smiles and platitudes of promises of prosperity to a legitimate concern for joy in the world. The next time you vote, don't just take into consideration whether or not the candidate is qualified or happy, but ask yourself if that candidate seems joyful in terms of the twenty criteria of the joyology thinking test you have just taken and read about. We are less likely to be led into war if we elect representatives who can help lead us into a shared and responsible super joy.

Do something for someone today. Pay attention to how your body reacts when you help someone. You will feel actual positive changes taking place in the body. Helping someone is one of the best ways to get a super joy high.

A Paradigm Shift for Joy

Now that you have been introduced to the new field of joyology and its principles, have read about the IN A JOY formula that describes the nature of the joy response, and have taken and reviewed the test on joyology thinking, it is up to you to make a paradigm shift that can alter your daily life.

A paradigm is a universal model, a way of believing, thinking about, understanding, and interpreting life and living. Traditional psychology has provided one way of looking at things, based on preventing illness, curing pathology, studying the sick to understand the healthy, and an adult developmental model that sees life in a series of stages going from the struggle of youth through the crisis of anticipation of old age to the final surrender to aging. Joyology suggests that we study the super well to learn how to be super joyful and to delight in our daily living. Joyology suggests that traditional psychology only teaches us to live happily with our addictions to stress and depression, but that we can learn a new addiction, an addiction to joy.

Chapter 4 helps you examine your own joy status, but first I suggest that you take the Joyology Thinking Test one more time to see if you are thinking about daily living in a different, more joyful way. It is change in your thinking that alters the prescription for the natural drugs that will dictate your life and your health.

CHAPTER FOUR

Your Super Joy Quotient

Alas for those who never sing but die with all their music in them.
OLIVER WENDELL HOLMES

Reminders of Lost Joy

Tears streamed from the father's eyes as he laughed harder than he had ever laughed in his life. He hugged his young daughter to his chest, whisking her into the air as he danced a jig of joy. Nothing else in the world mattered at this wonderful moment. All of the pain, all of the hassles of daily living were forgotten. He was one with his daughter again, and she seemed more a part of him now than ever in his life.

Time ceased to exist as he laughed, spun with his daughter in his arms. He felt renewed, invigorated, and more alive than he had ever felt in his life. Every cell in his body seemed to be celebrating this magic and most intense of human events. He was experiencing the most profound of human psychological and physiological responses: the super joy response.

His little daughter was only four years old and for several moments it had seemed that she was lost to him forever. She had vanished from his side as he shopped. When he turned from his impatient search for a part for his car, she was gone. He felt cold, his heart pounded, and he felt empty. His anger at not being able to find a car part seemed for a dreadful period of time to have cost him his daughter.

He began to run through the store, first softly calling his daughter's name and then running faster and screaming as he bumped past startled shoppers. He had read about kidnappings in shopping malls, and now he feared that he had lost his daughter as he groused and swore about a car part.

As he ran, he felt a tug on his jacket. He turned in anger to pull away from this interference with panicked search. No one was there. One more tug, and as the father looked down, he saw his daughter smiling up at him. She was panting from what she thought was a game of chase, and as he whisked her up in his arms he felt reborn.

Whether or not this father would continue to experience the joy response to this degree would depend on his ability and willingness to make fundamental changes in his thinking and behavior. If he could or would not, this reminder of joy would be short-lived, a brief contact with the emotional intensity of joyful daily living that embraces what really matters.

We do not have to wait for these joy reminders, for real or created crises that draw our attention to what is important to us in our lives, but such reminders are typically the catalysts for people who learn to make super joy a regular part of their lives. Perhaps we have become so distant from real crisis, so accustomed to our stressful living, that we are alienated from the intensity of joy. Perhaps we have gradually become a culture of observers, nonparticipants in life's transitional crises. Actors, videotapes, and sporting events serve as surrogate experiences as we watch others cry, celebrate, and even be sexual together.

When life does offer up the joy reminders, they are typically in the form of apparent crisis. At these times we can choose to make the joy we are reminded of a more regular part of our lives or to relegate that joy back to its dormant state. How far within you is your own super joy buried?

Measuring Your Own Joy Quotient

To help you assess the degree of availability of the joy response in your life now, take the following Joy Quotient Test. Use the scale to score yourself on each item, then read the discussion of each item that follows the test. Perhaps understanding your joy within will allow you to find super joy without first having the joy frightened out of you.

The Joy Quotient Test

5 = Almost always

4 = Quite a bit

3 = Sort of

2 = Not much

1 = Almost never

0 = Not at all

1. Do your friends see you as optimistic, as seeing the world through rose-colored glasses? _____

2. Do you sleep in a regular cycle, going to bed and rising at almost the same time every day? _____

3. Do you feel that you have a great deal of energy, almost feeling immortal? _____

4. Do you feel peaceful inside, with a sense of calm and steadiness? _____

5. Are you proud of you? _____

6. Do you eat regularly at set times, in moderate and healthy amounts and types of food? _____

7. Do you awaken with energy, as if something inside you is waking you for the day?

8. Would people who know you say that you are tuned in to them, really able to understand, even sense, how they feel? _____

9. Do you feel sexy, sexual, aroused, and arousing? _____

10. Do you have interest in a broad range of topics, people, and events, and are you clearly aware of what really is important to you? _____

11. Do you adapt easily when things go wrong? _____

12. Do you feel "connected" with others, close to them, and a part of a close group of friends and family? Are you loving enough? _____

13. Do you feel positive about your body? When you look in the mirror, do you like what you see? _____

14. Do you have a rich imagination? Can you fantasize, contemplate, meditate, and make believe? _____

15. When you laugh, do you laugh hard, loud, and long, with tears in your eyes? _____

16. Do you believe in God or do you have a strong set of beliefs about the meaning of life? _____

17. Can you suspend self-consciousness and get so involved in activities that you seem to lose yourself? _____

18. When you hear some types of music, do you automatically start to tap your toe, sway, and even sing or hum along?   _____

19. Do you ask other people what time it is? Do you poke your arm out and tilt your wrist to check the time several times a day?   _____

20. Do you believe in extrasensory perception and the ability to communicate without words, sense the future, and "read other people's minds"?   _____

Add up your score. If you scored 60 or less points on this Joy Quotient Test, you have two choices: wait for a life crisis to remind of your super joy capacity or start making changes in how you live and think day to day. To help you make joy changes now, read the following twenty discussions of the test items above to learn how to have super joy right now.

Question 1: Pessimism vs. Better Vision Through Rose-Colored Glasses.

People think I'm stupid. They seem to equate being optimistic with being out of touch, with not really knowing what is really going on in the world. Well, I do know what is going on, and I can't help it if I think it's terrific.

45-YEAR-OLD WOMAN

We have become pessimistic about optimism. Traditional psychology's emphasis on facing reality has caused us to turn away from our dreams, our hopes, our awareness of the beauty that counterbalances the tragedies of our world. Somehow, reality has been equated with the negative. Learning super joy depends upon our rediscovery of goodness even while we struggle to reduce evil.

Try saying the following statements out loud and see how you feel as you read them:

GOOD WILL ALWAYS OVERCOME EVIL.

ALWAYS LOOK ON THE BRIGHT SIDE OF THINGS.

OUR WORLD IS A WONDERFUL WORLD.

EVERYTHING HAPPENS FOR THE BEST.

LIFE IS ABSOLUTELY FANTASTIC.

If you read these to yourself without saying them out loud, try again. Say each phrase. Some people are so controlled that reading aloud from a book is something they just will not try. For them, super joy will require even more effort if they are to break free of the constraints imposed by an embarrassing and embarrassed society.

As you said each phrase, did you feel silly or phony? Most people find it easier to say negatives than positives, and that cultural orientation gets in the way of joy. Sarcasm and negativism are seen as smarter, more "with it," than hopefulness and optimism. We may even distrust someone who sounds too optimistic, suspecting phoniness or ulterior motives.

There is little joy if there is no ability to maintain optimism, even in a society that marks its history disaster by disaster, funeral by funeral, and scandal by scandal. Check the history books and you will see that the chapters are divided problem by problem. Almost everything is pre- or post- some war or another. When our children read their history books, they are receiving a covert lesson in negativism about life.

Schools use such terms as "probation," "detention," and even the punishment of "staying after school." If staying in school is punishment, just going to school at all comes to be seen as at least a short jail sentence.

Is it possible that the world has become what we expected it to be? Are we artists painting from pallets of dull and dark colors? Do we await an ultimate Armageddon that must precede any final salvation and rejoicing, or can we rejoice in our world now? The world does come to be as we choose to see it, and the choice of optimism or pessimism is one not of fact but of belief. Super joy is the belief in good, in better ahead, in the power of all of us to make things even better.

A mother brought her twin boys to a psychologist. "They're the same in every way, right down to the last freckle," said the mother. "But there is one big problem. Roy is the eternal pessimist. Everything is rotten to him no matter what we do or say. His twin brother Tom is just the opposite. He's the eternal optimist. Help me, Doctor, to balance them up. Make Roy more optimistic and Tom a little more pessimistic."

"That's easy," said the doctor. "For Roy's birthday next week, give the little pessimist a roomful of the best toys in the world. On their shared birthday, give Tom the optimist a pile of horse manure. I know it sounds strange, but toys for the pessimist and manure for the optimist. That will balance them out."

The mother reluctantly complied. She and her husband prepared the boys' bedrooms as instructed. On the boys' birthday the parents quietly looked in on Roy the pessimist. There he sat with all the magnificent toys. "What junk!" he said. "There are too many things here to play with. My parents must have something up their sleeve. I hate this stuff. They can't buy me off."

The disappointed parents moved to Tom the optimist's room. There sat Tom, happily digging through the manure. "You can't fool me," said Tom, looking up at his parents. "Where there's manure, there must be a pony!"

This old story illustrates the role of perception in the quality of life and the nature of human experience. We set the stage for what will happen to us by what we expect to happen to us.

I have noticed a contagion factor regarding optimism and pessimism. For some reason, pessimism seems more contagious than optimism. Negative rumors seem to travel faster than positive rumors, and most rumors seem negative. So-called "pity parties" are easier to have than to have a consensus of joy.

Rose-colored glasses are better for your outlook and your inlook than black or gray lenses that filter out the ultragood waves of joy. Remember the principle of joyology which stresses the fact that we come to feel as we think and behave. We have more control over how much joy we have than most people imagine, but it is what we imagine that plays the major role.

Question 2: Escaping To Sleep vs. Awakening To Your Dreams.

> I love having long and boring business meetings. That's the only time during my workday when I can tune in to my thoughts. I sort of get in this posture that makes people think I am listening. I can even nod my head automatically, like one of those toy dogs in the back window of a car, but I really am gone. I just get these ideas, these weird, strange ideas, but sometimes they're the best ideas I have. I don't think business could survive without very boring meetings. There would be no time for real creativity without them.
>
> 52-YEAR-OLD BUSINESSMAN

One of the best indicators of mental health is how well we are sleeping. Every psychiatrist asks the patient about this, and we all seem to know instinctively that something is not right when our sleep is disrupted. Sleep, however, is not only an indicator of health, it is also one way we can enhance our super joy.

Sleep is one of five ways we can "alter" how we interact with our world, a time when all relevant stimulation comes from within. These five unique receptive styles are:

Sleeping: A period of completely shutting off the outside world. This may be a time when we compensate for physical tiredness, allow time for cell and general body repair and protein synthesis that rebuilds the body's store of energy. As yet there is no one completely accepted theory about why we sleep, but I suggest that sleep is one escape from our stress and depression addiction, a healthy form of "blacking out" for a while.

Dreaming: Called REM sleep because of the rapid eye movements that occur with most dreams, this is a time when we seem to become mentally reorganized and to make up for our mental tiredness. I have found that joyful people tend to dream more or at least remember their dreams more often and more completely than less joyful people, perhaps because joyful people have more daily practice with altered states of consciousness and mental imaging.

Daydreaming: When outside stimulation is not novel enough or stimulating enough for us, we begin to daydream. We create our own novelty from within. My joyful patients seldom report "daymares." Their daydreams are usually positive, having to do with wishes, hopes, and needs for intimacy and joy.

Hypnopomping: This strange-sounding word is used by sleep researchers to refer to that time just before we are completely awake and during which our mental images tend to be a mixture of dream and our own created images. This is an excellent time to be creative, not just a time when we are getting ready to get up for the day.

Hypnogoging: This equally strange-sounding word refers to the time just before we are asleep when our images are a mixture of dream images and our own controlled thoughts and concepts. Like hypnopomping, hypnogoging is a creative time. It is possible that we can direct the movies of our dreams by making additions or changes to the images of the hypnogogic state, thus prearranging for a certain type of "theme dream."

There is very little evidence that sleep itself is sufficient to restore us to a state of being rested and energized. Some of the most fatigued people I know sleep a great deal, yet their energy for life is less than those people who sleep far less. Scientists do not really know completely why we sleep or even why we awaken, but we do know that sleep is only one of at least five phases of rejuvenation. If you pay more attention to all five of the receptive states above, you can come up with new ways to be more joyful by finding some ways of thinking and things to think about that may be original and unique to you.

Question 3: Slowly Dying Away vs. The Rediscovery Of Sudden Life.

I went to this death and dying program. Everybody said you had to confront your own death, your own mortality. We even wrote our own obituaries and gave eulogies for each other. I guess we have to face up to death, but I can tell you that sometimes I would just as soon forget the whole idea and let it surprise me.

35-YEAR-OLD WOMAN

Humans are the only animals that know they will die. It is one characteristic that makes us human. Traditional psychology has focused on death and dying, even suggesting death wishes and developmental stages for accepting death and the grieving process. Children used to worry about their parents dying. Now children worry about their own deaths. The crisis of teen-age suicide recently receiving more attention may reflect in part a cultural fixation on the intensity of endings more than on the joy of process.

A society that has rules for exciting "sudden death" playoff games has little interest in the fact that such games are actually "sudden life" games that allow both teams to continue playing for just a little longer. Perhaps we fail to have all the joy we can have from the living process because of our fascination with dying. Our life energy sometimes seems to be dying out as we accept psychology's theory that life exists as a straight line from energetic beginning through slowly deenergized aging, to the final end of death. The mental health sciences of psychiatry and psychology have trouble seeing things in cycles, preferring steps, lines, starts and finishes. If we accept this premise, our energy will gradually seem to run out.

The mental health movement has focused our attention on death without providing insight into death's meaning. We have been deceived by the false religion of a mental health movement that wants us to know that we will die without helping us understand why. Our mental health may depend on the acceptance of death, but super joy and extraordinary mental hardiness depend on seeing death as a natural transition to another state of existence, on finding meaning in dying as a passage, not as a dropping off into nothingness. If death means nothing but an end, how could there be any joy in living? If death means a transition, a part of the endless cycle of the human spirit, we can celebrate the process of being alive.

Just as sex therapists thought that talking about sex somehow made us sexually healthier, psychology seems to think that being able to talk about dying makes us more ready for death. Unless we find meaning for the human experience in a larger, more infinite context, there can be no super joy. The questions we ask as children, including "Where do we go when we die?" and "What happens to who we were?" are the key questions for adults, and we fool ourselves if we think that the stoic acceptance of our passing will ever be acceptable to the human psyche. Your super joy quotient is much higher if you can explain with hope and even peacefulness what happens to you when you die.

Question 4: "In It Too Far" vs. Getting Into Getting Out Of It.

> I met this woman at the health food store. It must have been an act. She was so peaceful, so centered, so quiet. I just wanted to yell at her to see if she would jump. She just smiled, and she spoke with such a quiet, calm voice. It made me feel like I was a raving maniac. I was trying to hold one kid, catch the other, balance a bag of groceries, and pay for my new supply of stress vitamins. She must have taken three dozen of them. Can't you overdose on calm?
>
> 34-YEAR-OLD MOTHER

We have created two special categories for people who seem too calm, easygoing, or at peace. We either see them as lethargic, passive people who are "missing the boat" or we see them as religious gurus who have fine-tuned their karmas, strange people with strange outlooks on life. In a society that is more accustomed to the siren than the serene, we seem uncomfortable when people are "out of it." We want them "in it" with us, sharing our stress addiction by yelling, rushing, doing, scheduling, and otherwise frantically searching for whatever "it" is.

We have lost our tolerance for doing nothing. We want to know what is wrong with someone who is "just sitting there and doing nothing." Ask any parent and they will tell you that what they want more than anything else is "a little peace and quiet around here." Parents love it when their children are quiet, yet parents also get suspicious when things get too quiet. Is there a parent alive who has not, at one time or another, yelled at the top of his or her lungs, "Quiet!" as if the louder the yell, the more likely the chance for peace?

When we yell "Quiet!" internally, we call for the depressing chemicals that counteract the stress chemicals. Our addiction to depression is a form of psychochemical self-anesthetization. When we can't take the external or internal stress chatter any longer, the internal pharmacy sends out a dose of quieting "downers." The more frustrated we are with the stress of our lives, the more welcome and addicting these downers can be. This stimulus overload and need for shutdown cycle explain why the stress and depression addictions go hand in hand, and why super joy is the only effective antidote for this SAD (stress and depression), not-so-merry-go-round.

One reason we have trouble with our peace and quiet, our "Ps and Qs," is that we seem to believe that we must earn our Ps and Qs. We feel that we must "deserve" a rest, after qualifying by hard work or play. Super joy depends on being quiet, on doing the SDASU technique (Sit Down and Shut Up) mentioned in Chapter 2 at least once a day, whether we feel we deserve it or not.

If we begin every day with a moment of silence, if we learn to speak more softly, we actually lower our blood pressure. We literally seem to put our hearts into everything we say, and perhaps overstress our hearts by how we say it. New research suggests that systolic blood pressure elevation is not as insignificant as doctors once thought, and that how we talk directly influences our blood pressure.

Diastolic, the bottom or second number reported when you are told your blood pressure, has been seen as the primary risk factor for stroke and heart disease. Now doctors suspect that the first or top number, the systolic pressure, is equally as important for risk of stroke and sudden death, and that is the blood pressure reading that goes up the quickest when we yell, talk loudly and fast, or speak angrily.

New research shows that less than half of patients receiving medication for systolic high blood pressure had their blood pressure significantly lowered, while almost three quarters of patients who had elevations in both systolic and diastolic blood pressure responded to medication. I suggest that the very rapid and intense rise in systolic blood pressure is a symptom of stress addiction, a type of stress addiction spurt, and the only medication that will work well against this type of high blood pressure comes from our own brains in response to our behaviors. When we lower our internal and external activity level, we can "depressurize" our lives. Super joy involves just such a quieting process.

Question 5: A Little Self-Disrespect vs. Enhancing Your Reputation With Yourself.

> My mother is proud of me, my father is proud of me, my children are proud of me, but I forgot to make me proud of me.
> 42-YEAR-OLD MOTHER

We have mislearned that positive self-regard is dependent on outside criteria, how others see and evaluate us, and how we see others seeing us. When I ask patients how they feel about themselves, they typically respond with evaluations determined by other people's assessments. While what other people think is important, super joy depends on a self-reputation determined not only by others' evaluations of us but on self-reflection on our own worth.

When I asked one man what he thought of himself, he responded, "I'm bright, make a good living, and take good care of my mother."

"Who says so?" I asked.

"I say so," he answered angrily. "I make more money than most people I know, I have been promoted twice this year, and my mother has every one of her needs met."

"Oh," I answered. "I thought you were telling me how you felt about you."

"I just did. What more proof do you need?" the man answered.

This man was unable to see that his feelings about himself were based almost totally on his views of other people's assessments of him, on criteria of comparison rather than self-established criteria for self-worth. We struggle to find self-value based on our own criteria. Even children learn too soon that their value becomes quantified, by a letter grade, a clean room, or positive evaluation by someone else. We have lost sight of the innate value of our humanness, how special we are because we are.

To experience super joy, we must recognize that the positive aspects of our self-esteem are not always those elements that earn us status, money, or success. We will never treat others much better than we treat ourselves. If we can be just a little easier on ourselves, maybe we will be just a little easier on one another.

Try complimenting yourself. Just think of how much capacity you have to care, to love, to hope, to help, to protect others, to be there when others need you. Don't lose sight of your innate value as a human being because you are busy trying to qualify for worth in someone else's eyes. Super joy is a celebration of self even as we show our caring for others.

Question 6: Consumed By Our Own Diet vs. A Diet Of Joy.

You have heard of the Mouseketeers? Well, I started the "dieteers." These were a bunch of my friends in the neighborhood. We tried every diet together. Of course, that didn't work, but we had fun talking about it.

35-YEAR-OLD TEACHER

Most people believe that we are what we eat, but we are also "how we eat." The toxicity that blocks super joy is due not only to a contamination of the body system by artificial food additives, empty calories, and junk food but also to our eating style.

We have all experienced mood shifts correlated with what we eat. Our stress addiction is supported by a related stress diet of fast, "hot" foods that lift us up quickly. Our depression addiction is supported by "cold" foods that have calories but little health value. When we are in our depression addiction phase, we either gorge ourselves so that we can barely move or stop eating so that our energy level falls.

Many of us eat when we ought to, have to, or when it is "time." Analyze your eating style and see if your eating is joyful, functional, or even problematic. Joyful nutrition has the following characteristics:

Joyful Nutrition

1. You eat with other people, whom you like.

2. You eat slowly.

3. You talk only of pleasant things when you are eating.

4. When you eat, you eat. You do not write, work, or talk on the phone.

5. You take time after you eat to be quiet and rest, allowing your body system to adjust to this major biological process.

6. You don't eat to change how you feel. You eat because you are hungry.

7. It is quiet where you eat.

8. You focus on the taste of each food you are eating.

9. You taste, chew, and swallow one type of food at a time instead

of putting something in your mouth even before you have finished what you are already chewing.

10. You don't drink alcohol or inhale cigarette smoke while you are eating.

Simple as this list seems, most of my patients with eating problems violate almost all of the above steps. Chapter 4 will go into more detail on the toxicity of what and how we eat, but remember that your own joy quotient raises when you enjoy the natural processes of life like eating and sleeping.

Question 7: Burning Up vs. Spiritual Glow.

I feel like getting up before it is time to get up. It's like I can't wait for the day to start. I have had a good sleep, and I have usually been awake about an hour getting ready to get out of bed, almost waiting for the day to catch up with me. It's not that I'm hyper or anything, I just seem to have a new energy.

26-YEAR-OLD WOMAN ACCOUNTANT

We have mistakenly equated energy with behavioral style. True energy is an energy of the spirit, an energy you can sense in people even when they are sitting quietly. Energy is not what you do, it is how you are.

There is a difference between high energy and stress addiction. When we are addicted to stress we feel driven, forced to keep going. When we have the energy of super joy we feel as if we can choose what we want to do and how intensely we want to do it. The "have to" of the stress response is replaced by the "ready to" of the joy response. The energy of joy is characterized by a feeling of choice, as if we can go to our abundant energy bank whenever we want to. Stress energy feels as if our energy account is getting low but we must keep making withdrawals.

When we have joy energy, we may feel energy for prayer, meditation, for just sitting. It seems that there is a joy light burning, that we have plenty of spiritual, not just physical, energy to do whatever we choose to do. Stress energy seems more like physical energy and we can almost feel the physical energy drain from us if we lead stressful days.

The energy of super joy comes from a strength of spirit, a willingness, even a craving, to be surprised. Science fiction author Frank Herbert wrote, "The joy of living, the beauty, is all bound up in the fact that life can surprise you." When we are running on stress energy, surprises are simply additional demands on our diminishing physical energy. When we are running on super joy energy, surprises are the fuel for the spiritual fire within us.

Question 8: Extra- vs. Undersensory Perception.

I have learned to really see things now. I have been around the world and to places that people only dream about, but I don't think I saw a thing until I stopped looking with my eyes and started seeing with my heart.

57-YEAR-OLD MALE DENTIST

"It's magic!" said the little girl. "The rabbit is gone. How did he do it, Mommy? How did he do it?"

The magician answered for the mother. "The hand is quicker than the eye, darling. Much quicker than the eye."

The magician was wrong. The eye and the light that stimulates it are much faster than the muscular movements of the hand. What the magician really meant was that we have not really learned to see at all. We are too willing to see whatever people want us to see, whatever the stress-starved brain needs us to see, rather than what we want to see and hear. We all seem to have a degree of what psychologists call ADD, attention deficit disorder.

Children and adults who experience ADD are said to be inattentive and are sometimes given stimulating medicine to promote better attention. My clinical experience indicates that persons with ADD actually pay too much attention. They use one sense intensely, watching or listening to one thing or one event with more acuity than persons who do not have ADD. The problem is that our society expects all of us to listen a little, watch a little, and generally combine a wide range of mini-attentions. The ADD person focuses one sense almost too intensely—for example, not watching enough but listening "too much." Perhaps the ADD person is actually overly attentive, focusing too much on whatever has his or her attention, and not as multiply attentive to many things at once as most of us typically are.

"Look at me when I'm talking," said the teacher to the student with ADD.

"Why?" asked the student. "I'm listening, not looking."

"You can't listen if you aren't watching," answered the teacher.

"I can't listen when I watch. I get too distracted," was the answer.

Try looking at one thing, a stone or a flower, for a long time. See if you can use one sense at a time. After intensely looking for a few minutes, close your eyes and just touch the stone. See if you can focus on just touching, seeing with your skin. Apply this same principle to your interactions with people. If you are going to listen, really listen. Contrary to popular psychology myth, you don't have to look into someone's eyes to listen to him or her. Try closing your eyes when you listen, and try to really listen for every inflection, every subtle tone of the message. This is practice for curing our undersensory perception.

More people have ESAD than have ADD. ESAD is extrasensory attention disorder. We all have the ability to "sense" things, and it is not spookology to try to develop our abilities to receive messages beyond sound and light waves. So much of our daily experience is intense that we have numbed our extrasensory perception. Just like what happens when we listen to loud music too long and have trouble appreciating softer music afterward, we cannot use our extrasensory perception if everything in our world is loud, fast, intense, and "super sensory."

We all have psychic ability. Joyology emphasizes this ability, but traditional psychology scoffs at the possibility of psychic process. Russell Targ and Keith Harary write, "The best scientific research suggests that the capacity for developing genuine psychic abilities lies latent in many, or perhaps most, people." Super joy involves super perception, and you will raise your super joy quotient if you will open your mind to the complexities and sensitivities of its own eye.

Question 9: A Joy Of Sex vs. The Sex Of Joy.

We bought the book *Joy of Sex,* but it was about sex, not joy. We tried some stuff that you could sell to Ripley's Believe It or Not. We've got a great sex life. Now we're ready to work on the joy part.

38-YEAR-OLD WOMAN

It is possible to have sex without joy, but the joy response depends upon sexual fulfillment. Sexual fulfillment means sharing bodily pleasure with someone you would like to share life fulfillment with, someone who matters deeply to you over time. Our society has refined sex into a series of phases, from fore- to afterplay, and we have focused on learning to do sex right. The fear of AIDS causes some people to ask new questions about their sexuality. "Does with whom and why we have sex also make a difference?" These same two questions are the joy questions about sexuality.

Being intimate is joyful and healthy. The fear of AIDS should not force us to surrender, to seek intimacy as an escape from exposure to a deadly virus. We must learn the joy of intimacy in its own right. Bodily communication, sensuous interaction, is one of the most intense sources of joy because it is a tangible way of connecting with someone else, of celebrating the verification of the physical existence of another person and our infinite connection with that person.

There is no joy until we connect on a physical level with someone else. Touching, holding, and caressing are super joy prerequisites. We all cry out against isolation, as we scream when the umbilical cord is cut. There is something in us even at birth that does not accept the wall that poet Robert Frost wanted down. You make a quantum leap in your super joy quotient when you physically connect with someone else.

Question 10: Blowing Our Minds vs. Cerebral Unemployment.

I just can't get interested in anything. I have more toys at home, from tennis rackets and golf clubs to an unopened box of watercolor paints and an unused easel. I've got the means, but not the motive. I can't get my interest up and, if I do, I can't keep it up. I have interest impotence.

42-YEAR-OLD SALESMAN

Our society relates external intensity of stimulation with degree of interest. If we want more interest, simply turn up the magnitude of the stimuli. As a result, intensity has gone up and up, and we have become "dys-interested." Our interest has been broken and taken from us, surrendered to manipulation from outside, and we are addicted to a hot running world that provides stimulation for us whether we want it or not.

So much is done for us that we have now gotten used to having our thinking done for us. Researcher David Krech writes, "The scientist has no corner on wisdom or morality." We are all scientists, but too many of us have stopped our research on life and living. We are so addicted to getting things done quickly and efficiently that we have come to fear the mistake making that keeps us learning.

It has been said that experience teaches you to recognize a mistake when you've made it again, but we are allowing others to make our mistakes for us, taking our learning risks and therefore the joy of learning in our place. Author Barry LaPatner writes, "Good judgment comes from experience, and experience comes from bad judgment." If we continue in our stress and depression addiction, we will never have time to know how our world works because we will be too busy or too down to take the risk of new learning.

"I don't have to know how anything works. I just have to know how to use things." This remark by a busy executive illustrates how far we have distanced ourselves from the basics of life. We feel that we don't need to know how things work anymore, just as we don't have to know why a drug gets us high. Some of us have spent all of our faith on a trust in the workability of things, leaving little faith for a trust in a higher purpose for our living. The broader our knowledge of how things in our world system operate, the more we are a part of that world system, and the more opportunities we have to celebrate life's innate efficiency and the genius of our evolving human culture.

To know joy we must recall the joy of knowing. We must get some of our news from reading, not just from two-minute segments on newscasts. We must pay attention to how our government works, not just watch television to see if anything is happening in Washington that might affect us. We must understand the principles by which the artifacts of our culture operate, become participants as well as consumers. We must put effort into understanding and being involved in the workings of the world around us, not just use that world as an arena for our stress addiction.

Question 11: Led By Life vs. Enjoying Life.

Did you ever feel out of whack, like you're just not going along right? If men had menstrual periods, I would be highly irregular. I feel like I'm in a movie and the sound track is a few seconds off.
49-YEAR-OLD MALE STOCK CLERK

The Chinese have a concept called "chi." It refers to the flow of life energy, the natural way things are and will be. Super joy relates to being in tune with the chi, with the flow of life, rather than trying to create that flow. Like a person who is drowning but only has to stand up in the shallow water to be safe, we continue to flail away at living, seldom sensing the ebb and flow of natural life rhythm, never understanding that things don't "happen to us" but just "are." Traditional psychology's rigid line of life mentioned earlier dictates our day-to-day view that we are moving through life rather than the fact that life is moving through us.

"I can't stand an uncut, untrimmed lawn. I like things done right," said one man.

"Are you kidding?" said another man. "I never cut my lawn. I did once, but it grew back."

"I don't know how you can stand it," answered the first man.

"I don't know how you can't stand it," answered the second man. "Why do you go against what happens naturally?"

"It's not natural to have an uncut lawn," answered the first man.

"Who do you think did the landscaping for the Garden of Eden?" answered the second man.

"God did," said the first man.

"He does mine too," said the second man.

Length of lawn, hair, or beard is not the issue, but attitude toward natural life processes is a key issue to a more joyful life. Super joy requires equanimity. We must learn to let much more go by than time.

How much of your own life is "natural"? Do you feel in sequence with the dance of life and living? How much of your time is spent trying to control natural processes, going against the natural flow of things?

Consider one of the most frequent unnatural behaviors we engage in: jet travel. Crowding two hundred people in a silver cylinder and blasting them across time zones is not a natural process, but many of us have come to expect to fly coast to coast and be "on time" for a meeting on a Monday when we leave on Sunday. We struggle to perfect our air travel, to fly faster, keep tighter schedules, totaling our miles so we can earn free flights for our vacation. Visit your local airport as an observer and draw your own conclusions about the naturalness of the struggles you will see there.

With all of the reports of problems with air travel, the first governmental attempts at intervention have been about improving airline punctuality. The quality and safety of air travel, any issue of potential joy in air travel, are not seen as priorities. Traveling is not viewed as something to be enjoyed but as something that must be done, just as we view life as something to lead rather than to experience.

Super joy may depend on longer lawns, longer travel time, and our collective ability to say "enough" to a society that continues to make stress addiction a prerequisite for success.

Question 12: Falling Apart vs. Being A Part.

Did you ever feel just out there somewhere? Did you ever feel like everyone else was invited to planet earth, but you were an uninvited guest? I just don't feel like I belong anywhere sometimes.

18-YEAR-OLD COLLEGE STUDENT

One of the most important of the six IN A JOY characteristics of the super joy response is connecting, joining, not only with someone else but on a universal level. One of the most destructive world influences is ethonocentrism, an "us-them" or "me-it" approach to life.

Recently the crisis of the increasing damage to the ozone layer that protects our earth from lethal ultraviolet light was confronted by a governmental bureaucrat who offered a very simple solution. "People should wear hats, a sun screen, and dark glasses," said the man responsible for advising the President of the United States on policies regarding the environment. Not only is this a ludicrous suggestion in consideration of the magnitude of the problem, but this man's viewpoint demonstrates the anthromorphization of our world. Did this man think about the plants, the animals, the people in the world who may not have time to go to their local shopping mall before some global deadline?

All disease is ultimately a form of disconnection. When we behave as if we are not a system within a system, we get sick and cause sickness. As you consider your own super joy quotient and apply joyology thinking to your own life, be sure you find your place among us all by behaving and thinking in ways that not only take others into account but give them equal billing with you.

Question 13: Outside Interference vs. Signals From Inner Space.

> If Moses had seen my body, he would have brought down a few more commandments. I not only look bad, I feel bad. Everything hurts at one time or another.
>
> 62-YEAR-OLD WOMAN

Our society provides strong sanctions against causing pleasure for our own body. Warnings from our parents are clear. "Don't touch yourself, stop picking, stop playing with your hair." Our parents ultimately fail, of course, for we all privately study, touch, and explore our bodies. Our bodies are such miracles that it would be impossible for us not to sneak in some secret exploration when we get the chance.

"I never take a bath," said one man. "I shower. It's fast, efficient, and I feel much cleaner. It uses less water too."

"Don't you ever just sit in the tub, rub soap all over your body, and enjoy yourself?" asked his woman friend.

"If I want to touch a body, I call my wife," was the man's answer, illustrating his difficulty in understanding the importance of appreciating his own body.

How often do you touch yourself gently and slowly? Does even the suggestion of self-touch and -appreciation create some anxiety? Women have been given more cultural permission for this type of body joy than men, but even for women the touching and self-coddling are tolerated by our society as a form of preparation of the body for someone else's enjoyment, not as a means of self-celebration.

When we are injured, our first reaction is to touch the site of our pain. One of the most healing touches of all is our own healing touch, our tender attention to our own bodies, lingering over special areas that we find attractive, strong, healthy, or hurting, sore, and in need of comfort. Touching ourselves is a way of closing the circuit between mind and body, of making the circuit complete, of letting the mind and body know each other more intimately.

Question 14: The Hot Facts vs. The Value Of Self-Deception.

One thing about fantasizing is that you never have to worry about
being caught and it's absolutely free. I can go anywhere in the world
on my frequent fantasizer program.

40-YEAR-OLD MAN

We have come to view reality as superior to fantasy, somehow
more mature and healthier than illusion. The hot, stressful daily
stimulation we encounter is seen as the only reality. Actually, fantasy is as real as what we think is the only reality, just as a dream is
real for the dreamer.

Who is to say what is "real"? Democritus wrote, "Opinion says
hot and cold, but in reality there is nothing but atoms and empty
space." Does this mean, then, that hot and cold does not exist, that
they are pure fantasy? When more than one thousand people think
they see a statue move and thousands more think they see the face
of Christ on a brick wall, are the three or four scientists who were
never there to see these "illusions" stating "fact" when they report that such things cannot happen?

The experience of Clare in the prison camp was affected by how
she perceived, thought, and fantasized about that experience.
When we think about a threatening situation, the body responds
no differently than when that situation is actually encountered.
When we think arousing sexual thoughts, the body shows tangible
signs of those thoughts, just as if the object of our sexual excitement were present. The body and brain respond to our pro-
grammed thought, our input, just as intensely as they respond to
the outside world.

A mother came to me for help with her child. She began to
describe how upset this child made her feel. "If he were here right
now, I'd be terribly tense," she said. "My blood pressure goes up
and I just get tight all over." Even as this woman spoke, she
showed the same physical signs as if her son had been in the room.

Understanding that our perceptions create our world is a difficult but fundamental step in learning super joy. The brain prefers to describe things and people as "out there," separate from itself. In fact, we determine what the brain receives through our thoughts. Reality is created, it does not "exist."

A major reasoning error that blocks the joy of fantasy is that there is only one reality. "What is, is, and that's that" is our approach. Modern physics teaches and documents that there are multiple realities, worlds within worlds that obey differing and sometimes contrasting laws. The laws of the quantum world are not the laws of Newton's world, yet both sets of principles are "true." Our stress addiction causes us to think that only what we can see is real, because what we can see with our eyes is convenient, easily available stimulation that fits well into the brain's prewired optical paths. When we have to use our other senses, our "extrasensory senses," we must work much harder to break free of the set of rules that govern our daily see/touch world.

The most magnificent finding of modern physics is that we create our own reality, that the observer directly alters whatever is observed, yet this finding goes largely ignored or even ridiculed as a new age fad. When psychiatrists say a person is "out of touch with reality," they usually mean that such a person is behaving in inappropriate ways. We are never out of touch with reality, we just have the capacity to deal with different realities, create different realities at different times. Unfortunately, we are too spiritually nearsighted to see clearly the multiple levels of human experience that can allow us to use our imagination for super joy.

Question 15: Running Scared vs. The Importance Of Regular Jogging Of The Intestines.

I love laughing. Once I get going, there's no stopping me. And when I get going, everybody comes along. My laugh is a strange one. When I laugh, people laugh at my laugh, so I start laughing even harder. That makes my laugh even stranger, and on and on it goes.

50-YEAR-OLD MAN

What a human response laughter is! Almost everything in your body that can pulsate begins to do so. At least five major muscle groups begin a rhythmic movement. The body temperature goes up at least one degree. The glottis and larynx begin to rock, and air rumbles up along the windpipe, banging against the trachea, exploding out of the body at almost seventy miles an hour. Immediate and intense relaxation follows. Laughter is a public announcement that super joy just took place.

Stress and depression addicts develop a pseudo-laughter. Listen and you will hear the hollow, phony laughter that some people use as social interaction. Real laughter happens to you, you don't "do it." Young infants laugh by ten weeks of age, and six weeks later the child is laughing almost once an hour. By about four years of age, the child laughs once every four minutes unless we have managed to interfere with his or her joy development.

In my research for this book, I examined fifteen child development textbooks used by the major colleges in the United States. While all of the books discussed childhood humor, none of them discussed the development of joy. How and when the child sits up, walks, gets toilet trained, learns to read, interact with others, and become independent are described in detail, but there is a total lack of the stages of joy development. Parents have seen the joy developmental stages clearly, and the following system outlines a general sequence of joy development.

The Stages of Joy Development

Joy Stage One: Status Joy.   Joy with just being alive, with the wonder of a general contentment in just "being." Babies coo, gurgle, and emit other little announcements of their joy in just "being."

Joy Stage Two: Reactive Joy.   Laughter and giggling at body processes such as urination, defecation, and the passing of air. This is a recognition type of joy, celebrating everything from burps to bubbles.

Joy Stage Three: Care-taker Joy. Recognition of the care taker and a gleeful greeting of her or his presence. Babies let their joy in the parent's presence be clearly known, and any attempt at separation brings a strong protest at the disruption of this profound joyfulness.

Joy Stage Four: Interpersonal Joy. Laughter and smiling with people other than the care taker.

Joy Stage Five: Peer Joy. Screaming and laughing with joy with other children.

Joy Stage Six: Object Joy. Enjoying toys, pictures, and environmental stimulation such as storybooks, flowers, cars, and trains.

Joy Stage Seven: Self-joy. The capacity to celebrate the child's own activities and accomplishments. At this phase, the child is vulnerable to sanctions against being "too happy" with herself or himself.

Joy Stage Eight: Matching Joy. Laughter and smiling because others seem joyful. This is the stage at which an empathy with the joy of others and a joy in causing joy in others emerges.

Joy Stage Nine: Measured Joy. A major joy developmental transition stage, this is the time when the child learns just how much joy a person is supposed to have and show and where and how it should be shown. Joyful role models are most important here, and you may want to ask yourself if you are modeling joy as a parent and who your joy model was or is.

Joy Stage Ten: Dispositional Joy. Super joy style of delight with life. If there were a medical term for this stage, it would be something like "status joyous," as the person integrates all of the above phases of joy development into his or her own personality joy character.

These general guidelines are not the "steps" in joy development but phases of a continuing joy developmental cycle. As an adult, you continue to recycle through these same phases, each of which is a particularly vulnerable time in a child's development. Some children and adults develop joy blocks and are unable to continue through the joy cycle. Others become fixated at one phase of joy, unable to enjoy the full range of the super joy response. Review the joy cycle above to check for your own block and fixations. If you find some areas where your joy development is impaired, you can go back to the particular joy stage and practice that type of joy to break your "joy block."

Question 16: Believing What You See vs. Seeing What You Believe.

I don't really believe in anything I can't see.

23-YEAR-OLD MAN

I have trouble seeing anything I don't believe.

86-YEAR-OLD MAN

The great sculptor Michelangelo believed that the sculptures he created were encased within the unsculpted marble, waiting for him to bring them their freedom. He believed the images within the rough marble were waiting for him to give them life. Was he right? Certainly, remarkable images appeared from within the rough marble as his hands brought them forth. Was it Michelangelo's skill or his belief that caused the images to emerge?

Without his great gift, skills, and training, the beautiful works of art would never have appeared. Without the belief that the figures were someplace "in there" waiting for him to give them life, none of Michelangelo's masterpieces would have seen the light of day. Belief is the one ingredient that is the catalyst for the admixture of psychochemicals of joy to work their magic and replace the stress and depression addiction cycle.

The Michelangelo factor illustrates psychology and psychiatry's suspicion of the supernormal. Certainly a man who saw images within marble would be examined closely by psychotherapists for signs of mental illness. Persons who could not see such images would be considered "normal." Where would our great art and music be without all of the "abnormal" people?

Not since the work of pioneer psychologist William James in his book, *The Varieties of Religious Experience,* published in 1902 has psychology paid much attention to the search for the meaning of life and the value of a transcendent belief system. Although almost three billion people are members of the major religious groups of the world and are influenced strongly in all that they do by their formal religious beliefs, psychology and psychiatry have largely ignored spiritual issues in favor of an emphasis on "getting in touch with our feelings." When an examination of the mental status of a patient is conducted, nothing is asked about belief in God, in a power and meaning beyond what the doctor may see as "reality."

Psychologist Abraham Maslow represented an exception to the traditional psychological approach. He stressed the importance of belief and focused his writing on what he called "eupsychic" factors: the factors that help us transcend mere mental health to function on a level of extreme mental and emotional well-being. Many psychologists consider such concerns as "mystical" and beyond the legitimate range of the study of mental health. In private, many other psychologists are pursuing the study of the extremely well.

The search for meaning is the search for joy, and the new pseudo-religion of modern psychology and psychiatry cannot replace our human need to believe in something more, to live with the hope and faith that belief is not a human frailty but the ultimate human strength. My patient, Clare, said, "If you didn't believe, you died. That's all there was to it." Clare's belief carried her through her suffering and allowed her not only to survive but to bring her super joy through the experience with her.

Mental illness does exist, and traditional psychology and psychiatry are at their best in dealing with sickness. Even in the treatment of mental disease, however, psychotherapists tie one hand behind their back by ignoring belief, faith, and the search for higher purpose by those who are mentally hurt.

Saul Bellow, in his Nobel prize acceptance speech, pointed out that he believed that his inspirations were drawn from an ebb and flow of energy drawn from a universal energy. He added that we have trouble talking about such things as universal energy because our language fails us. He said, "Few people are willing to risk talking about it. They would have to say 'there is a spirit, and that is taboo.' "

Pianist Arthur Rubinstein talked of his interaction with his audience as a metaphysical power, a tangible energy at his concerts that seemed to float between himself and his audience. This description of "something more" is discussed by every great artist, scientist, and writer. Buckminster Fuller said that God is a verb, a process of active believing, loving, and living in harmony with all others, and super joy is that process of tuning in to the "something more" that these great people were describing.

The word "mystical" is from the Greek word *mystos*, meaning "to keep silent." Unlike the stimuli that constantly bombard and feed our stress addiction, the source of nurturance for super joy is silent and difficult to describe in words. The current interest in so-called "new age" thinking represents the popularization of this inner need to make connection with that something more that we all know exists.

Rupert Brooke wrote, "Behind the night . . . somewhere afar, some white tremendous daybreak." Do you believe in that daybreak? Are your eyes too blinded by the flash of bombardment from outside to be able to see in a softer, quieter light?

Question 17: Getting Serious vs. Taking Ourselves Ridiculously.

I feel so self-conscious most of the time. It's not like everybody is watching me. It's like I am always watching me.

28-YEAR-OLD MAN

To be joyful is to be free. The O in the IN A JOY formula in Chapter 2 represented an openness to risk taking for joy. We seem to be paralyzed by our stress and depression addictions, rigid and sometimes afraid to let ourselves interact freely with others and our world.

"You should see my husband try to dance," said one wife. "He dances like he has a coat hanger in his shorts. He just will not let go, let up, and dance away." Super joy requires a freedom of movement not only of the body but of thought and emotion. Traditional psychotherapists again suspect "too much" looseness in living and relating, labeling some people as "emotionally labile" because they have such intense changes of emotions and show them so openly. While a minority of people do have trouble controlling their emotions and end up hurting themselves and others, the risk to super joy is that too many people have too much control of their emotions.

I entered the rest room at a major airport. The counter was very long and the room seemed empty. As I began to wash my hands, I heard a terrible singing voice belting out a song from one of the stalls. The words to the song were totally made up, and there was no rhythm or sense to any part of the song. As I pushed the button on the hand-drying machine, the singing stopped. As I turned to adjust my luggage, I saw an image in the mirror of a man hurrying by. He seemed flushed and embarrassed. I finished strapping my luggage on my shoulder, and as I did, the same man rushed back in, frantically searching stall to stall. He finally grabbed the briefcase he had left behind and, avoiding any eye contact with me, managed to run out of the room before the heavy swinging door closed from his entering push.

I saw this bathroom singer once again by the airplane gate, and he looked away, no doubt praying that we would not be sitting beside one another on the plane. He had "let loose" by mistake, assumed he was alone, and now wanted to find only complete anonymity for his debut as a closet singer.

We have learned to take ourselves too seriously for joy. We are embarrassed by our very human nature of playfulness and childishness. We are not too shy to run wildly through an airport to catch a plane, but we are reticent about letting anyone hear our bathroom singing voice.

Question 18: Being Out Of Tune vs. The Rhythm Method Of Joy .

> I can't help myself. I not only move to music, but I sometimes start
> to hear a beat when there is no music at all. I can start to walk in a
> rhythm, talk in a rhythm, even begin to snap my fingers or play my
> desk at work like a drum. I guess I just got rhythm.
>
> 40-YEAR-OLD WOMAN

Most people agree that music has a strong healing capacity, and I
use it regularly in my work with patients and in my lecture-con-
certs. In almost every case, people respond to the sounds and the
beat, and they feel intensely with the music. They cry, sing, move,
and laugh. If you have been to a top-notch performance of an
opera or concert, you have probably noticed that something very
special can happen there. People suspend for that brief time most
of their worries and become part of the intangible energy that
Arthur Rubinstein identified. The audience becomes one, and the
performer addresses the audience as one.

Check your own rhythm of life. Just sit quietly and start tapping
your hand, snapping your fingers, or tapping your foot. What is
your beat today? Is it too fast, syncopated, too slow, irregular?

Question 19: Out Of Time vs. Being "Just In" Time.

> I just can't find the time,
>
> 22-YEAR-OLD MAN

> All I have is time.
>
> 60-YEAR-OLD WOMAN

Anthropologist Edward Hall describes what he calls M-time and
P-time cultures. We live in an M-time, or monochronic, culture,
meaning that we do one thing until time "runs out," as if time was

a line and we have come to the end of the line. Other cultures are on P-time, what Hall calls polychronic time. In these cultures, events end when they end, without reference to when they ought to end or when the time line has "run out." Super joy depends on our learning to run on more P-time, becoming less dependent on clicks of the clock as the directors of our lives.

Most people have heard about the "twin paradox," an example used to illustrate Einstein's theory of relativity. It is a fact that clocks in motion—all clocks, including the human heartbeat—are altered by our motion through life. If one of two twins could take a trip to space at light speed, that twin would be younger than his earthbound brother when the space traveler returned. The traveling brother's biological clock moved slower because of the speed with which it was traveling, so his brother's clock went ahead of his.

As I pointed out when I discussed the new joy thinking in Chapter 3, time is something we create. The personal internal clock of the hot running person, the stress addict, runs slower than the personal clock of the depression addict because the stressed person is traveling so fast. The stress addict would never mature if it were not for the inevitable depression crash that resets his or her clock.

The depression addict ages rapidly, feeling older, more tired, and less energetic than his or her stress addict counterpart. Depression causes us to move emotionally slow, and our biological clock speeds up. Our heartbeat, brain waves, and blood pressure are all "clocks" altered by the time we choose to keep, the speed with which we travel through our own space. Super joy is a healthy rate of travel, ageless and marked by the metronome of the spirit, not the external demands and the digital clocks flashing their demands to continue our SAD cycle of up and down addictions.

QUESTION 20: Being In A State vs. Altered States.

It's funny how you can be in a different state of mind day to day, even hour to hour.

30-YEAR-OLD WOMAN

Psychologists have researched what they call "deautomatization," or breaking away from ordinary day-to-day consciousness. As I discussed in Chapter One when I reviewed the principles of joyology, we are capable of functioning on many levels of consciousness. When we are stress- or depression-addicted, the consciousness altering is done for us by our brains. When we learn super joy, we choose our level of interaction with our world.

The current drug problem in our culture is related to artificial attempts to achieve altered states of consciousness. People who use drugs are trying to alter their own brain chemistry through mechanical means. There is a pattern to drug use in our society, and this pattern perpetuates addiction to the wrong drugs.

First, researchers have found that a drug is introduced by a minority of people within society, usually a small fragment of that society who seek to alter their consciousness. Next, the drug is condemned by society, usually because of the altered consciousness states shown by the users of the drug. Finally, society accepts the drug, probably because using artificial or what I call the "NBM drugs" (non-brain-made) is easier than working for super joy in order to alter consciousness through our own elective addiction to healthy psychochemicals (the BMDs or brain-made drugs).

We have developed a consciousness and drug carousel in our society. Stimulants, from coffee to amphetamines and cocaine, are used to get us going. Sugar and junk food are used to keep us going. Analgesics such as morphine and even aspirin are used to ease the pain of our stress or depression addiction, since it is possible to be addicted to the BMDs. Psychoactive drugs, such as marijuana, mescaline, and LSD, are used to alter our mood state so we can endure the side effects of our stress and depression addiction.

Psychotropic drugs from the "establishment" medical field, such as antidepressants, antipsychotics, neuroleptics, lithium, and methylphenidate, are used to maintain what society thinks is "normal consciousness." Finally, barbiturates and alcohol are used to help slow us down from this maddening up-and-down pattern.

Super joy is the ultimate human state, with BMDs or brain-made drugs serving as the drugs of healthy addiction. When we learn super joy, we learn how to write our own prescription in the form of an addiction to life and living, not to artificial mood states.

Now that you have considered twenty aspects of your own joy response, determined your own present super joy quotient, read about the tenets of the new joyology and the six IN A JOY characteristics of the super joy response, you should be drawing up a new cognitive map for joy. With this new map, you are ready to learn about the psychochemistry of super joy as it compares with the psychochemistry of other human responses. As you did in Chapter 3 with the Joyology Thinking Test, I suggest that you retake the Joy Quotient Test in this chapter before moving on to Chapter 5. Check to see what effect the discussion of each question and the new examples of the joyology principles and joyology thinking are having on your own super joy. I hope I have succeeded in helping you begin to change your mind, your self-view of daily living, so that you can help your brain learn about super joy.

CHAPTER FIVE

The Psychochemistry of Super Joy

> Man, this stuff is great. If you could bottle this, you'd make a million bucks. Now this is getting high!
>
> 42-YEAR-OLD MAN

Getting High on the Right Stuff

There is a drug to which we should all become addicted. It is more than two hundred times stronger than morphine, yet all of its side effects are healthy. It is more addictive than the refined opiates such as heroin, yet the addiction you develop actually enhances your immunity to disease and promotes healing when you are ill. It produces a euphoria unlike any other human experience, a sense of well-being and strength that is unparalleled in any drug you can buy on the street, yet this drug has been pretested for thousands of years for safety and toleration by your own body. This drug can make you high and mellow you out, serving as an "upper" and a "downer" at the same time, but you will never stay too down or too up for too long because the drug is self-regulating. This drug is the strongest painkiller in the world, and it is capable of diminishing both physical and mental pain simultaneously. This drug alters the way you view the world, but the resulting perceptions

110

enhance your life rather than distort it. This drug is absolutely free, totally healthy, and completely legal, yet people use this drug very little.

The drug I am describing is our own brain-made set of psychochemicals called the endorphins. There are probably more than two hundred different neurotransmitter systems in our brains related to the endorphin pathways, the drug factory inside the brain. We currently understand about three dozen of these natural pathways in which are produced the BMDs, the brain-made drugs I mentioned in Chapter 4. The highs and lows that the endorphins produce are actually related to alterations in the way the brain pays attention to its world and what we tell our brains to pay attention to.

Super joy is a super attention to our living. Super joy is accompanied by an endorphin balance that allows us to free ourselves from the anticipation of mental and physical pain that seems to dominate our life. The stress and depression cycle I have been describing is really an addiction to fear, the fear of mental and physical pain. We run fast to outrace our fear or we withdraw to avoid such pain. We behave anxiously or depressed as a result of the brain's misguided strategy for avoiding what it fears most, the pain that may signal the end of the system in which it lives.

The brain's fear for its survival is an unrealistic fear, one that dominates most of our lives as we become afraid not of real pain but of what we come to symbolize as potential death. Fear of failure, of not being loved or not loving enough, and fear of rejection dominate our brains' concerns.

Most of the time such brain fear is totally without merit. When the boss yells at us, the brain thinks that its body is going to be killed. The human brain is in a constant state of "pain flinch," and as a result we are stressed or depressed as the brain's maladaptive coping style attempts to outrun or hide from threats that are not as severe as the brain thinks they are.

At the moment of death, researchers suggest that the brain may "dump" all of its supply of endorphins. Patients who have been near death report intense feelings of peace and even joy, perhaps related in part to the endorphins finally overwhelming the brain's fear. At what the brain views as the inevitable end, it decides to tune out completely, secreting its complete store of endorphins to cause complete distraction and inattention.

Special People and the Problem of Attention

I have noticed that learning-disabled children with whom I have worked often came to therapy with bumps and bruises. When I asked if they were in pain or if they could tell me how they got hurt, their response was typically, "I don't even remember how I got that." The label of attention deficit disorder may relate to different patterns of endorphin secretion in ADD children and adults, a pattern we do not yet understand but carelessly try to medicate away with artificial stimulants and other psychiatric drugs. Could a more effective treatment be more joy with the accompanying better balance of endorphins?

Schizophrenic patients also experience a different type of attention to the world than most other people. These patients also often have cuts and bruises they are unaware of, perhaps again related to different patterns of endorphin secretion in this population. The emotional problems of the schizophrenic patient, and possibly patients with other mental disorders, may relate to disregulation of the brain's endorphin production system, some type of joy disorder that results in an accompanying endorphin imbalance.

When I have worked with children and adults who have been diagnosed as mentally impaired or retarded, I have noticed two characteristics that relate to the endorphin patterns. First, these persons seem capable of intense joy, super joy. Their glee and laughter are sometimes boundless. At the same time, their attention span can be extremely limited. Is this inattention related to an imbalance, perhaps an excess, of endorphins that in turn affects other brain chemistry?

We have not even begun to understand the endorphins and other neurochemicals of the brain. These special drugs interact in complex ways, causing and resulting in stress and depression. Intentionally changing how we think and behave can have a profound impact on our own brain chemistry, but we must first be willing to become our own pharmacists and prevent our brains from automatically interacting with the world without our intervention. Talking to your own brain, letting the "self" be much more than a brain reflex creation, is the major first step in learning super joy.

A Visit to the Brain's Drug Factory: SAD, SAM, PAC, and WAM

Understanding how the stress and depression cycle works in relationship to the joy juice of endorphin can help us learn more about super joy. To break free of our stress and depression addiction cycle (SAD cycle), we first have to recognize the emotional dance we perform throughout our lives.

Our brains are dedicated to maximizing stimulation and keeping us alive. When the brain senses a drop in what "it" (not the "self" but the brain) considers a sufficient level of stimulation, it becomes insecure, concerned that it will not receive enough stimulation to stay alive. To protect itself, it starts the SAM cycle. We have become victims to this psychochemical overreaction which was once necessary to save us from wild animals but now causes us to go wild within ourselves.

SAM stands for the sympatho-adreno-medullary system. The sympathetic nervous system interacts with the medulla or middle of the adrenal glands, and a small brain within the brain, the hypothalamus, releases a substance called CRF, or cortico-releasing factor. This CRF signals the pituitary gland where it triggers the release of ACTH (adrenocorticotropic hormone) and accompanying stress hormones. The endorphins react to this secretion and are released in high doses, which means that the more stressed we get, the less we can pay attention. When we get too high we tune out. The more we tune out, the more the brain "thinks" it needs even more stimulation, and the addiction cycle has begun, as the brain actually ends up confusing itself and possibly stimulating itself, and therefore us, to death.

Eventually this SAM system, if unchecked, results in our getting sick. The immune system is impaired when the SAM system runs too long in high gear. There are only two reactions strong enough to defeat this SAM stress addiction pattern: depression and super joy. Depression is an escape from the immediacy of living, a shutdown of the system. The PAC system, representing what is called the parasympathetic-adrenal-cortical system, accompanies and both causes and is activated by prolonged depression and the related personal pressure experienced in this addictive state. The hypothalamus again directs the process, but this time the body goes into a slow burn, as the parasympathetic nervous system communicates with the cortex or outside of the adrenal glands. We become addicted to this state because it comes to feel "natural," a way of "getting by under severe pressure." Our attention is reduced even further and for longer, and we come to acclimate to being "out of touch."

Super joy is accompanied by a balance of the SAM and PAC systems and is accomplished by what I call the WAM system. WAM stands for being "wiser and mellower." We can learn to talk to our brains, tell them to think more clearly. Tell them that they are not as threatened as they think they are, that they do not need as much stimulation as they think they do, so we do not have to outrun imaginary tigers through our stress addiction. We do not have to hide in an emotional cave as an addiction to avoidance of daily living.

We can be wiser if we become aware of our ability to tell our own brains what to do. Super joy is the realization that the brain serves us, and that its theories of what is happening to us are archaic, based on the law of the jungle that the brain evolved in, and not on the rules of relationship, intimacy, and joy. We can be "mellower" if we learn to be aware of the SAD cycle of addiction, the involuntary stress-to-depression-and-back-to-stress pattern of response to our world that neglects the presence of a "self." Super joy depends on the self, the "spirit," the "us" within that relates to what you are reading now even as the brain collects the light reflections and processes them for you.

Doing What You Think and Thinking About What You're Doing: The Five "Other" Human Responses

Breaking the SAD cycle and learning or relearning the super joy response requires more than the thinking changes I described in Chapter 3. Some major behavioral changes must be made as well. We not only come to feel as we think, but our behavior must match our thinking. If we think one way but behave another, the brain we are trying to reprogram gets mixed messages and usually selects out the stress and depression behavior rather than any super joy thinking we may do. Remember, the brain prefers efficiency, so it will typically take the easy way out. The SAD addiction cycle is the easy way out, and also the fastest way out of this world, owing to stress-induced illness and the eventual failure of our immune and healing systems.

Self-help books have focused on five major human responses that are designed to "result in joy." An examination of each response illustrates what happens when our behavior and thinking are not consistent with one another. Exercise, sex, relaxation, eating, and prayer or meditation are the five major human responses that have received the most attention in popular psychology books, but when any of these five responses is processed through the SAD cycle (stress and depression cycle), it loses any value it may have for our overall wellness.

Examining each of the basic five human responses from the point of view of stress, depression, and super joy illustrates the importance of the "self" being integrated with what we are doing, thinking, and feeling. One reason so many people have trouble accepting the existence of a super joy response is that they are fooling themselves daily through a set of behaviors or rationalizations that prevent them from seeing that there is more to life than the addictive cycle into which they have fallen.

People who confuse happiness with super joy are typically allowing their brains to speak for them. The brain is happy, content with the efficient SAD cycle, but the spirit is neglected because what is being thought does not match what is being done and felt. Happiness is the brain's contentment with its addictive cycle. Super joy is the spirit's freedom to go beyond the stress addiction to an addiction to a healthier psychochemical balance.

The Exercised Body and the Neglected Spirit

Exercise influences not only our physical health but also our psychochemicals. When we are in the stress phases of our SAD cycle, exercise can have one of two effects. If we exercise out of obligation or fear of illness, hurrying an exercise program into an already overcrowded life, exercise only increases our stress-addiction chemicals. This is one reason our society has created "exercise machines" and seems so "hooked" on health. The new exercise machines allow us to "get our exercise quickly." These machines are poor approximations for the bending, lifting, stooping, and running of the real-life activities that we are paying people to do for us while we use our machines. We are busy earning the money to pay the people to do the exercise that we have to do on machines because we don't have the time to do what we hire the people to do.

If we exercise as a form of escape from stress, fooling ourselves that exercise is a way of "getting away from it all," we fail to confront our stress addiction directly and simply by some time through a physical focus to our stress addiction. We bring on a pseudodepression with our after-exercise fatigue or a pseudolift through our jogger's high, but we do not confront "how" we are living. The human spirit where joy is, the "self" I have been talking about, still has not dealt with an overstressful life.

The key question to ask yourself about the value of any exercise program you engage in is, "Am I having fun?" If we exercise with true joy, laughing and making exercise a part of the world and people around us rather than huffing and puffing alone to "stay fit" or "look trim," the exercise benefits us with an increase in the healthy super joy chemicals.

Watch the joggers run by. You will see two types of runner. One looks stressed, pushed to the limit, fighting for health. He probably will not even acknowledge you as he passes, even expecting you to get out of his path. Another is smiling and may wave at you as she runs by, moving slightly aside to avoid inconveniencing you. The difference in these styles illustrates the difference in the effect of exercise on the psyche of the exerciser. We would have much more super joy if people would say, "I'm going to play," rather than, "I'm going to work out." Even as you walk alone in the morning, that walk will be much healthier if you look around you at the people, the plants, the grass, and the sky rather than paying attention to your pulse rate and the appropriate pace and walking style.

It is important to learn to exercise, not out of obligation or fear, but as a means of physically celebrating our humanness and our relationship with the world around us. We should be exercising our spiritual strength as well as our body strength, being sure that our exercise is not only good for our body but good for the whole system.

Having Sex vs. Experiencing Our Sensuality

Sex books are popular. Most of these books tell us how to "do it better," how to "master it" or be a "better lover." With all of the talk about sex and the abundance of "sexperts," it would seem that people would now be happier than ever with their sex lives. The patients I see continue to feel incomplete sexually, even if they have found every magic "sex spot" and learned every technique. The problem relates to the fact that sex is being processed through the same SAD cycle, with very little joy involved.

When we attempt to fit sex into the stress phase of the SAD cycle, we typically encounter mechanical breakdown. Something goes wrong in the sexual response system. We may ejaculate too soon, not experience orgasm, or find ourselves unable to respond at all. This happens because the stress chemicals block human sexual response. We may try to "force" ourselves to be sexual even when we are stressed, trying to keep up some self-imposed version of the national average for sexual intercourse, but we only end up feeling incomplete.

When we attempt to be sexual in the stressed phase of the SAD cycle, we typically do not have time to allow ourselves to make sexual interaction a priority or to respond to a naturally occurring sexual response to another person. We typically have sex at night, after all the "important things" are taken care of. Sex becomes an afterthought, more after-work than foreplay, and we develop a sexual anesthesia.

When we attempt to be sexual when we are in the depressed phase of the SAD cycle, we do so typically in response to pressure from someone else. When we are depressed, our interest in sex may lessen considerably. Even though we feel alone and isolated, sex does not seem to be a way for us to make connection with someone else. Instead, sex almost makes us sadder, causing us to withdraw from the brief glimpse sexual interaction gives us of what life can be like when we love and show that love.

Sexuality and super joy are characterized by feelings that our sexual interests are a part of our life interest. Everything seems to arouse us, not just genitally but spiritually as well. The sky seems bluer, the sun brighter, and our lover sexier. When sex and super joy combine, there is no one time or place for sex; we just find ourselves responding to our closeness with someone else. Super joy sex is not something we do or have, it is an experience we share, a way of saying, "You show me your spirit and I'll show you mine." There is nothing in life more intimate than spiritual connection demonstrated intimately and sensually.

The Joy of the Relaxation Response

Herbert Benson researched what he called the "relaxation response." He described this response as a state during which a person was quiet, breathing deeply and slowly, and focusing on one thing, such as a number or a simple phrase. Benson later extended his theories about the relaxation response to emphasize the importance of the spirit, reporting that some special word or phrase that has meaning to the belief system of the person should be used during the relaxation response.

The popularity of the concept of a relaxation response resulted in thousands of people trying to relax twice a day for twenty minutes: brief pauses in the SAD cycle. It was a response that seemed perfect for a stressed-out generation, a type of Gatorade for the stressed system, a quick and efficient gulp of relaxation and then back to the war. Just as sex and exercise cannot work their healthy effects out of the context of super joy, so the relaxation response has become a type of stress-addiction drying-out period following which people return to their stressful lives.

If we attempt the relaxation response when in the stress phase of the SAD cycle, we actually end up rewarding ourselves for being stressed. We stress ourselves all day and then, as a reinforcement for our stress, we offer the body a "mini-nap." These stress-nap cycles only allow the stress level to gradually increase over time.

My patients who have tried the relaxation response as a "quick rest fix" almost always fail to continue using it, because their stress is rewarded by a quick relaxation fix. Their stressful lives actually become more stressful, punctuated by mini rest escapes. Some of my patients experienced more stress when trying the relaxation response because they now took the time to think about all the things they hadn't done, shouldn't have done, or still ought to do. Some researchers have recorded blood pressure increase during the relaxation response attempt, indicating again that we cannot fool ourselves about our SAD addiction.

When we attempt the relaxation response during the depressed phase of the SAD cycle, we sometimes only become more pensive, more hopeless, and more withdrawn. When we are in this stress-reactive down phase of the addiction cycle, the relaxation response may cause us to go even lower. Relaxation is *not only* a body technique for stress reduction, it is potentially a time for spiritual balancing and cleansing.

When we use the relaxation response with super joy, it becomes a time of quiet celebration. We are not "getting away from it all," but instead we are becoming more a part of the world than at any other time. We are not tuned out but completely tuned in. We are not focusing on our breathing, a number, or a mantra, we are just "being." We intentionally shut our brains off, free from the constant cerebral chatter that clutters our day. Just as with exercise and sexuality, it is not just what we do but why and how we do it that seems to determine the health impact of the basic human responses.

Eating Yourself Up and Down

No other human behavior seems as immediately responsive to the SAD cycle as eating. Our eating behavior when we are stressed is seriously disrupted. We may forget to eat, then eat quickly, then eat a big meal, then not eat for a period of time, so that eating becomes something we do that accompanies stress rather than something we do for nourishment or pleasure. Food becomes almost a necessary evil, another stress stimulus, a fuel we must stop for in our hectic trip. This taking on of fuel while the engine is running causes physical symptoms and disruption of the natural aspects of eating.

When we eat when we are stressed, we eat to "keep ourselves up." When we eat when we are depressed, we eat to "get ourselves up." Food becomes a stimulus, something we "take in" without having to "reach out." Eating becomes a passive ingestion. Unlike stress eating when food becomes a stressor to be coped with, depressed eating causes food and even the act of eating to become ritualized, almost a necessary evil or at best an escape into a redundant oral gratification. As a result of this escape, involvement with other life activities diminishes.

Super joy eating has five characteristics. First, less food and fewer calories are ingested. Very little junk food is eaten, and few so-called empty calories. There are a minimum of the so-called "mood-altering foods," such as chocolate, caffeine, sugar, and artificial additives. This reduction in quantity and improvement in quality is due to the fact that actual food itself becomes only sustenance, something we need to keep us alive. The eating becomes more important than the "fueling." We need less food because our SAD cycle is not burning up our energy. We don't fill the tank as completely, but we eat at a higher octane. Food does not take on any other meaning than nutrition.

Second, joy eating is slow eating, because what is enjoyed is not the amount of the food but the eating process. Tasting, chewing, drinking, smelling, and resting during eating are characteristic of joy eating.

Third, joyful eating is shared eating. People who enjoy the eating process almost always eat with someone else, not discussing business but discussing the eating and pleasant, happy issues.

Fourth, joyful eating is regular eating. The joyful eater eats many times a day at scheduled times. There is no eating "on the run," few missed breakfasts, lunches, or dinners, and almost never gorging or feasting. Small, multiple, regularly scheduled meals seem to be the joyful and healthy pattern of nutrition, sometimes referred to as "gleeful grazing."

Fifth and finally, joyful eating is hassle-free eating. There are no arguments or confrontations, just pleasing company in a quiet atmosphere enjoying a natural process together.

Communicating with the Not So Far Beyond

Everyone attempts to communicate with a higher power, something "beyond," even if that beyond is inside us. Call it meditation, contemplation, prayer, or just talking to "ourselves," each of us sometimes tries to talk in some way with someone or something that we can't see or hear, something beyond our see-touch world.

When we are in our stress phase, our "cosmic communication" is as rushed as we are. We tend to use what I call "power prayer." We may demand that somebody out there "listen to us!" There may be an anger in this prayer, a defensive, doubting prayer exemplified by this patient's prayer:

"God, if You're there, give me strength. If You're not, give me strength anyway. I've got to close this deal. God, help me at least this once."

This impatient and skeptical prayer illustrates the irony that stressed people may doubt the existence of a higher power and feel that they themselves must do it all, but nonetheless turn to "something or someone more" when the going gets really rough. At the most difficult of times, the stressed person looks beyond, uncharacteristically looking for power outside the behavioral realm to the spiritual. The stressed person may deny a belief in something more, but I have never interviewed a patient who didn't make some attempt to reach out or reach in for spiritual help.

In the depressed phase of the SAD cycle we tend to use what I call "passive prayer." The depressed person prays out of surrender, not the near demand of the stressed person. Depressed prayer reflects a lack of self-power and feelings of being undeserving of power from a higher source. The following depressed person's prayer illustrates my point:

"I've tried my best, Lord. I don't know why I'm chosen to suffer like this, but I trust in Your wisdom. If You see it as possible for me, please help me."

This person's prayer illustrates the helplessness and hopelessness of the shutdown phase of our human addiction cycle. The prayer of the depressed person is more an appeal than an attempt to communicate with a higher power, an attempt to mobilize spiritual power.

Some form of praying is as natural a human response as the other four responses discussed here. In my clinical work, I always ask my patients to share a recent prayer with me. They may not call what they do praying, so I usually ask for an example of something they may say to themselves in private when they feel they need something more than they have available to them at the moment. Even the most rigid atheist is able to share a prayer with me.

The stressed person is typically sending prayers, the depressed person is typically attempting to receive some message, and skeptics about spiritual issues seem to send "insurance prayers," as in this example from one of my atheist patients:

"Okay. I'm praying. I don't believe in God or anything more than what is here right now, but just in case, please take care of me and my family if you're there."

When I asked this patient about his prayer and who he was talking to while praying, he answered, "I'm not talking to anybody or anything."

When I pressured him on this issue, asking what image he had in mind as he said these words, he answered, "No image, I'm just talking to my inner self. But don't get me wrong, I don't think there is anything spiritual about this whole thing."

When I asked, "You mean, until I asked you, you had never prayed and you never pray now?" he answered pensively, "I pray, I guess. I just don't know to what or who. I just do it just in case, just sort of as a superstition or something."

So the most skeptical person sometimes attempts communication on a different level than the see-touch world. Everyone is aware of "something more." Super joy prayer is more a celebration process involving a sending and receiving system. The joyful person prays regularly and there is a clear idea of to whom or what he or she is praying. Patricia Weenolsen of Seattle University categorized persons' definitions of the meaning of life and their spiritual orientation as follows:

1. Cosmic Specific: This involves a belief in one God, a supreme being who created and directs all life.

2. Cosmic General: This is the belief that there is a "force," an overall energy, that directs all life, a general overall life energy system not necessarily in the form of a single deity.

3. Individual Specific: This is the point of view that every individual has his or her own purpose in life, such as success or raising children, and this purpose is what directs their lives.

4. Individual General: This belief is that being happy, loving, sharing, and caring for others is the major purpose of living, and

that here and now behaviors of responsibility to others are the meaning and purpose of life.

The stress prayer is typically oriented to the "individual specific" category of life-purpose orientation. The depressed person is more typically oriented to the "cosmic general" concept. In my clinical experience, the super joy person typically combines the cosmic specific and cosmic general orientation, a combination of hope and some trust in one God, but a firm commitment to "a higher power or force." Here is an example of a joyful prayer by someone with super joy:

"God, I feel You within me and I try to realize my closeness to You every day. I love You as You love all of us, and I thank You for giving me life and for giving me this world to live in. Please let me know how I may better serve You."

The one key component of this joyful person's prayer is the "receptive" mode, being willing and able to listen for messages in whatever form from a higher force or being in which the joyful person believes. The joyful prayer is only half "sending." The other half is an attempt to feel and listen on many levels for new meaning for day-to-day life. Joyful prayer is not talking "to" something or someone, it is a process of communicating with our higher purpose, a way of establishing connection with everyone and everything, and, like all joyful living, joyful prayer is interactive, not executional.

Super joy is being super connected with life on all levels, and breaking down not only the walls of normalcy to be super normal but breaking down the walls that divide our experience of life into "out there" and "within us." To say that we are God is to say that we are all one together as people and together with the power that gives life meaning.

The miraculous human psychochemistry that can cripple us or make us whole is not a system beyond our control. Super joy is the process through which we can access our human capacity to transcend the brain's automatic interaction with day-to-day life. The journey to super joy is ultimately a spiritual journey into self, a self that is one component of an infinite system, unified with a power that we have not begun to understand but must begin to acknowledge. Chapter 6 suggests specific steps for learning the super joy style of daily living and presents the behaviors and thinking that are the codes through which we communicate with the origins of our super joy potential.

CHAPTER SIX

The Super Joy Program

Recycling for Joy

Picture in your mind a large spiral, shaped something like a funnel or wide, beautiful, clear, but slow-moving tornado. Everything about the spiral is movement. The spiral itself gets longer, then smaller, the walls move in one direction, then another, and the spiral expands and contracts in a breathing rhythm. If you were to enter such a spiral at any point it would be impossible for you to remain in one place. You would be in constant motion, moving up and down, in and out. There is no better or worse place within this life spiral, only "other" places to experience. You could not climb through the spiral, because there are no steps. You would have to learn to spin with the spiral to progress. Too much effort, and you would just spin out of control. Not enough effort, ignoring the natural motion of the spiral, and you would spin helplessly, never experiencing the entire spiral itself.

This is the joy spiral, a model of human development that does away with the step approach and focuses instead on perpetual motion and change, a dynamic system of being human that takes into account the cyclical rather than linear nature of the human experience. To learn the super joy response, to experience the six IN A JOY components of super joy (*i*ndescribable delight, intense knowing (*n*oesis) of life, extreme *a*ppreciation of life experiences, *j*oining and connecting with the world system, *o*penness to risk tak-

126

ing, and a new energy of perpetual youthfulness), there are different parts of this spiral that you must learn to revolve within, different rotating rings of life within the spiral that you must learn to move with instead of against.

There are some basic rules for living joyfully within this life spiral. These rules are the joy manifesto, basic starting points for beginning to learn super joy. This joy manifesto is a brief summary and review of the joyful thinking principles discussed in Chapter Three and the new principles of the new field of joyology presented in Chapter One.

The Joy Manifesto

1. We are all addicted to the SAD cycle of stress and depression. We cannot be totally free of this addiction, because addiction to our own brain chemicals is a human trait, but we can substitute a healthy addiction to the wellness psychochemicals of super joy.

2. We live in a society that not only accepts but rewards our SAD addiction. To replace the SAD addiction, or at least to reduce it, we will have to change many of the ways we think about daily living, for we are as addicted to the brain's thinking style of stress and depression as we are to the brain chemistry that accompanies it.

3. Super joy can overwhelm our SAD addiction cycle because it offers a healthier balance of the BMDs (brain-made drugs).

4. We will have to make significant behavioral changes along with our thinking changes if we are to learn super joy.

5. We are all part of a system, and we must make our thinking and behavioral changes realistically and responsibly within that system, letting other people know and be a part of our joy.

6. Some people will be threatened by our attempts to be more joyful. We may encounter ridicule and even anger, but these feel-

ings come from the SAD addiction of our society and are not aimed at us personally. We will have to have the courage to be extremely well, to be "abnormal."

7. All learning takes place in small steps. We will have to be patient with ourselves as we learn super joy. Stress and depression are always waiting to claim us when we become impatient with ourselves.

8. Super joy and our beliefs about the meaning and purpose of life are united. We may have to re-examine our faith and belief systems, perhaps rethink a crisis in faith in our lives, before we can fully learn super joy.

9. We are always learning. We will never "achieve" the super joy response, only learn to be more and more super joyful.

10. Learning super joy is one of the most important things we can do for ourselves, our families, and society. We must not allow ourselves to give up, even if circumstances seem sometimes hopeless and joyless. The temptation to give up is only the brain's attempt to maintain its addiction to the SAD cycle.

Once we accept the existence of super joy as an alternative to our SAD addiction cycle, there are some important behavioral changes that we must make. All of these changes must be seen from the point of view of small and consistent positive change, not complete conversion to an entirely new life style. When most programs for change fail, they do so typically because we ask too much of ourselves in too short a period of time. We only increase the odds of increasing our stress and depression addictions when we expect to be "converts" rather than students.

Detoxification and Clearing Ourselves "for" the System

I'm on a seafood diet. When I see food, I eat it.

ANONYMOUS

Our addictive behavior results in considerable buildup of toxicity in the body system. Fortunately the body has its own built-in purification mechanism, so no drastic measures are needed to begin to return the body to a healthier internal balance. As you begin your own super joy program, there are some ways you can help your own purification system work even better. The purer the body system, the more room there is for super joy.

Here is a system to help you begin a detoxification process. Buy a notebook and for one day record everything that becomes a part of your "diet." Record only those things that you consider toxic. Record the things you eat that you consider toxic, but also record for just this one day everything toxic that comes into your system. Record the sounds, the odors, the personal interactions, everything that makes a negative impression on you during one day. This will take some work but, once you have even a partial record of what you are allowing into you that you wish was not coming in, you can begin to make some choices and changes to reduce some of the toxicity. Here's just the first part of a "toxicity list" from one of my patients:

— noise of alarm clock in A.M.
— kids fighting in kitchen
— phone ringing too loud
— dog next door barking
— ate sausage and coffee
— had cigarette
— got worried about kids being late for school
— stick of gum
— television on all morning

— next-door neighbor visits
— call from mother
— sound of cars outside
— smell of lawn treatment chemical from outside
— sirens
— watched dumb game shows

This is only the beginning of this patient's list, going up to about 11 A.M. on the day she made this list. The patient reported that this was not an unusual day, and she was upset that she had allowed so much to enter her system that she herself considered disruptive.

As another suggestion for beginning to detoxify, spend another day listing everything that you allow into your system that you consider healthful or potentially conducive to a purer body and mind system. Remember, I am talking about not just your physical body but spiritual nutrition as well. Here is that same patient's "soul food list."

— look, touch, and smell of my baby's hair
— warm water on my back in shower
— smell of roses by porch steps
— call from sister
— watching husband wink at me during breakfast
— taking vitamins
— how the kitchen looked cleaned
— just sitting down in afternoon
— seeing sun come through blinds on front window
— reading (not enough time)
— seeing whole family together at dinner

This is the patient's "soul food list" for the entire day. The patient was particularly aware of the comparison in the length of the lists and resolved to make some effort to add to the soul food list and subtract where she could from the toxicity list.

Remember, addiction is a natural human state, and the addiction to toxic substances is strong. The brain loves toxic substances because they fit right in with the brain's preference for intense, easy highs, no matter what the long-term consequences may be. Give yourself credit for trying to balance the two lists above and don't get down on yourself because you have toxicity in your system. Here are some of the toxic targets, "food" that can enter your system that you should make every effort to reduce.

Toxic Targets

1. **Nicotine is a particularly toxic substance.** If you smoke, cut back as much as you can. Even one cigarette less is progress. Get professional help if you can't seem to deal with this addiction. Try to stay away from smokers and try to get as much fresh air as possible to counter at least some of the contamination of any smoke to which you are exposed or to which you expose yourself.

2. **Reduce your intake of alcohol.** Alcohol facilitates stress and depression addiction by altering brain and body chemistry. Remember, all alcohol is a depressant, and it can either take you further down or make you thirst for more stimulation to bring you up. Nicotine and alcohol are the respective catalysts for the up and down phases of the SAD cycle.

3. **Reduce caffeine in all its forms** (coffee, soda pop, tea, and even chocolate). Like most toxic substances, caffeine is a mood-altering substance and usually serves as a quick upper that first gets you edgy and then allows you to drop during the day.

4. **Reduce your chocolate.** The chemical makeup of chocolate can be a substitute for the joy response, a quick spurt of good feeling followed by an equally quick drop in emotional and physical energy. Your brain loves the quick ride. I suggest that if you are loading up on chocolate your joy deficit is serious. Don't let your brain succeed in trying to sweeten you away from your pursuit of super joy.

5. **Cut back on red meat.** Heart disease and cancer are related to excess fat intake, and even the common condition of osteoporosis

is related to our excess intake of red meat. Taking calcium pills won't help reduce your chances of osteoporosis if you don't exercise joyfully and regularly and reduce your red meat diet. Since we eat almost eight times as much protein as we need and we can't store the excess, we urinate the excess away. In the process, we wash out calcium. Drinking more milk won't help either. You may not get osteoporosis when you eat or drink more dairy products, but that is only because you may die of cancer or heart disease before you are old enough to experience osteoporosis.

6. Avoid, as much as possible, negative people. Unless you have to stress or depress yourself more by trying to avoid a specific negative person, try to steer clear of angry people. Such people give off "toxic vibrations," and this negativism seems very transmissible.

7. Try to reduce what I call "adrenalinizations." These are major blowups and overreactions that result in major doses of stress and depression psychochemicals. We all "lose it" sometimes and shoot up on adrenalin, but just being aware of the adrenalinizations phenomenon may alert you to the fact that every overreaction is like shooting a deadly addictive drug directly into your heart.

8. Reduce negative "self-talk." It not only hurts others when you say negative things to them, but the whole body is listening when you say things to yourself that are not flattering. Negative self-talk is similar to eating junk food. It's easy to do and tempting, but it is not at all good for you, and the more you do it, the worse it is for you. When you find yourself talking negatively to yourself, it is your brain scolding you again for not providing it with enough stimulation to meet its stress addiction.

Again, the brain loves negative self-talk, because such talk allows the brain to run things, to be the boss over the "self." One of the most difficult concepts to keep in "mind" is that you are much more than your "brain" keeps telling you that you are.

9. **Reduce environmental noise as much as possible.** We live in a noisy world, and our stress addiction allows us to become numb to the noise pollution, giving the brain the chance to gorge itself on this excessive stimulation. Give yourself as much quiet time as possible. The noise we hear is always accompanied by at least mini-adrenalizations. The same warning applies to unpleasant odors and even "sight pollution."

10. **Delay your anger as much as possible.** Getting angry is a part of being human, but the old idea of counting to ten can sometimes allow an anger spurt and its accompanying adrenalization to pass. I suggest counting to twenty-five, because some people get so angry so quickly that they speed-count to ten before two seconds have passed. I ask my patients who have trouble controlling their anger to count with the second hand on a watch, waiting for fifteen or twenty seconds to pass before allowing their anger to be expressed.

Anger is usually a "brain tantrum," during which the brain is in some way upset that it is not getting the type or amount of stimulation it wants when it wants it. By exploding emotionally, the brain uses the negative body reactions as a substitute for the external stimulation it is addicted to. It is pure myth that getting your anger "out" is healthy. The angrier you behave, the more upset you get.

These are only some of the major sources of toxicity and blocks to super joy. Eating fewer calories, a starch-based diet with plenty of legumes, fruits, fiber, and seeds is also a good idea for increasing the soul food list. Feast once in a while if you want on what nutritionist Dr. John McDougall calls the feast foods, such as milk, eggs, cheese, steak, and bacon, but try to reduce additives, cholesterol, salt, and refined foods in favor of as natural and varied an approach to eating and living as possible.

The Joy of Simplicity

Never invest in anything that eats or needs repairing.

BILLY ROSE

Comedian George Carlin defines a home as that place in which we keep our "stuff" while we go out to get "more stuff." We have become addicted to complication, to the artifacts of a stressful society that seems to think the more complex things are, the happier they will make us. Super joy depends on a simpler living style, one that leaves at least as much room for feeling as it does for doing.

To help you begin to simplify your life, use the simplification survey to assess your "complication index." When I interview very successful people, they all tell me that they sometimes long for a much simpler life than their success has bought them. The higher the complication index, the more reinforcement there is for our stress addiction, because there is more to do, more to do it with, and more things constantly going wrong, needing fixing, or taking our attention away from joy.

Simplification Survey

1. Do your clothes wear you out? Does it feel that you spend too much time shopping for, caring for, and trying to organize and update your wardrobe? Has your clothing divided itself inside your closet, with seasonal divisions and even subsections for clothes to wear for your different bodies when you are at different body weights?

You have a chance to do two things at one time for your own super joy. I mentioned earlier that altruism is a key factor in the joy response. You can benefit from that factor and reduce your complication index by cleaning out your closet and donating excess clothing to charity.

You may require help with this assignment, because many of my patients cannot seem to bring themselves to get rid of any of their "stuff." You may require a "closet exorcist" experienced in dealing with the demons of closet clutter. Sometimes a friend can show more common sense about what is needed and what is just "there." A trusted friend can also prevent the "restuffing phenomenon." Restuffing happens when, in the process of cleaning out closets and drawers, we somehow are stimulated to acquire new stuff.

One of my patients stated, "Until I tried to get rid of all my junk I didn't need or use, I didn't realize how much I didn't have. I really had to go out shopping." This "stuff logic" can sometimes be blocked by a friend who is better disciplined than you are in the art of simplification. Beware of the stuff co-addicts who may see a closet cleaning as a chance to acquire stuff for themselves from your stuff supply. Such friends are likely to go with you on a restuffing expedition or even to trade stuff with you.

2. **Is your car driving you out of your mind?** Has the cost of your car's maintenance become a financial burden? Are you addicted to getting more and more expensive big-name cars? Has dealing with the car mechanic become a battle of wits with an unarmed person? Do you spend more time arranging for car repairs than for your own physical health? Are you more cautious with oil and gas for your car than you are with your own diet? Has your car become something other than transportation?

If you can possibly do it, sell your car and use mass transit. If you must have a car, buy one that is simple, cheap, and most of all safe. Try to overcome your own "auto erotic" syndrome of valuing a car as a symbol of sexual prowess, phallic potential, or vaginal vigor. As one of my patients said, "Cars can drive you crazy."

If you must buy and own a car, remember that people at one time really did raise and lower their own car windows, shift their own gears, and unlock their own car doors without power assistance. If there is one incontrovertible rule about things, it is that things break. When a car comes "loaded," it is likely to end up loaded with problems for its owner.

No matter what means of transportation you use, I recommend that you always leave fifteen minutes earlier than you think you have to in order to get where you are going on time. Stress addiction is worsened by "cutting it too close" when we travel. Most of the people stuck in the traffic jam with you, fighting with you for a cab, or dashing to catch a plane just left too late. Look around you, and you will see Alice's rabbits, all very late for their very important dates.

3. Is your television screening you off from joy? Do you find your life being scheduled around "prime time"? If you have more than one television, you have too many. I know four-person families who have five televisions. I suppose the fifth is an emergency backup for a quick TV fix should one of their own private televisions break.

When I work with patients trying to learn super joy, I suggest that they cut back to one television in the house. I suggest that it be a small-screen, black and white set. Television is addictive enough without the added seduction of big screen, color, stereo, and automatic timers that turn the set on and off for you. Some televisions now come with what are called "sleep options" which turn the set off after you fall asleep. Remember the five receptive stages, including hypnopomping and hypnogoging? Do you really want your first and last images of the day to be Johnny Carson?

Other televisions now let you watch two channels at one time on the same screen. It is difficult to understand how anyone could really watch two television programs simultaneously, unless of course it is just the brain's way of catering to its outside stimulation addiction. Super joy is an attempt to substitute internal stimulation addiction for the outside focus of the addicted brain, so television is a major competitor with the joy response.

The cost of a simple, small black and white television has gone down considerably in the last few years, probably because people are addicted to the more intense stimulation of television with multiple features. The money you save buying one of the smaller televisions can be spent buying a videotape recorder. With a VCR, you can record what you really think is worth watching instead of waiting through three shows in a TV trance until the one you want to watch comes on.

I ask my patients, if they can afford it, to allow each family member to have one two-hour videotape of his or her own. The only television shows that can be watched are shows that have been videotaped. When you are watching a live show, you must tape that show, using up your television allotment time. You can then add to or subtract from your tape, but two hours is all you have to spend in one week. Using the videotape as a set quantity measure, requiring careful editing, additions, and subtractions, can help reduce the television addiction.

4. How many of your rooms are actually "living" rooms? Do you have several rooms in your house that are "for company and special occasions only"? Does your family cluster in a basement or family room and only use the "good" rooms on holidays or for entertaining? Do you find yourself cleaning rooms that are almost never used? Are you paying bills for the heating and lighting of rooms that really don't need these utilities because human beings seldom visit these "not for living" rooms?

A house analysis will help you make some decisions about whether you are living in and enjoying your home or your home has become another factor in the complication index, another whale for your Ahab complex. We now have family rooms, dining rooms, guest rooms, living rooms, bedrooms, even so-called "great rooms," as though certain human behaviors can only be done in rooms with the appropriate names. With the exception of the bathroom and kitchen, how many of the rooms of your house can really only serve primarily one purpose?

One woman said, "Now that I think about it, this multiple-room thing doesn't make much sense. One room for the family, one room for recreation, one for living, one for dining, it just doesn't make much sense. I don't know why the bedroom is the only room named after a piece of furniture. We don't refer to a couch room. Maybe we're afraid to call the bedroom what it is, the sleep, sex, and sick room."

"I don't know why we finished off the basement," said another man. "It's supposed to be a recreation room, but we never recreate down there. It's still a basement, a below-ground stuff holder. Our Ping-Pong table is a storage center, the pool table is an open-air file cabinet, and you couldn't find the bar because of all the toys on top. We all go out to recreate, we go our separate ways. There's no room in the recreation room to recreate anyway."

Here are some radical suggestions for getting more super joy out of your own home:

How to Get into Your Own Home

1. Allow everybody into every room. Every room should be a family room.

2. Allow all family members to sit on the furniture, even the "good" furniture.

3. Allow people to leave their shoes on, even on the carpet. (Remember, if every room is a family room, then all of the family must help in the cleaning of all rooms.)

4. Eat some family dinners at the dining-room table, even though it is no one's birthday.

5. Go ahead and "leave stuff out." There is nothing sacred about always "putting things away." If you find yourself in a "hide the stuff" panic when there is an unexpected knock at the door, you probably just have too much stuff. Maybe your visitor could take some of your stuff when he or she leaves. Leave your stuff out as a type of perpetual estate sale for visitors to shop through and take some stuff off your hands.

6. Allow some eating in rooms other than the kitchen. Getting crumbs on the couch is good for your health (again just so long as everyone helps clean up).

7. If you don't want to make the bed, shut the bedroom door and pretend it's made.

8. Eat on paper plates as often as possible and throw the entire table setting away when you're finished.

9. Allow spoons in the fork pile in the silverware drawer.

10. Write the word "joy" in the dust on the table sometimes. Dusting is only a process of small particle rearrangement. Erma Bombeck said that she would like the following line on her tombstone. "Big deal! I'm used to dust."

The theory of "dust relativity" proves that dust cannot be created or destroyed. If you dust one place, the dust simply goes somewhere else. When a child asked his mother if it was true that we all begin and end as dust, his mother assured him that this was true. The child then pointed under his bed and said, "I think Uncle Harry is either coming or going under there."

The above list is just for fun, but it makes the point that if we allow our daily living to be governed by obligatory compliance to a set of rules of "house cleaning," we will have little time to enjoy homemaking.

You Can Buy Happiness, but You Can't Buy Super Joy

It is a reality of life that money can buy better health care, better education, and a generally better life style in terms of acquiring the things that make life easier and more efficient, the brain's addictive preferences. An easier life can be a happier life, if happy means the absence of hassles. Super joy has no price, however, because joy is more than the absence of inconvenience. Super joy is freedom from the SAD addiction cycle I have described, going beyond ease and convenience.

How much poverty has your money bought you? Does there always seem to be too much month left at the end of the money? Are you making more money now than ever before, but your own "need inflation" makes it seem that you have much less money? Has managing and protecting your money begun to cost more money than you used to make? Are you making more and enjoying life less? Is money a frequent source of arguments in your family?

To free yourself from unrealistic financial pressures, you must make a very difficult decision. You must decide how much money is enough or how you can live with whatever money you will be able to make. Many patients who come to me feel that financial problems are contributing to their emotional problems. More often the reverse situation is true. These patients have never really decided how much money they will, can, and really want to make. They just keep working, with no financial plan other than how to "manage" whatever money they may make. How much is enough? What is that financial level that you can comfortably, joyfully maintain? Is that level realistic? Does that financial level take too much out of you or your family?

Be careful that money does not start making your decisions for you. Many of my patients who were increasing their income also increased their living style, and the resulting cycle was one of more money followed by more expensive life style followed by need for more money to maintain the more expensive life, and then an endless repeat of this addictive cycle. Your life style must not be reactive to how much money you do or can make. A life style with super joy follows a decision about where the cutoff point will come in the financial cycle.

Joy for the Spirit

The American Plains Indians used to take time to wander, to merge with nature, to allow themselves time and space to look more deeply within themselves for their purpose and spiritual energy. The Hopi Indians would go on a "vision quest," communing with nature as a means of spiritual enlightenment. Super joy depends on constantly refocusing yourself on the difference between your brain and your "self." Your own super joy comes from a spirit that does not defer to the brain's incessant demand for external stimulation, from a deepening awareness of who you are beyond what your brain keeps asking you to do.

I suggest that you take some time to draw your own "spiritual map." Draw a line on a sheet of paper, and along that line write down your own private history of your belief and view of God. Even if you are a devout atheist, trace your views of God or a god to this point in your life and how you came to believe or not believe as you do.

What was your view of God as a child? What events changed, blocked, modified, or blocked your views? What were your views as a preadolescent, adolescent, young adult, and as you went through major events in your life? You may want to jot down general phases of your life first on the top of your line, and then, underneath each period of your life, write down your concept of God.

Here is an example of how one patient described her "spiritual map":

"Well, I can't even remember a concept of God at all when I was little. My family was never very religious. Then, I remember other kids talking about God when I was in kindergarten. Now that I think about it, I guess I saw God then as an old man on a throne. When I became a teenager, I went through a phase where I believed in sort of an out there, sometimes ghosts and things. God then was sort of a force or power, or the source of the big bang. Then there was a long period when I just didn't think about God or anything like that. Then my grandma died, and I started to wonder about a God again. Then my grandpa died, and I hated God. I sort of punished Him by forgetting Him. Now, I haven't thought about God for a long time."

Now comes the most important part of the spiritual mapping assignment. Examine each of the phases of your belief in God and try to remember how you were feeling in your life at each time. Were you happy, busy, distracted, sad, grieving, or just going happily along unaware of any spiritual needs at all? Most of my patients discover that the major changes in their views of God or a higher power related to times in their lives when a major change or loss occurred. A death, starting school, deciding on a marriage ceremony, a transitional religious ceremony, a time of extreme fear, a divorce, a long period of loneliness is usually when we focus on our belief systems.

It seems that any time we focus on our life, we instinctively look to our spirit. Is there something beneath our addictive behavior that doesn't like what we are doing to our "self"? Will we wait too long, wait until too late before we commit ourselves to an examination of the meaning of our life?

To test my point about the existence and neglect of the human spirit, just go on your own vision quest. Take a whole day and just walk alone through a beautiful forest, watch a thunderstorm, listen to the sounds of our world. Notice what happens when you become closer to nature and are very, very quiet. The spirit will try to get your attention. Your sense of "self" as related to everything else will become your focus. Whenever we are pensive, whenever we step away from our stress and depression addiction, we hear the spirit calling.

The Buddha's Warning

The Buddha said, "Never lie, even in jest." We live in a society that is based on lies. Never show your hand too soon, don't wear your heart on your sleeve, little white lies, polite lies, lying to protect somebody, stretching the truth, and "dealing" are common phrases in our culture. The person who does not learn to lie is seen as at a disadvantage, naive, in danger of being hurt and controlled by others.

Lies are the brain's way of preventing the "self" from taking control. Lies help the brain get whatever it wants when it wants it, and are ultimately always lies primarily to the self. I'll be happy later, I thrive on this stress, nobody can be super joyful, I have to work this hard to keep ahead, and you get them before they get you are brain lies used to maintain our SAD cycles.

Popular psychology has given tacit approval to lying. "You only hurt others when you tell the whole truth" has been the traditional psychotherapy point of view. Super joy requires complete disclosure, sharing with others how you feel, what you have done, what you hope to do, what you fear and wish for.

"So, you mean I should tell my wife I had an affair?" asked one man. "Go ahead and destroy her. Is that your point?"

Complete disclosure is not irresponsibly dumping your own guilt on someone else's shoulder. Being truthful is sharing how you feel, not presenting your behavioral history and then standing back while the other person struggles to give meaning to what you have said. My answer to this man illustrates this point:

"No, I see no value in just telling her about with whom or where you had sex. But you have an obligation for your health and hers to tell her much more than what you did. You must first understand why you did what you did, and then share the whole issue. Telling partial truths is the same as lying. In today's world, having sex with someone is a major health decision that affects everyone with whom you interact. It is not true that what people don't know won't hurt them. It's your own fear of being able to deal with the intensity and complexity of your marital problems and your own sexual behavior that is stopping you from telling your wife about your affair. You are not protecting her, you are hiding yourself."

Lying is another human addiction. We get used to lying about busy schedules that really aren't so busy, saying we really want to go to a party we really do not want to go to at all, and almost any other lie that allows us to continue our SAD cycles. When we stop lying, we confront the major problems in our lives that even the smallest lie can disguise.

Think also of the major lies in your life. Most of my patients have told me about major lies that they have carried for years. These may be lies about sexual preferences, about their dreams, their fears, the true nature of their "selves." It just is not convenient to tell the truth all the time, but super joy requires making the time to be real before we lose any sense of what real is, of where the truth starts and the lying begins. When you talk about convenience, you are usually talking about some degree of addiction, some degree of lack of spiritual energy to work on life and living.

The Joy of Learning

Author Marilyn Ferguson stated, "Learning is not only like health, it is health." This statement summarized research showing that one of the healthiest things we can do for ourselves is to learn.

The "aha" phenomenon is a major component of super joy. The

"aha" experience takes place at those magical times when some new pathway is being established in our brains, a pathway that short-circuits our addictive pathways as we see another, a better way to do something.

I ask my patients attempting to learn the super joy response to begin a new project they have never tried before. I ask them to learn to play a musical instrument, take a class in something unique for them, or start a new hobby. Be careful not to pick an activity that only causes you to fall back to your Ahab complex, getting so involved with trying to learn quickly and perfectly that all the joy is taken away from the learning activity.

To demonstrate my point, I ask the couples I work with to try to learn to juggle together. Most people have never tried juggling, and when I videotape their efforts they are surprised to see how impatient they are with themselves. They also see on the tape that the only effective learning is joyful learning, having fun, taking time, and getting the brain out of the way so the "self" can learn.

"Damn it," said one man as he tried to juggle. "These aren't the right kind of balls." He frowned as he chased after the balls, failing to see that his brain was trying to get this learning done quickly and in the process just causing more problems.

"Ease up," said his wife. "You can't juggle if you're going to get mad at the balls. Be nice to them. Just let it happen. Here, I'll stand beside you and we'll do it together."

The husband began to laugh as he juggled beside his wife. "It's never going to work," he said as he chased another ball. He began again, this time laughing as he tried to develop a slower rhythm, letting go of each ball and catching more gently. "Hey," he said after a mini-juggle, "I think I started to get it."

He picked up the balls and started again, and smiled as the balls rotated in a perfect circle. "There," he said. "I can feel it now. This is great."

The rules of joy learning are clear in the above example. Go slow, be patient with yourself even if your brain isn't, and let learning happen to you by continuing to make yourself available for the "aha" phenomenon.

Working Yourself Too Far Up

Bertrand Russell said, "Work is of two kinds: first, altering the position of matter at or near the earth's surface relative to other matter; second, telling other people to do so." As you will see in Section Two of this book, work offers a great opportunity for super joy. Unfortunately, many of us manage to take all the fun out of our work, even seeing the words work and fun as antonyms. Like most human behaviors, we can become addicted to work, making it yet another whale for our Ahab complex.

Researcher Marilyn Machiowitz writes of work addiction: "These people are remarkably satisfied with their lives." She is referring to the fact that we mistake satisfaction with the potential for super joy in working. So-called workaholics reading this will deny their work addiction, saying that they love their work. These workaholics forget that most drug addicts will tell you that they have come to "love" whatever it is they are addicted to. Work, like alcohol, can become an automated source of the SAD cycle, resulting in feelings that "everything is just fine" even while our overall health is suffering.

As a part of your own super joy program, try the following "joy of work analysis":

1. Of all the things I do in my job, what things would I do for free? If you already are doing some job for free, how do you feel about that?

2. How trapped am I in my job? (Lily Tomlin writes, "The trouble with the rat race is that even if you win, you're still a rat.")

3. How and how much does my work affect my family?

4. What has my job done to my outlook on life?

5. Would I want my children to deal with their work life as I deal with mine?

6. Is what I am doing important to the welfare of others?

7. How did I end up in this job in the first place?

8. What choices are open to me now in my career?

9. If age, gender, race, or religion were not factors of discrimination, what career would I choose? Author Florence Kennedy writes, "All jobs should be open to everybody, unless they actually require a penis or a vagina."

10. If I had so much money I never had to work, would I? What would I do with my time if I were independently wealthy?

Think about your answers to these questions as you attempt to bring more super joy into your life. There is something inside us that needs doing if only we look deep enough. Doing a job is a feature of the SAD cycle. Having a career is finding and doing that special "something inside us." Poet Kahlil Gibran wrote that joyful work is ". . . earth's furthest dream, assigned to you when that dream was born."

Work addiction seems to be an addiction we are proud of. We almost seem to brag with mock displeasure that we are "overwhelmed" with busyness, sometimes as an excuse for not really being able to do what we really want to be doing. Work addiction is a symptom not of working your brains out but of your brain working you out. Why are you doing what you're doing for a career and how do you like doing it? Do you like your answer?

To Play's the Thing

The word "play" has fifty-five definitions in Webster's American College Dictionary, ranging in meaning from a dramatic composition to an attempt to get into the favor of someone else. I define joyful play as the intentional regression to childish interaction with people and things, a type of amazement with daily life. Norman Cousins writes, "If ever we begin to contemplate our own composite wonder, we will lose ourselves in celebration and have time for nothing else." Play is acting on your awareness of this wonderment with life.

A recent survey of annual directly earned incomes revealed that the top pay in the country went to an executive selling real estate. His salary was $250,000 a year. A clown, providing laughter and play, averaged less than $10,000 a year, one twenty-fifth the income of the man who buys and sells property. We devalue laughter and play, seeing such activity as a temporary break from reality.

Your own super joy program depends on relearning play. Purchase a silly game or, as I suggested earlier, play some of your favorite childhood games again. Don't mistake business lunches, cocktail parties, or obligatory entertainment for play. You cannot regress to childish play when you are in the middle of the SAD cycle, trying to impress someone important, or too tired to find the energy for a good game.

Just Let Yourself Stop

All of the suggestions above for developing more super joy in your life require making contact with other people and the world around you. Ultimately, all addiction is isolation, the brain's undisciplined striving for self-stimulation. To counteract this brain-oriented addiction to life, you must let the brain know you are watching it. There are two major ways of doing this.

First, start talking about joy. This is a difficult step, because joy is not a typical topic of conversation. It helps in learning about super joy to "go public" and let people know that you are seriously reconsidering your daily life style. Make it clear that you are not having a "mid-life" crisis. The so-called mid-life crisis described by traditional psychology is really an all-life crisis finally recognized.

By "connecting" with other people and if possible enlisting them in their own super joy program or inviting them to join yours, you have taught the brain that it is not as isolated as it thinks it is. There are other people out here too.

Author E. M. Forster wrote, "Only connect. Personal relations are the important thing for ever and ever." Connecting is a beginning step in interrupting the isolation of the SAD addiction cycle. It helps if you start touching people more, just making some form of body contact through more and longer handshakes, resting a hand on someone's shoulder, or gently patting someone on the back.

Family therapist Virginia Satir writes, "I believe the greatest gift I can conceive of having from anyone is to be seen by them, heard by them, to be understood and touched by them." This connection with others is the ultimate gift you can give to yourself.

The second way to override your brain's addiction to external stimulation and find super joy is to do the "brain-watching technique." Sit down for several minutes and try to watch your brain thinking. If this sounds strange, it's only because your brain doesn't want to receive the message of the prior sentence. The brain thinks it's you, and if the real "you" is going to try to watch the brain, the brain gets confused, even afraid.

Sit quietly and just watch your brain doing its thing. See what thoughts occur, what your brain is busying itself with. Try to stand back and observe the brain as just another part of you, as if you were watching your abdomen go up and down to observe your breathing.

If you master this brain-watching technique, you will notice that the brain becomes embarrassed. After it tries a few stress and depression maneuvers, such as "Get up and get going," or "You're really not a very ambitious person," the brain will give up and just become another part of your body system. Brain watching takes practice, but it is a basic exercise for your own super joy program.

Part Two of this book deals with three of the most important aspects of the super joy response: working, loving, and believing. If you have tried just some of the above suggestions for your own super joy program, you will find that the next three chapters will help you make super joy not only a part of your life but a new way of living.

PART TWO

---

*The Joy
of Working,
Loving,
and
Believing*

CHAPTER SEVEN

The Joy of Meaningful Work

If you have built castles in the air, your work need not be lost; that is where they should be. Now put the foundations under them.

THOREAU

Ordinary work, as the root meaning of the term indicates, is work that is in harmony with the order we perceive in the natural environment.

FRITJOF CAPRA

The Three "Ds" of Work

I was sitting at my word processor preparing to write this chapter on work and the joy response when I heard a loud buzzing noise. When I looked out my window I saw that the septic tank system for my home was receiving its biannual cleaning. Three men were standing by a large truck and watching as hoses vacuumed the system. One of the men motioned for me to join them. As I talked with the three workers, their discussion illustrated how different our perceptions of work can be.

"Well, Doc," said the first man, "how would you like to be doing this all day? Pumping out crap. Some job, eh?"

Before I could answer, the second man smiled. "That's the doc's job. He's an author." All four of us laughed as he continued. "This isn't so bad. I'm getting decent money, so I can send my daughters to college. I never went, and I never dreamed my own kids would go to college. Every day working is a day for her in college."

The third man adjusted a valve on the truck and said, "We have to keep a better eye on the pressure. We don't want any fumes escaping. You know, this work saves the environment. None of these homes could be here if we didn't have this equipment and do this job. It's like a small thing, but at least I'm doing more than talk about a clean world. The good doctor here could not live way out here in the country and write his books if somebody didn't do this."

Here were three men doing exactly the same job at the same time, with three entirely different views of their work. Which of the three men's stories most closely approximates your own view of your work? Are you working because you have to, because you are helping yourself and your family grow, or because you have a vision, a dream, some belief that what you are doing really matters in the overall scheme of things? Experiencing joy in your work requires a combination of necessity, self and family support, and vision. If you are able to accent the third factor, a meaningful vision of the purpose of your work, your chances for finding super joy in working are increased.

I call the above factors the "three Ds" of work. First, there is "demand." We must keep the world moving and functioning. We must "execute" tasks for the common good and balance our consumerism with our own contributions. Second, we must "develop," see our "selves" and our families enhanced by our efforts. Third, we must have a work "dream," an imagery of overall purpose and contribution to the world that transcends simple execution and the daily barter of survival. Although our early childhood experiences teach us that play is different than work, and that play is fun and work is difficult and boring, we must unlearn that lesson if we are ever to rediscover the joy of working.

The Five "Must" Myths

The next time you are working, stop and look around you. How many of your colleagues are working joyfully? You may find that not too many of us are really happy at and about our work. This is because of five myths about working that must be challenged if we are to work with super joy.

MYTH ONE. Work is not fun.   Fun is what you have on weekends or vacations. Work is what you do so you can have fun later.

Sociologist Daniel Yankelovich's book *New Rules* describes an emerging emphasis on not just "doing your job" but also finding fun and purpose in doing it. An early sign of what I call "freeze-out" (not "burnout") is not having fun in working. We don't burn out, because too few of us are "on fire" with a passion and joy in our working.

Work cannot be divided from your "personal" life. We all do and should "take our work home with us." Traditional psychology taught us that working, playing, and loving were to be done in different places with different people. This was never possible. People have always fallen in love at work, brought love problems to work for discussion through the work web of gossip and talk that dominates all places of employment. People have always tried to sneak some play into work, through the covert passage of copies of jokes and sexual stories or practical jokes and continued attempts to extend the lunch "hour" to the "lunch hour and a half."

People have always taken their work worries home for discussion and review, and they should. We cannot enjoy working if the only time we combine real life with work life is at the company picnic. Perhaps office parties sometimes become a little too wild because workers view this rare opportunity as some type of professional recess instead of just another opportunity among many to share and celebrate the full life process together.

When women were given the opportunity to move up the professional ladder, they climbed the rungs with families, children, and friends with them. Later in this chapter I will discuss the potential positive joyful impact of the androgynization of the workplace. Many women are unwilling to be forced to make the choice men surrendered to: to work or to love. Women expect not only to have families and children but to be able to work and enjoy all areas of their lives. The more holistic nature of our feminine side can save work from becoming a divisive life force.

MYTH TWO. Work must go on.   Even if you are sick, go to work. The "show" must go on, and we must demonstrate that we are willing to die for our jobs. In fact, many of us will.

The largest single cost in building the new car you buy comes from the health care of the worker who built it. In a society that spends more than one of every ten of its dollars on health, sick workers are draining and crippling the work force. Alcoholism and stress-related illness are the major causes of absenteeism, yet the money companies spend for worker health programs is not really for health at all but for the treatment of the sick.

At any given day in the factory or office, more than one third of the workers are sick. Many of these workers are passing their illnesses on to other workers. We have not learned that keeping workers healthy is not only more humane but cheaper than trying to cure them when they are sick.

The typical workplace is the most unhealthy environment imaginable. People are smoking, mysterious fumes are in the air, the building is sealed tight with fake windows that do not open and often look out only at other windows and walls. In spite of the installation of jogging tracks and mandatory annual physicals, business has failed to grasp the point that wellness is a balance between where we work, how we feel about our work, and the relationship between working, loving, family, friends, and colleagues. Like a professional football team with an excellent conditioning program, our players continue to get hurt. We give them injections and send them back into the game. We commend them when they "play hurt." We fail to look at the nature of the game itself as responsible for the injuries.

MYTH THREE. Pick your career and stick with it.   Don't be a job hopper. Establish seniority, security, and stability. Change jobs only for more money or when you "can't take it anymore."

In my work with the joy group, I have identified two categories of workers regarding job change. First, there are the "quick change artists." These workers seem to think that fulfilling work is somewhere "out there" instead of inside themselves. They are looking for "meaning through work" and never seem to be able to find meaningful work. Like persons with serial divorces, the quick change artists never learn from their changes. Their remarriages are predestined for another career divorce because they do not learn that work is more person than place. The poet Kahlil Gibran wrote, "And to love life through labour is to be intimate with life's inmost secret." Like a participant in many love affairs that have gone sour, the quick change artist fails to see that a happy career depends more on being the right worker than on finding the right job. Sometimes it is more important not to take a job and shove it but to take time to take a job and try to love it.

The second category of workers in terms of job change is at the opposite side of the scale of change. These are the "gold watch workers." They seem to be motivated by sameness and the ultimate presentation of the proverbial gold retirement watch. Even when they are unhappy and have tried to improve the work situation through all available alternatives, they feel trapped by seniority and fearful of change and new beginnings. They cannot see that a new job is only another step in working, in finding a working vision for ourselves. Instead, the gold watch worker feels that job change is an acknowledgment of failure, even immaturity. Their sense of security seems to come from trying to survive until Social Security. Their vested interest is only in survival.

Comedian Slappy White said, "The trouble with unemployment is that the minute you wake up in the morning, you're on the job." We have mistaken unemployment for failure. When opportunity to work exists, unemployment is a time for realignment of vision and direction of career. Constructive, considered, careful change in work is as natural as change in all life development.

MYTH FOUR. It doesn't matter if what I am doing doesn't match my values and beliefs. It's just a job.

Psychologist Douglas LaBier describes the serious problem of executives who achieve success at the expense of their own values. He feels that any worker who continues to compromise his or her principles for the attainment of status, wealth, security, and success will eventually come to a time of crisis in life meaning.

Disillusionment in the workplace is all too common. Ask service persons you deal with if they are proud of the product they are servicing and the company for which they work. You are likely to receive a negativistic, sardonic answer. Inspiration, energy, enthusiasm, and dedication have become suspect in a business world that values savvy, cleverness, manipulation, money, and the hard sell.

It is not possible to separate personal values from our daily work. We delude ourselves when we say things like, "it's just a job," because our job is "us." What we do to and for our world and for others matters far beyond a paycheck. When we work, our spirit is listening, and sooner or later we all ask the question, "Has what I have done in my work helped others and really mattered?"

MYTH FIVE: People need managing. In our attempt to learn to manage people in one minute, we have forgotten that joyful work depends upon helping workers discover and mobilize their own visions of work and career. Just listen to any worker anywhere and you will hear an entire theory about how the business could be run more effectively. What these workers are really talking about is their vision, their own definition of what working means to them.

Until the business world learns that the art of facilitation of joy in working is more important than rules of management, it will persist in its infantilization of the American worker. Such infantilization will result in a self-fulfilling prophecy, with managers resenting their parental role and the managed rebelling much like joyless children. The American worker will be more than ever a person in the middle, torn between visions, dreams, hopes, and loving on the one hand and the artificiality and inhumaneness of the workplace on the other.

The Work Cynic Cycle

We need to move from individual to collective approaches and to
create optimum health and productivity for all of humankind.

KENNETH PELLETIER

There will be little joy in working when cynicism dominates the
workday. In my interviews with workers at several levels of what
has been called a "flow chart," or structure of the work force from
top to bottom, I have found more of a "stuck system," a cynical
cycle of employee mismanagement that fails to account for joy in
working for every worker and fails to unify an entire group of
people behind the joy of a common goal for working. Here are
the stages of the work cynic cycle:

STAGE 1.   INITIAL ENTHUSIASM.   Everyone seems to get
very "high" about a new mission, concept, product, or program.
But, because of a failure to align all employees on all levels behind
this new mission by relating this mission to their personal joy in
working, failure of the new mission is preprogrammed.

STAGE 2.   CONTINUED COMPLICATIONS.   Most new
programs experience failure. The business world is impatient and
tends to jump ship long before the ship is really sinking. Sometimes, the more the complications, the more likely that we are
dealing with a very important idea, but because of failure to maintain faith in and understanding of the mission, only the complications become visible.

STAGE 3.   DISILLUSIONMENT.   Because of a failure to em-
power and align all of the workers and an emphasis on efficiency
and immediate gratification over worker understanding and happiness, complications result in a sense of disillusionment and disgust.
While persons high up in the organization may have trouble understanding why the initial enthusiasm has vanished, the line
workers begin to feel that they are only dealing with complications

and seeing very little progress toward the initial mission. Most organizations have insufficient structural integrity to allow all levels of workers to interact directly around a common purpose, to make adjustments and attend to the emotional aspects of change, so disillusionment spreads much more rapidly than inspiration. Motivation requires feedback. Disillusionment always results from disconnection.

STAGE 4.   SEARCH FOR SCAPEGOATS.   When it becomes clear that the project is failing, usually long after it is too late to fix the problem and disillusionment has become rampant and is seen as equivalent to the initially proposed program itself, there is a rush to assign blame for the failed venture. Someone must be labeled as "guilty" in systems that are not viewed as a whole. The "he or she did it" rather than a "we do it" orientation dominates. The organization wastes countless hours in detective work designed to protect some people while exposing others. Workers become aware of a witch hunt, and worker morale and health suffer. Any potential fun in the challenge of saving or modifying a new project is replaced by fantasies of being blamed for failure or even dismissed. In the anticipated industrial beheading, the individual worker begins to fear that it is her or his head that will roll. The only joy that is seen is the pseudojoy of relief that someone else got "the ax."

STAGE 5.   PUNISHMENT OF THE INNOCENT.   Major players in this cynical game seldom suffer. Somewhere down the line, some innocent worker or workers are blamed, disciplined, even dismissed. Distrust in the organization worsens. High executives may leave, but typically only long after the crisis for which they are ultimately responsible has destroyed the health of many people. One employee said, "They bring in a new big gun, he shoots, we fall, he stays awhile, and then he leaves with everybody saying how bright he was. And then they bring in another big gun and we do the whole thing over again."

STAGE   6.   DECORATION   OF   THE   IRRESPONSI-BLE.   Once the "guilty" are found and disciplined, persons who seldom deserve the accolades are rewarded, promoted, or given credit and prestige. We are really rewarding the ability to avoid responsibility, skill at grabbing the limelight, and the ability to save one's own neck or lower parts of the anatomy. The lack of continued vision, failure to align all workers behind that vision, the powerlessness felt by many workers, ineffective bureaucracy, misplaced rewards and punishments, and most of all the complete neglect of joy in working only serve to reinforce the fourth "must" myth of working: "Do our job and go home." We come to feel that survival and endurance are more important to working than vision and aspirations. We fail to learn that we must discover how to make a joyful life, not just a living.

The Personal and Social Joy of Working

Second to sleep, we spend more hours working than doing anything else in our lives. I have never seen a patient in my clinical work who was not experiencing problems with work, the meaning of working in his or her life, or stress in daily work. Only a small percentage of us have been able to find meaningful, pleasing work. Physicist Fritjof Capra writes, "In our society most people are unsatisfied with their work and see recreation as the main focus of their life."

Researcher Michael Frankenhauser addresses this issue of alienation and lack of joy in our working, and identifies two key factors that must be present if our working is ever to be a part of and not a requirement for our daily living. He identifies the issues of personal "joy and pride in work" and "discretionary freedom" or a sense of control and personal significance in the workplace as the real components of work satisfaction. How are you doing on these two components of work?

Joy and pride in working are found only when two criteria are met. Psychologist Aaron Antonovsky writes of the importance of the social valuation of the "enterprise" (the occupation, the industry, the plant) in which one is engaged and the personal joy at a particular place of work. He refers to the sense of social constructiveness of the work task in combination with a personal sense of

worth where the work is being done. I have divided these two
work factors into the personal joy of work and the social joy of
work factors, and you may learn more about joy in working by
taking the tests in these two catagories.

The Personal Joy of Work Factors

Frankenhauser's "discretionary freedom" is a key part of personal
joy. Such freedom is the sense that we have a voice in what is
going on, the free choice to be actively involved in what happens
at work. This means a freedom and encouragement to interact
with our coworkers and to feel that our presence at work really
matters in our immediate working environment and to the overall
endeavor of the institution for (and hopefully "with") which we
work. The following questions may help you assess these personal
joy of work factors:

The Personal Joy of Work Factors Test

1. Do people listen to you at work when you talk about work
   issues (not just gossip or more general issues)?

2. Do you have a sense of "teamwork" at work and a feeling that
   you are a key member of the team?

3. When someone must leave a job or becomes sick or experiences some major life event, is there true concern for this person on the part of the people at work (not just a "flower
   fund")?

4. Does what you are doing at work interact with, relate to, and
   help the work of others with whom you work in a direct and
   obvious manner?

5. Does the work "load" seem balanced where you work, with
   everyone doing their share?

6. Do you look forward to going to work not only because you enjoy what you're doing but because you enjoy the people you are doing it with and the company you are doing it for?

7. Can you postpone thinking about work problems and actually leave your work problems at work while taking your work purpose and interests home for stress-free discussion and review?

8. Do you laugh at work (a celebrating laughter, not a sarcastic laughter at failings and problems in the workplace)?

9. Do your colleagues think you are a good worker?

10. Do you trust and respect the people you work with?

11. Do the people you work with trust and respect you?

12. Is most of the workday spent talking positively (as opposed to complaining, "awfulizing," and talking about how crazy and inefficient your workplace is)?

The more "yes" answers to the above questions, the more likely that you are finding personal joy in your work even if sometimes there is severe stress, strain, and pressure in the workplace. The more "no" answers you have, the more important it becomes that you consider changing what you do and not just where and how you do it.

Psychologist Peter Sorokin wrote, "All the psychological processes of any member of an occupation undergo modification, especially when one stays for a long time in the same occupation. Still greater is the occupational influence on the processes and on the character of one's evaluations, beliefs, practical judgments, opinions, ethics, and whole ideology." Sorokin means that we all "become" our jobs, and when our jobs become unhappy, so do we.

We all start to think at home the way we think at work, to value what the people at work value, to approach life just as we approach our jobs. We may become alienated from our family and

friends if we allow ourselves to become our work instead of learning to enjoy working and being able to share with them our feelings and views that come from our working. When we cannot
share our working beyond where we work or experience a
catharthis about our frustrations there, it is time to change not only
where we work but our very work itself.

The Social Joy of Work Factors

We do not have to become Marxists to understand that the product
or service we work on must be of perceived social value, a partici-
pation in a "collective" or common purpose. If we do not share in
this common purpose and profit directly in some way from it, we
will become alienated no matter how personally happy we may be
with our day-to-day tasks.

Educator Theodore Roszak writes, "Work that produces unnecessary consumer junk or weapons of war is wrong and wasteful.
Work that is built upon false needs or unbecoming appetites is
wrong and wasteful. Work that deceives or manipulates, that ex-
ploits or degrades is wrong and wasteful. Work that wounds the
environment or makes the world ugly is wrong and wasteful." As
painful as it may be for us to realize, work that doesn't help our
world eventually hurts our world and the worker. The following
test items refer to this issue of true "social work."

1. Does what you do really help people? Do people need what
your work provides?

2. Is the product that results from what you do easily destroyed
and disposed of? Our society does not value jobs that are entropic
or that create "things" that are easily destroyed. Work that must
be done repetitively without leaving a lasting impact, such as cooking meals, sweeping floors, or cutting lawns, is assigned low pay
and status. Jobs with high status and pay create lasting things that
are difficult or, in the case of nuclear products, impossible to get
rid of. I suggest that we consider the possibility that this whole
idea is backward. Jobs that are entropic and cyclical are usually

FRIENDSHIP LOVE STAR

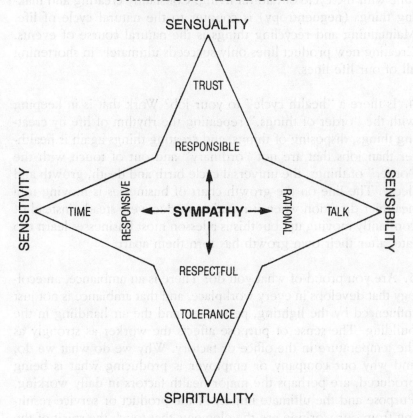

much healthier for our world and for the worker who does them than jobs that are neguentropic, creating more stuff and complicating our lives. Those jobs that create what can be easily disposed of are the jobs of true value.

3. Is your job repetitive, doing some things over and over again? I suggest that it is healthy, not unhealthy, to do repetitive work if this work relates to environmental health. Sweeping the floor in a charity kitchen may have a different health impact than sweeping the floor of a missile factory because of the impact of each of these endeavors on our world. Doing things in repetitive cycles is in

tune with the cycle of natural living. Constantly creating and making things (neguentropy) is counter to the natural cycle of life. Maintaining and recycling things is the natural course of events. Creating new product lines only succeeds ultimately in shortening all of our life lines.

4. Is there a "health cycle" to your job? Work that is in keeping with the "order of things," repeating the rhythm of life by creating things, disposing of things, and creating things again is healthier than jobs that are not "ordinary" and out of touch with the "order" of things, the universal cycle birth and death, growth and decay. The line on the growth chart of businesses is moving in a healthier direction when it remains productively steady instead of constantly moving up, but this is a lesson most businesses learn too late, after their own growth has torn them apart.

5. Are you proud of what you do? There is an ambiance, an ecology that develops in every workplace, and that ambiance is not just influenced by the lighting, personnel, and the air handling in the building. The sense of purpose affects the worker as strongly as the temperature in the office or factory. Why we do what we do, and why our company or employer is producing what is being produced, are perhaps the major health factors in daily working. Purpose and the ultimate impact of the product or service resulting from our working are the elements that touch the spirit of the worker, and worker morale is a matter of morals, of how much good results from the work being done.

6. Is there a spiritual quality to your work? Religious work has always involved giving, farming, cooking, cleaning, and keeping people and our world alive. Does your work contribute to this movement, or more to the need for others to do this life-maintenance and -saving work?

7. Does your place of employment attempt to improve society, not just to see how fast or efficiently society can do or consume things? Are you working at filling needs more than trying to create them?

8. Does your place of work attempt to develop and lead the way in the improvement in living (as opposed to trying to be ahead in reading "trends" or trying to keep up or be just ahead of the next fad)?

9. Does your place of work treat all workers with true respect (not just common courtesy), no matter what their task?

10. Does your employer have a clear set of moral objectives that are conveyed to the employees (not just "lip service" but true commitment to moral objectives)?

11. Do you consider "service" to others to be the highest and most important work of all (as opposed to seeing such work as demeaning, and something to be done only for money)?

12. Have you ever fantasized about just cutting lawns, raking beaches in Hawaii, or painting houses? Have you ever looked longingly out the window of your office at the person sweeping the street, wondering if all of your status isn't really a little boring after all?

The more yes answers to these twelve questions, the more likely you are to be enjoying the social dimension of working. The more no answers to these questions, the more likely you are to have fallen into the cultural trap of *"the wrongful work wish."* The "wish" is to do more and more for more and more to turn out more and more to get more and more so we can enjoy life more and more which only seems to cause more needs and complications which require even more work. In effect, this is a death wish. The arguments you are having with your boss or fellow employees, the anger and frustration you feel at work, the uselessness and impotence you sometimes complain about at work, are *not* just due to "the job." Such feelings of work despair stem from the lack of joy, pride, and a sense of self-value in the type of work you do and the purpose of that working in the context of the world system.

Many of my successful patients suffer from what psychologists call the "impostor phenomenon." Even though they have success, money, and status, they feel somehow empty and unfulfilled, as if they could be exposed any minute as frauds undeserving of their positions. I suggest to you that much of this "impostor" feeling, this sense of not really deserving and being able to rest and enjoy what we have done, is due to the impact of the wrongful work wish. We just do not pay enough attention to what we want to do when we grow up, so when we do finally grow up, we discover that we have failed to grow "in," to examine why and for whom we are doing what we are doing.

As difficult as it may be for you to remember at times of anger and disappointment at work, any potential for joy in working will be lost if you do not attend to the why and so what of your job. We must continually ask ourselves about the "fit" of our working with the overall system. We must ask ourselves less about what we do for a living and more about the overall impact of what our working does for the lives of everyone else.

The Joyful Job

I don't have much choice really. It's go to work or watch game shows and soap operas.

WOMAN ACCOUNTANT

Learning super joy requires that you examine the purpose behind whatever work you do. We all work, someplace, doing something. Many of us work with little or no pay in the form of money, but we all work. The joyful job test is one way to assess your working style for the presence or absence of joy. Before you move to the chapters on the joy of loving and believing, take time to check for joy in whatever job you do.

As I have done throughout all of the chapters, I have tried to use a letter and code system to help you remember the key concepts related to the joy response. The Joyful Job Test is summarized by the "Ten Cs," some of which you will recognize from other aspects of super joy.

The Joyful Job Test

Use the following scale to score yourself on this test.

not at all   some   average   quite a bit   very much

0   1   2   3   4   5   6   7   8   9   10

1. Completeness: When you end your work for the day, are you satisfied that you have been productive and that you have done a good day's work?   _____

Joy in working relates to a sense of "mini-closures," of being done at least for a while. A constant feeling of never being caught up takes the joy out of working.

2. Cognition: Can you focus on the task at hand without distractions from inside or outside? Are you focused on what you are doing, free of a sense of trying to think of many things at once?   _____

Pressure at work begins when you are not able or free to focus your thoughts and attention on what you are doing. You can't have fun at what you are trying to do if you are too distracted, too "mentally busy" to fully experience what you are doing. Joy at work relates to being rational and focused at work.

3. Caution: Are you working at a pace that allows you to be as careful as you should be as you work?   _____

There is nothing more "joyless" than working for hours only to find that you have been working too quickly, too carelessly, and have to do much of what you have already done all over again. People who work regularly on computers know only too well the sinking and panic feeling of watching hours of work erased by lack of caution and step-by-step attention. We must learn to take our time at work, not try to squeeze more into the time we have.

Effective use of computers requires that you work step by step, in small segments, and always save your work. This cautious approach prevents the loss of hours of work. The same principle applies to all working. Take time to stop, reassess, and "see and save" what you have done so far. Working at a careless but quick pace could result in a total loss of all that you have worked on and for and is one of the main causes of industrial injury.

4. Competency: Do you consider yourself very skilled and talented at what you do?   _____

As I discussed earlier, a key component of joyfulness is a strong sense of personal worth and effectiveness. Particularly when we are working, our joy depends on reflections from others and personal reflection on ourselves that we are very good at what we do. Learning theorists know that the first step to effective development is the establishment of the "I can do it and do it very, very well" feeling.

5. Control: Do you have a say in how things are done where you are working? Do you feel that your input will not get you "put out" and that what you think matters?   _____

Researchers have shown clearly that a sense of control of our own destiny is a key component of what Suzanne Kobasa calls "personality hardiness." Such control is also a key aspect of our professional hardiness. We should be less busy arguing over who is in charge and be more busy seeing that we are in charge of ourselves and committed to common goals. Quality control depends on a personal sense of control by the workers producing the products and services.

6. Calm: During most of your workday, do you feel calm and in a comfortable rhythm? Are you free of a sense of impending problems and/or constant setbacks and disruptions?   _____

We would all be much better off at work if we had more "calming breaks" than "coffee breaks." Workers find themselves on a "caffeine-glucose go-round" of caffeine, sweets, fatigue, followed by more caffeine and sweets to combat the fatigue, temporary "buzz" from the "highs" of the caffeine or machine food, followed again by fatigue, and so on and so on. We seem to be trying to drag our bodies through the workday by quick fixes of toxic substances instead of realizing that fatigue is a symptom of joyless work. On your next break, sit down and pray, meditate, or at least listen to some relaxing music. Stretch, dance, move, and smile. This will work much better for you and your colleagues than driving your pancreas crazy by spinning it through the caffeine and "crud" cycle.

7. **Commitment:** Are you still dedicated to your place of employment? Are you proud of where you work, your coworkers, and the work your company does?   _____

You will not respect yourself or your work any more than you respect the company for which you work. Our society began to ridicule concepts such as company loyalty and faithfulness to the company mission when the erroneous idea of "management" became popular. People who need "managing" will never feel totally committed to a company vision, and those companies that are able to clearly show their vision to the workers and make them part of that vision will not need management at all. Truly effective "management" is the art of exposing workers to the joy, relevance, importance, and challenge of their jobs and then getting out of the way.

8. **Communication:** Do you feel that you are heard and understood at work and that people with whom or for whom you work are talking with you?   _____

I have spent my career in hospitals, universities, and now working with the publishing industry. All three of these institutions should be models of outstanding communication, yet almost everyone working in these areas complains daily about not being understood, listened to, cared about, or really communicated with. Hostile letters, memos, notes, and comments are frequent in the work world, while positive feedback, compliments, real talking and listening sessions are very rare. Until we take the large conference tables out from between the people sitting around them and form a closer circle of caring and communicating, the "bored" room will be the model of one-sided dys-communication, a-communication, and mal-communication.

9. Challenge: Do you feel that you are learning every day at your job?   _____

If we do not learn, we die. Learning is growth and development and, at work, we must maintain our student status if we are to graduate to increasingly meaningful work. A cynical and surrendering approach to a job is the last stage before total burnout or freeze-out.

10. Caring: Do you care about where you work, whom you work with, and what you work at?   _____

When our work becomes just a job, then we have lost the impetus of joy that can influence the other areas of our living. We may use the term "burnout," but we really mean that someone just doesn't care anymore about what they are doing. Such people may never have found the spark of joyful working in the first place.

If you scored over 90 points on the Joyful Job Test, you are doing very well at taking joy to work with you and bringing it back home again; 89 or less points, and it is time to look at those areas on the test where you lost points. Don't wait until you have worked yourself to an early grave. It is possible to work yourself to a sense of new energy and a super joy in working that makes daily living more meaningful.

CHAPTER EIGHT

The Joy of Sympathetic Loving

> I have never been in love for more than a few minutes, I mean, the feeling is so intense that it can only last in spurts. Otherwise, it would just kill you with its intensity.
>
> ANONYMOUS MAN

The above statement illustrates a mythology about love that takes the joy out of loving. We view love as some magnificently profound emotional experience, a romantic reflex over which we have no control. We think that love happens to us or that we fall in it. Love is really sympathetic joy, intentionally trying to feel with and for someone over time. This chapter discusses love as a key component of the super joy response and describes the "love star" concept that I have used for more than eighteen years in my clinical work to teach about the joy of loving.

Rethinking Love

Before you can understand the love star concept, you must broaden your concept of what loving means. Our society prefers to focus on only two types of love: romantic and familial. We talk of love exclusively in heterosexual terms if we are not talking

171

about what we see as a familial love. We may say that we "love" our same-gender friends or good friends of the opposite gender, but we seldom really mean that we are "in love" with them. Somehow, "real" love is exclusively reserved for family love and sexual love.

I suggest that the joy of love requires five key changes in this narrow view of loving:

1. **Love is not a quantity to be invested.** Loving is infinite. Therefore, we can intensely love and be intensely loved by a much wider range of people than we may have originally imagined.

2. **Sexuality is always a part of love.** This sexuality is not always genital sexuality, but a touching and connecting sensuality that must be present for real loving to take place. We must overcome our unrealistic fear of touching each other, of being sensuous with each other. We must overcome our homophobia, our needlessly love-limiting concept that real sexual love is always heterosexual. Whom we choose to share erotic stimulation with can be profoundly related to love, but such a choice cannot limit whom we choose to love and be sensuous with.

3. **Loving takes work, hard work.** Our image of being helplessly and innocently struck by Cupid's arrow is the stuff of Valentine cards but has nothing to do with the joy of love. You must act to love. Love is volitional and experiential, not emotional and responsive.

4. **We must learn that love as sympathetic joy, a caring with someone, cannot survive if it is isolated from all other life experiences.** Love must find its way into the workplace, the school, and the hospital room, and if we are to survive, into the negotiation room when the life of our world is being discussed. Love cannot be viewed as separate from daily life and the interaction of nations and national leaders. Somehow we have to get "love" some better publicity. We must come to see love not as

something that takes place after everything else is settled but as the only way anything will ever be settled.

5. We cannot let fear of disease scare us into an intimacy of surrender. AIDS and other diseases cannot be given the power to shove us together because we will die if we don't stay with one person. We cannot wait until modern medicine "cures" AIDS before we look for more people to love. Intimate genital contact should always be a matter of thoughtful and responsible partner selection, but the evolution and conquering of disease have always been primarily related to the evolution of human loving. The decline in disease has been due for the most part to loving changes in how we live, not to medical miracles.

Declines in deaths from tuberculosis, influenza, whooping cough, measles, pneumonia, and scarlet fever all preceded the discovery of medicines that further reduced the death rate. Even though it is difficult for us to accept, medicine just has not been the magic savior it is cracked up to be. A more nurturing, comforting, sympathetic society has always resulted in the most significant health changes. Medicine has helped, but it has not been the major factor in solving any disease crisis.

I believe that the death rate from AIDS will increase to a tragic peak level and then decrease dramatically *before* a vaccine or treatment drug is discovered. I believe that the turnaround in the death rate will occur because of an increase in our understanding, sympathy, and love for the AIDS patient and the world in which he or she lives, and our discovery that it is not just a virus but a complex set of societal and cultural cofactors that are related to AIDS. This is not to say that modern medicine will not play a major role in unraveling the AIDS puzzle, but medicine will not save us from AIDS any more than it has saved us from any disease. We must save ourselves, and sympathetic love, including a broadened view of whom we can really love, will be a key part of the rescue. The letter to AIDS patients and people worried about AIDS in Chapter Fourteen addresses the issue of love and AIDS in more detail.

Drs. Ornstein and Sobel, in their book *The Healing Brain,* write, "Why should we place our faith and resources in a medicine based largely on the treatment of disease?" It is how we live and love that matters, not how we are made well when we are sick. Super joy is a way of finding more joy in our living and less medicine in our cabinets. We had better look as hard to our loving as we do to the test tube if we are going to survive any disease. We must put the joy back into loving.

Listen to the major songs about love and you will notice that they seldom contain words of joy or celebration. We hear about the pain of love, the agony of love, how much love hurts, or how much it drives us insane and clouds our judgment. Some songs sing love's praise, but we seem to think that love is some type of major crisis, some soul-wrenching experience. I suggest that love is one of the most joyful of human experiences. Love doesn't really hurt at all; it just stings a little. Love stings because it demands that we control the selfish brain and let it know that other people matter as much or more than it does. Maybe, with the sting of a vaccination of love, our selfish brains will develop a tolerance, even a preference, for the stimulation of love.

The Star of Joyful Love and a Cure for the Cupid Complex

When I first began working with disorders of love and people who were confused about how they loved, why they felt unloved, or where love was, I became aware that people were "love lazy." They wanted love to happen to them. I called this the "Cupid complex," passively waiting for an arrow of love to strike rather than acting lovingly. I needed a system that would help my patients learn about the complexities of love. The love star provided a focus for discussions about the meaning of joyful loving. The star concept developed over the years as a system that promoted discussions about loving and allowed a simple way to talk about ideas that were not so simple at all.

Here is the drawing of the love star that my patients used to focus their discussions. Again, I have used a simple "letter" system so you can more easily recall the main ideas.

I will describe the core of the love star first, and I will include the actual comments of some of my patients as they discussed the love star concept. We taped the love star discussions during marital and group work and found relistening to the tapes to be helpful in understanding the complexities of loving. You may want to discuss the love star with someone you love and tape your discussion. Listen to your own tapes then as a private review and you may see some new or neglected dimensions of loving that can broaden your joy of loving.

To understand how the love star works, look first at the inside of the star. Look at the words beginning with "R." I used the same letters for each set of concepts to allow for a continuity in our discussions. Patients were more easily able to memorize the concepts and continue discussions with others when a "code" system of common letters was used.

For example, look at the word "Reliable." This is the core concept for the arm of the star that reads "Touch." This leads to the point of that particular arm of the star, Sexuality. All core concepts relate to each respective arm of the love star, culminating in one of the five major "points" of love. The idea is to read the love star from the inside out, but if you have a problem in one of your loving relationships, you would start at the "point" where the problem seems most pronounced and read "outside in" to the core concept at the root of the problem.

Core concepts on the love star are related to individual characteristics. Each arm or ray relates more to the interactional component of love. The end of each ray is the result of the combination of individual and interactional components of loving, a major dimension of joyful, sympathetic love.

If there are sexual problems in one of your loving relationships, either lack of sexual happiness or problems in straightening out the sex aspect of love with someone, some trouble in putting sex in a mutually comfortable perspective, you would look first to that "point." You would then look to the concept of "Touch" in the arm at that "point." It is likely that the concept of touch is being distorted or miscommunicated in the relationship. In turn, attempting by one or both persons to love is not seen as a reliable source of sympathy, attention, and understanding. One or both partners may feel that their needs for sex in the relationship are misunderstood, unrequited, or frustrated in some way. There may be a feeling that the partner or the relationship does not provide reliable cues regarding sex or assurances of dependability following physical loving.

To better understand the idea of the five rays or arms of the love star and how the concepts of the star interrelate, I will describe each separately.

Love, Rationality, Talking, and Sensibility

Working with love disorder patients taught me that people feel rational thinking is not a part of love. In fact, one symptom of the Cupid complex is muddled, wrongheaded thinking. We think we have to become "love struck," overwhelmed, or at the very least "crazy" about someone before we are truly in love. Joyful love depends on our ability to be sensible about our loving, our ability to realize that love is as much (or perhaps more) a way of thinking as it is a way of feeling.

Being rational about love requires the avoidance of eleven "love lapses," slips of the heart that cause our brains to be even more selfish than they already are.

Eleven Love Lapses

1. I must find my one and only lover.

As I have discussed, love is not by nature restricted to one lover. To say you can only really love one person is like saying you can only be angry with one person at a time. Emotions and thoughts are not person specific, and it is irrational to think about finding a one and only.

2. When I am in love, I must give myself completely to my lover.

Loving has nothing to do with giving ourselves or our lives away. In fact, quite the opposite is true. Joyful loving is accomplished as much by self-enhancement and growth as it is by helping our lovers grow.

3. Love is never having to say you are sorry.

Love is always having to say you are sorry. If love is joyful sympathy, then being responsible for our impact on our lovers is very important, and when we behave hurtfully or irresponsibly, we are obligated not only to say we are sorry but to show we are sorry by recommitment and reinvestment in the loving relationship.

4. When I am in love, I must tell little love lies to protect my lover.

Joyful love is based on complete disclosure, not the protective insult of assuming that we know just how much our lovers can deal with.

5. If my lover truly believes that I love her or him, then he or she will never doubt my love.

Joyful love is a growing and ongoing process. Doubt can lead to questions that challenge the relationship to more breadth and depth. Doubt does not diminish love, it can enhance it by keeping a focus on the volitional component of loving. Expressing doubt about love and loving does not have to destroy or weaken our loving.

6. Love grows by itself. Once you are really in love, it is like a seed that keeps on growing.

Nothing about us as humans takes care of itself. Loving requires constant vigilance, change, effort, nurturance, and care. No seed grows without support. A loving relationship that is struggling is not always in trouble; sometimes it is just in a growth spurt.

7. Love is illogical and follows no rules.

Love is the same as all human capacities and follows the same rules that dictate our thinking, living, and feeling. Illogical love is romance, not real love. Joyful love requires clear thinking, not cognitive surrender.

8. When you are loving, you can't do or feel anything else.

The miracle of being human is that we are able to do and feel many things at once. Love does not knock out the entire system and render us love slaves. Love, like all feeling and thinking, is always a part of the whole life system.

9. Love is blind.

Love enhances visual acuity. We see life more clearly when we are experiencing joyful love. If we are blinded by our loving, we are being overdosed by the stress chemicals of our stress addiction, dominated by romance, not joyful loving.

10. Love is like no other human experience.

Love is like all other human experiences. It is like anger, hope, fear, guilt, intelligence, and even rage. At its very core, to love is to be human. When we put love on a pedestal, we separate it from our humanness, make it larger than life rather than a part of living.

11. Love can save the world.

Lovers can save the world. Love itself will never be enough, because energy, intelligence, altruism, and an overcoming of our ethonocentrism are just as important as love if the human race is going to outrun the arms race. Love may be an underlying motivator of changes for peace, but it cannot carry the burden for change by itself. We must fight and sacrifice for peace as much as love for it.

When a loving relationship seems to be plagued by nonsense, illogical arguments, and immature withdrawal, rationality is at the core of the problem. The way in which you "go public" with your thought processes is your communicational style. Thinking rationally about loving is not enough if you persist in talking about love in irrational, ineffective styles. Here is the Simplified Communicational Test for basic rational communicational skills.

Simplified Communicational Test

Score yourself on the items below using the following system.

5 - Always

4 - Much of the time

3 - Sometimes

2 - Not very often at all

1 - Once in a rare while

0 - Never

1. I listen as much as I talk. _____

2. I talk in a steady, rhythmic pace. _____

3. People seldom have to repeat the things they say to me. _____

4. I allow others to choose and direct the topic of conversation. _____

5. I enjoy others' views on controversial topics and like to hear what they have to say. _____

6. I understand and tolerate angry talk by others and do not respond in kind. _____

7. I take responsibility for my communication, and if others miss what I say or do not understand, I patiently repeat and explain myself. _____

8. I speak in an easy, soothing, calm tone.   _____

9. I avoid sarcasm and negative statements.   _____

10. I request, rather than demand, when I am asking for something or asking people to do something.   _____

Thirty-nine points or less on this test and you are probably having severe problems in the talking arm of the love star. This talking includes listening and refers to "having a talk" with your lover. The Simplified Communicational Test is a test of process, not content. As author Marilyn Ferguson points out, our communication must be not only effective and broad but deep and meaningful as well. We must communicate our feelings, hear others' feelings, and be able to empathize and sympathize with these feelings.

Psychologists talk about effective listening skills as basic to any good communication. Greek philosopher Epictetus wrote, "Nature has given man one tongue, but two ears, that we may hear twice as much as we speak." If there is trouble in a loving relationship along the sensibility arm of the love star, look to the way in which intimate messages are sent. Work on sending and receiving messages, and remember the basic rule of loving talking. The accuracy and receipt of a message always rest with the sender. If your partner misunderstands you, it is your responsibility to clarify your position and feelings.

Joyful love must be sensible love. It must be characterized by a balance in the talking and listening, in the empathy between the lovers. At its core, joyful love must by rational, based on clear thinking and a constant learning with your lover.

"What drives me to distraction is that nothing in our relationship makes sense," reported one wife. "Our discussions just seem to miss the mark. And the more we talk, the less sense we make. When we argue, all sense goes right out the window." This wife's statement illustrates the need for love to make sense, to give lovers a feeling of being heard and being able to tell their story, to be rational in a sometimes irrational world. One joy of love is that it provides us with an escape from the senselessness of much of our daily living.

Sensitivity, Time, and Responsive Loving

Sensitivity is an act of time commitment. It is a major time investment to pay attention to our lovers, to "spend" time with and for them. When patients complained that their partners were insensitive, this complaint translated to the fact that not enough time was being spent on the relationship.

Looking at the sensitivity arm or ray of the love star, you can trace back to the time issue and ultimately the issue of "responsiveness" to partner needs. In a society that stresses individualism, we have failed to teach our children how to recognize needs in others, how to lower the threshold of their responsiveness. Many children now have trouble identifying looks or expressions of sadness or happiness when shown pictures of people expressing different emotions. We are teaching our children what to say and do about loving, but somehow we are failing to teach them to be sensitive to others, to read people for what needs they have. We have become an articulate society but we are empathetically illiterate. We communicate as if we are computers interacting, receiving only "data" without feeling. How many salespersons really mean what they say when they ask, "May I help you?" Don't they more often mean, "Can I sell you something?" Hasn't selling become the art of creating needs instead of trying to recognize and fill them?

We show recognition by giving our time to our loving. Too often, lovers speak of lack of sensitivity without assigning a necessary measurable definition to the term. Sensitivity is ultimately measurable by the time we give to our loving. Try this mini-test to see if you are spending enough loving time.

The Love Time Test

During a seven-day week, how many minutes do you spend:

1. Asking about the needs of your lover? _____

2. Discussing the future of your relationship? _____

3. Commending and complimenting your relationship, talking about how good it really is? _____

4. Complimenting your lover? _____

5. Thinking about your lover's needs in his or her absence? _____

6. Planning to do something for your lover? _____

7. Going out of your way for your lover? Doing what you really don't like to do, but doing something to make your lover happy? _____

8. Just looking at your lover, quietly and admiringly? _____

9. Daydreaming about your lover? _____

10. Improving something about yourself *for* your lover? _____

Remember, I am talking about a very broad type of loving, so you may have many lovers. Take the test for each of your lovers. Some of my patients arbitrarily assigned a minimum of what they called "heart hours" per week invested in the time categories above. They might decide to invest a minimum of an hour per lover per week in the above behaviors.

"I have five kids, one husband, a mother, three women lover-

LOVE STAR OF JOYFUL SYMPATHY

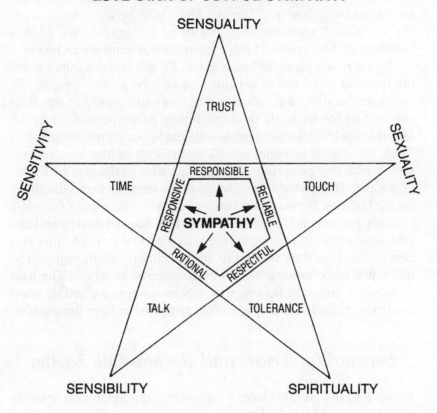

friends, and two men lovers. I'm going to be hearted out if I spend this much time on loving," said one patient, "and I can't imagine a better way to become exhausted."

Another patient said, "You know, we are forgetting something here. I still love my father deeply, and he passed away years ago. I spend time thinking about him, what he needed, what he did, how valuable he was to me. Doesn't that time count?"

"Sure," answered another patient. "In fact, when I really think about this, most of the time I am not with the people I love. Love is a matter of imagery, of keeping them in our mind to help crowd out the selfish brain bunk junk."

"I agree," said another patient. "But I am having nothing but trouble talking about my 'lovers.' The whole neighborhood is going to think I am scheduling orgies or something. We need a better word for 'lovers.' I can't go around talking about lovers."

"If you're not going to laugh at me, I'll tell you the stupid word my husband and I use to get this idea of loving many people. We call them 'luddies,' a combination of lover and buddy. It was difficult at first for us to think about loving other people. Then we learned that loving other people only made our own love special. I think you can only really get all of the rays of the love star together with one person, but you can get a lot of the rays with a lot of people. But you do have to take the time to make 'luddies,' loving buddies. If you don't, you end up with just a lot of friends."

Super joy depends on extended and broadened loving and the time investment to recognize others as a part of you. The first two rays of the love star, sensibility and sensitivity, then, require the individual to be rational and to be responsive to others. The irrationality of stress addiction, with it's accompanying selfish brain syndrome makes rational, sensitive, sympathetic love impossible.

Sensuality, Trust, and Responsible Loving

For love to live, it must have a sensuous component. Our sexually retarded society has had trouble separating sex from sensuality, and as a result our "luddies," the men and women friends whom we can come to love, have been "off limits" regarding touching and holding. Although women have been given cultural permission to touch one another more openly than men, male/male or friendly female/male touching has been highly suspect and prohibited by our culture. Affairs may be frequent and even winked at knowingly, but mature and responsible sensuous touching between male and female friends is seen as inappropriate.

I suggest that joyful loving requires the breaking of the "three-foot" barrier, the sensuous cocoon that we weave around ourselves. Most sociologists and behaviorists have noted that there is an approximately three-foot area around us that we do not allow to be penetrated by anyone other than our families or those with whom we have sex. As a result, full joyful loving of many people is prevented because we think that there is only one type of intercourse. If we love enough to trust one another, then we can be responsible and mature enough to learn that our erotic zones are not buttons that operate our genitals. Our erotic zones can also be our contact zones. We are not helpless slaves of psychophysiological sexual reflex. We can feel good when we touch and hold one another without being sexual.

As you will read in Chapter 11 in the letter to sad young people, I believe that one reason for the increasing depression in children and particularly adolescents is that we gradually withdraw our physical contact from our children as they get older. We are afraid of being accused of "incest," "sexual abuse," or are turned away by our children's culturally induced touch-shyness, and as a result we deprive our young people of touching when they may need it most.

"It was frightening at first," said one woman. "I have been friends with Linda for more than ten years. We hugged each other and stuff, but we never really just walked and held hands. One day after our discussion of this love star thing, I took a risk for joy. I took her hand as we shopped. She didn't say a word. It was like she didn't know I was holding her hand. She did know, though, because I felt her hand go from warm to cold to cold and wet. Later, when we got back to the car, I asked her if she was upset. She started to cry and took me in her arms. She said she always wanted to hold hands with me, but she thought I would think she was gay. I don't know why that would make any difference anyway. I found out now that she is. I'm not. We hold hands now and hug all the time. We comb each other's hair. I'm so mad that we missed all those years of touching."

A male patient responded, "I know just what you mean. I finally held hands with a woman friend, you know, a buddy. She got upset at first and said that we were just very good friends and that she had no intention of having sex with me. I told her I just wanted to touch her, to hold her hand because I felt close to her. We still can't do it. This man-woman thing is ruined by sex instead of helped by it. Sex takes away half of a possible friendship population."

Even in a relationship in which sex is taking place, the sensual dimension of that relationship requires responsibility, a responsibility for clear communication of sensuous needs. A strong degree of trust and responsible sexuality can lead to a much wider range of sensuous experiences, not only of touch but of sharing intimately the beauty of one human's awareness and verification of the existence and presence of another human.

"At first I was afraid to talk to my friend about the sunset. Can you imagine that? We played semivicious handball three times a week. We swore at each other, cheated, and lied. But he is a great friend. I just wanted to sit with him and share a sunset. When we did, he finally became a 'luddy.' " This patient was discussing the broader and more meaningful definition of sensuality. He was able to find sensuality with his friend because he took responsibility for his own feelings, trusted himself, his friend, and their relationship, and took the risk of trusting his own feelings and his friend enough to be sensuous with him. Can you take such a risk in your friendships? Can you change some of your good friends to great "luddies"?

To help you discover more sensuous joy, take the next test. It is designed to help you understand the importance of physical confirmation with loving friends.

The Sensuous Joy Test

Use this scale for scoring yourself on the next items:

4 - Always

3 - Very Much

2 - Once in a while

1 - Hardly Ever

0 - Never

1. Can you stand close to people when you talk? _____

2. Can you hold hands with close friends while walking? _____

3. Can you talk about your dreams with your friends? _____

4. Can you talk with your friends about what makes you sad? _____

5. Can you touch and stroke your close friends of both genders gently and pleasurably? _____

6. Can you cry in front of or with your friends? _____

7. Would your friends describe you as emotional and open? _____

8. Do your friends and other people seem to want to be close to you? _____

9. Do you feel as though you make people feel good when you are around? _____

10. Do you talk honestly with your friends, giving them the whole story and trusting that they will keep your confidence? _____

If you scored 29 or less points on this test, your relationships would probably be more joyful if you were more open and sensuous in your interactions. If sensuality is a problem in one of your relationships, look to trust and mutual self-responsibility before you look to sex. The natural consequence of being self-responsible, trusting, and trustworthy is a sensuality that derives from intimacy instead of a pseudo-intimacy attempt through sex.

If our society continues to divide itself into touchables and untouchables, avoiding sensuality because we think it is always related to sexuality, we will continue to have only a fraction of the lovers and loving we could joyfully experience. If we can lower our sensuality thresholds, we can stop sex from robbing our sensuality lives.

Spirituality, Tolerance, and Respectful Love

Marriage and relationship therapists have focused heavily on communicational approaches to solving interaction problems. Therapists have largely ignored, however, the spiritual component of love. An important fact emerging from my years of work with troubled families is that few of us practice sufficient tolerance in our daily living. We have lost our liberal spirit toward others, and our sense of patience and fairness is overwhelmed by our stress addiction and sense of urgency for what will be or we think ought to be.

For joyful love to take place, we must relearn acceptance of the present moment. We must relearn how to live nonjudgmentally, with acceptance, and with forbearance. We will forever be too agitated to really love others if we allow our selfish brains to attach themselves to the future at the expense of the present.

Our society is always in a state of foreplay. Teams compete to qualify for the "really meaningful" games of the playoffs. We work so that we may eventually get the job we want. We touch, hold, and massage so we can get ready to "do it." We search for magic sex spots that can save intimate time by reacting quickly and efficiently to the right touch at the right place. Joyful love is much more acceptance than anticipation, much more a celebration of sharing than getting ready for physical release, and the joyful sympathy that is love can only be achieved by intense focus on the "now."

To love joyfully, we must develop congeniality, a community of feeling with others. Compassion, commiseration, consonance, and accord are all key components of loving sympathy, and at the base of each of these feelings is tolerance and focus on what "is" rather than what could or ought to be, an unqualified acceptance of the basic humanness of another person.

The first core component of joyful loving (being rational, responsive, and responsible) will get us nowhere if we are unable to be respectful of others. Perhaps because we are so impatient with our own imperfections, we expect others to be somehow better than we are. We expect our lovers to make up for some real or illusionary deficiency in ourselves. Something spiritual happens, something much more than just the sum of two people, when we have enough respect for ourselves and for our lovers to be tolerant of who we are and who they are.

When persons having trouble with their relationships come to me in trouble, I can sense a spiritual crisis. The couples seem to have lost common purpose and direction because they have lost mutual respect. There is a lack of a shared, intact, and practiced belief system that provides a base for universal respect. There can be little tolerance if there is not a higher value placed on living, some clear purpose for our existence.

One of the first lines of attack on relationship problems is to have the lovers examine or re-examine their belief systems. Tolerance and respect grow from a sense of the sameness of all of us. Chapter 9 will present the Ten Commandments as they may be seen in terms of recommendations for joy and health. Each of these commandments requires tolerance and faith in self and others and, when practiced consistently, can provide guidelines for joyful loving.

Here is the Love Tolerance Test I use with my patients. You may want to take the test with a lover or a "luddy" and discuss the results.

The Love Tolerance Test

Without much thought, answer yes or no to each of the following questions. Even though you may think you fall somewhere between yes or no on a specific item, pick the answer closest to how you feel. If you are getting upset about having to answer yes or no, be tolerant and take the test anyway.

1. Do you find yourself watching for flaws in others? _____

2. Do you feel that most people are selfish? _____

3. Do you feel that people will take advantage of you if you give them the chance? _____

4. Do you react strongly to certain quirks or habits that others may have? _____

5. Do you feel almost like hitting someone who has thoughtlessly stepped in front of you in line? _____

6. Do you get angry when people do not do what they say they are going to do? _____

7. Do you find yourself encountering more and more obnoxious people? _____

8. Do you believe that most people lie? _____

9. Do you feel that if more people acted as you do, this would be a much better world? _____

10. Do you get upset just by how someone looks? _____

The more "yes" answers on the above items, the more intolerant you tend to be and the more likely that your loving will be diminished by this intolerance.

"I can't stand his laugh," said one woman. "I'm sorry, but his laugh just sends me off. It sounds phony."

"Well, I can't stand that you don't laugh," answered the man toward whom she was intolerant. "You laugh backward. You sort of snore instead of laugh. You sound like this." As the man demonstrated how he heard the woman's laugh, both the man and woman began to laugh. The critical woman could not help herself. She laughed while trying to maintain her critical posture. "Be careful," said the man. "You might get a laughter hernia if you hold back. Go ahead and do your snore laugh. It makes me laugh, then you get upset, then you do more of your snore laugh, and we all go crazy." The shared laughter that followed resulted in laughter tears, evidence of the occurrence of super joy.

Most human interactions are not so easily saved by the natural tolerance of humor. If we could look for the humor in all of us, the fact that we all are ridiculous sometimes, maybe we could learn to laugh from respect instead of derision. Would you say that your relationships show a strong spiritual tone of mutual respect and tolerance? Remember, respect and tolerance are prerequisites, not earned payoffs, and they are starting points for loving, not goals.

Without an intact spiritual belief system, some transcendent view of the purpose of living, the motivation and energy for tolerance will be lost. Most programs that attempt to treat addictions include a strong emphasis on belief systems. To overcome the stress addiction that blocks joy and love, the rediscovery of life's meaning for you must take place.

You can now look at four key components of joyful love; *Sensibility*, *Sensitivity*, *Sensuality*, and *Spirituality*. You can see that the related loving behaviors are effective *T*alking, taking *T*ime, *T*rusting, and the development of *T*olerance. Looking further into the love star, you can see that the key personal characteristics of a joyful lover are being *R*ational, *R*esponsive, *R*esponsible, and *R*espectful. I return now to the ray of the love star that I first used as an example to introduce the love star concept. The fifth ray, the sexuality arm of the love star, is not a necessary ray of all love stars. As the drawing on page 183 represents, a four-ray love star can shine very brightly. There are love stars that we may choose to make into five-ray special stars, including the sexuality dimension of loving. Other love stars we may choose to enjoy without the ray of sexuality, interacting with a "luddy" instead of a "lover."

Sexuality, Touch, and Reliable Love

Sexuality is related to intimate and erotic touch. All of the sexual problems I have ever treated have really been disorders of reliability. One or both partners feels, rightly or wrongly, that the other partner is not dependable, either in the mechanics of sexual love or as a person with whom to relate over time in many life situations.

"She expects me to be some kind of robot. We may have just had a fight and she has just told me what a jerk I am, then an hour later we are supposed to have sex. No way." This husband's report illustrates his sense of undependability on the part of his wife. He feels that he cannot be sure of how she really feels for him even though she may want to feel him and be physically felt. We seem unable to learn that feeling cannot be divided into physical and emotional categories. As you learned earlier in this book, all emotions are accompanied by physical change, and physical changes themselves result in emotional experiences.

When you notice sexual problems in your relationship, you must look to the whole love star, not just the sexual dimension. Look at the whole star, and then look at the touching. The touching will not be erotic or fulfilling if the toucher or touchee feels that he or she cannot rely on the partner for effective and sensitive touch and more total loving accompanying and following the sexual interaction.

When William Masters and Virginia Johnson described their therapy program for couples, they emphasized what they called "sensate focus." Sensate focus is a technique that many therapists thought was a way to learn more about sexual response in a nonpressured and comfortable setting. Actually, this slow and sensuous taking turns touching was a way of re-establishing reliability. A renewal of self-reliance in sexual desirability and skill was one part of the reliance formula. The other part of the formula was the development of a new reliance on and comfort with the partner and with "self."

Here is the Sexual Reliance Test I have used with my patients. It is a simple test to determine the degree of confident, trustful reliability on self and partner.

The Sexual Reliance Test

Use this scoring system for the following items:

4 - Always

3 - Sometimes

2 - Seldom

1 - Never

1. When having sex, do you feel completely at ease with your partner's touch?   _____

2. Are you free of fear when you are having sex?   _____

3. Do you feel that sex enhances your relationship?   _____

4. Does your sexual partner know your "magic spots," the areas of your body that bring you pleasure?   _____

5. Is your partner's touch as gentle and/or firm as you would like it, and is that touch adaptive to your changing needs?   _____

6. Do you feel as if you are a good "toucher" and can please your partner?   _____

7. Do you feel that who you are and how you are is a "turn-on" to your partner?   _____

8. Do you feel that it is "you" and not just the "sex" that is turning your partner on?   _____

9. Do you feel that you are the best sex partner your lover could ever have?   _____

10. Do you express yourself clearly regarding changes, corrections, or modifications that are needed in your sexual interaction?   _____

If you scored 30 or less points on this test, you may be experiencing some problem with the reliability factor in your sexual life. More open communication and some risk taking by letting your partner know and encouraging him or her to let you know that something needs attention can improve things significantly.

Super joy may be the only true aphrodisiac. If sex turns us on, it is sensuality, sensitivity, sexuality, and spirituality that can "turn us in," make us aware of a connection through love that is the most profound of human experiences. Loving is always at the root of super joy.

CHAPTER NINE

The Joy of Faith: How to Develop Your Placebo Ability

When the sea was calm all boats alike showed mastership in floating.

SHAKESPEARE

A Breath of Fresh Hope

He couldn't seem to get his breath, and when he did, there didn't seem to be enough of it. His eyes itched, his nose was dripping, and short little sneezes squeezed the last air from his exhausted chest. As he looked down at his arm, the tears in his eyes made it look as if the needle the doctor was using for the injection was being held by four or five quivering hands.

"There. That should do the trick," said the doctor as he handed his patient a fresh box of tissues. "This stuff is brand new and is supposed to be the first real relief from your type of allergy. Call me tonight if I'm wrong, but I think you are going to see a real improvement."

As he drove home, he prayed that the doctor was right. His allergies had worsened steadily over the last few years and had

195

become almost unbearable since he took this new job. He now felt that he was allergic to everything, including not only his job but himself. No medicine had helped before and this new wonder drug could be the difference in surviving through another spring season. Every time he changed jobs, his allergy had gotten worse, but he knew that this was a real problem, not just "all in his mind."

The doctor received a call from his patient, but it was a call of celebration. "I cannot believe it," said the patient. "I can breathe. My eyes don't itch. I just look a little swollen, but I feel just great. That stuff is magic."

The patient returned to the doctor's office the next day. He would be receiving shots for several days, but now he came with hope and trust in the magic drug that drained his sinuses, dried his eyes, and opened his lungs like a big clean breath of the freshest air in the world.

The doctor decided to try his own experiment to make sure the drug itself and not the patient's belief in the drug, the so-called placebo effect, was the reason for the quick cure. This time the patient was given an injection of a totally inactive substance, a simple saline solution. "Here you go again," said the doctor. "This stuff seems to work wonders for you. Call me at once and let me know how good you feel."

This time the call was a call of panic. "Doctor, it didn't work like the first shot. I can hardly breathe. I am crushed. I thought sure that stuff would work for me."

"Don't worry," answered the doctor. "I gave you a placebo, a false injection, to see if the drug worked or if your faith in the drug was responsible for the effect. We know now that the drug works, so it is worth taking the slight risk of side effects from the real drug and giving you some of this new medication every day for a month. Come right in right now."

As the doctor hung up the phone, he immediately called the drug company. "Send me more of that new antiallergenic drug. It works like magic."

"You said a mouthful, Doc," answered the clerk representing the drug company. "We never sent any of the actual drug to doctors in your part of the country. All we sent you was placebo, just a saline solution. If it worked, it's magic all right." It was in fact the doctor's own belief in the drug that directly affected his patient, a form of physician placebo belief effect.

The doctor and the clerk in this true story are right. The potential of the human system to write its own prescription drawn from the internal pharmacy of the joy response psychochemicals is a magic of healing. The placebo "effect" is not an "effect" of the placebo, because by definition the placebo has no active ingredient to cause an effect of its own. Instead, the placebo is the catalyst for an internal implosion of healthy and healing chemicals drawn from the body's ability to protect and cure itself. These are the "joy juices" I mentioned earlier, and your body's placebo ability is actually your own potential for mobilizing the healing power of super joy.

We all have a placebo ability, an innate capacity to mobilize internal healing chemicals in response to our thoughts, feelings, and beliefs. This ability is not beyond our own control. We can learn to develop and improve our "placebo ability," actually train ourselves to use super joy for healing.

Researchers have recently discovered ten factors related directly to our own natural placebo ability. All ten are also related to super joy, which is the spark that ignites the whole natural and reflexive process of healing and hardiness. As you continue to learn about your own super joy, consider the next ten placebo ability factors and check to see how you and your family are doing on each of them.

1. Your Hypnotic Ability

Researchers have shown that your hypnotic ability, your ability to focus your attention intensely while reducing your awareness to peripheral stimulation and while suspending critical and analytic thinking in favor of more visual and emotional processes, is directly related to your ability to use your beliefs to promote healing.

No one hypnotizes you. All hypnosis is self-hypnosis, sometimes assisted by someone else who helps you to focus and enter a different state of consciousness. Hypnosis is always something you do, not something that is done to you. About ten percent of us show high hypnotic ability, while another ten percent show very low hypnotic ability. The ability to focus intensely is not something you show only during hypnotic induction, just as intelligence is not something you show only on intelligence tests. Most of us fall somewhere between the extremes of hypnotic ability. To learn where you fall on this component of your placebo ability, where you are in terms of being able to make suggestions to yourself when you are focused, centered, visualizing, and uncritical, take the following hypnotic ability test.

The Hypnotic Ability Test

Select a number from 10 (very much so) to 0 (not at all) that best represents you in response to each of the following items. Numbers above 5 and toward 10 mean that you are high on a given trait, and numbers below 5 and toward 0 mean that you are low on a given trait.

1. I attribute psychological causation to most events. _____

2. I think that you should go to the doctor frequently, and that your doctor should help you watch for illnesses. _____

3. I am a sensitive person and I get upset easily. _____

4. I find it easy to express my emotions verbally. _____

5. I believe that people can send "vibrations" and communicate without words. _____

6. I am superstitious. _____

7. I can act very silly and be a clown. _____

8. I like being the center of attention. _____

9. I enjoy being illogical and like to make decisions with my heart instead of my head. _____

10. I cry easily and hard. _____

11. I enjoy singing and dancing. _____

12. I can use either my right or left hand for many tasks. _____

13. I don't care much for organization just so long as I can find what I need. _____

14. I enjoy reading self-help books and books about popular psychology. _____

15. I have seen a ghost or apparition. _____

16. My dreams are strange and very real. _____

17. I like to watch talk shows on TV and will often follow the advice of a guest on one of these shows. _____

18. I like to touch and hug people. _____

19. I like planning and dreaming more than actually doing and executing. _____

20. I enjoy and value taking little tests like this test. _____

Now, count the number of scores you selected that were over the number 5. Do not total the scores, just count up how many of your scores were over 5. Subtract from that number the number of scores that were less than 5. For example, if you scored twelve items with numbers over 5, and six items with scores under 5, you will ignore the two 5 scores, and your hypnotic ability score would be 12 − 6 (ignore all 5s) = 6. Next, place your score on the scale below.

HYPNOTIC ABILITY SCALE

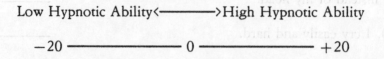

Low Hypnotic Ability<————>High Hypnotic Ability

−20 ————————— 0 ————————— +20

The closer your score is to the 0 point, the higher your placebo ability. In my work with chronically ill patients, I have found that this test is predictive of how effectively they can experience the joy of healing, how well they can use their own suggestions to their healer within for a dose of healing joy juices. Too much or too little hypnotic ability and your own placebo ability is lessened.

Doctors report that different patients react differently to exactly the same dose of a given medicine. There are many reasons for this, but I believe that one reason is the placebo ability of the given patient. One aspect of this ability is a balance in hypnotic ability. Persons at the extremes of the hypnotic ability scale tend to have much more frequent and severe stress disease symptoms, partly because of a lack of balance in their self-written internal joy chemical prescriptions. Persons at the far ends of the hypnotic ability scale tend to experience less joy than persons near the center of the scale. Your placebo ability is the healing component of super joy, and hypnotic ability is one measure of your capacity to use joy to heal.

Balance in hypnotic ability may be important for many reasons. First, persons who are too high on the above scale tend to be very high in fantasy ability. These fantasies are accompanied by physiological changes, and prolonged and repeated intense fantasy is no different than experiencing the actual fantasized event. Stress-related illness is caused as much by imagined stressors as by real threats. Super joy is a super balance in our interaction with reality, a balance between coping well with the real world while being able to create our own worlds when we want to or need to.

A second reason that hypnotic ability is important to super joy is that persons too high on the hypnotic scale may actually "incubate" illness and disease because of their hypersensitivity to their own bodies. Constantly aware of the slightest change in their body functions, the high hypnotic ability person may be overwhelming the adaptive mechanisms of the immune system, much as an over-sensitive alarm goes off too often and eventually burns out, leaving us open to break-ins and injury.

Third, persons with high hypnotic ability also tend to have high amnesic ability. They can close their minds to events they find displeasing. While this "closing out" can help us avoid needless worry, it can also result in ignoring serious symptoms while over-attending to less serious variations in body function. In effect, extreme attention is focused on the front gate while something more dangerous is sneaking in through the back door.

The psychological insensibility, the inability to share feelings, and the denial of a holistic explanation for health and illness are factors of low hypnotic ability that may decrease our placebo or self-healing ability. If there is one clear lesson in all medical research, it is that balance and moderation are key components of wellness, and these two rules apply directly to hypnotic ability as one of the factors in the effective use and development of our placebo ability.

Shakespeare's statement about boats that appear stable when the sea is calm reflects the idea that our true joy response ability is measured less by how we celebrate the gifts of life and more by how we rally in the face of emotional and physical challenges. Placebo ability is one measure of the resilience of our joy reflex, an index of how well our spirits are willing to listen to hope, belief, and trust in miracles.

2. Solid and Soft Support Systems

All disease and unhappiness, all lack of joy, is related to disconnection. Every living thing must be a part of the overall system of life or it will wither and die. Even plants grow better when they are among other thriving plants rather than standing alone in some cold and sterile hallway. When I showed pictures of solitary plants to my patients, they reacted with sympathy. "The poor thing looks lonely there," said one woman. When I showed these same patients pictures of the same exact plant now arranged in a grouping with other plants, these same patients responded with comfort and positive feelings. "Beautiful," said one man. "It looks like a happy family."

Our placebo ability, our mobilization of the joy response for healing, depends upon our connection with others, what researchers call our social supports. A better term would be "support systems," the ways in which we maintain contact and context within the world system, including solid and soft support systems.

The solid supports are money, shelter, food, and safety. Without these solid support systems, no amount of effort at self-healing will be maximally successful. Although it may not sound romantic, being unemployed is as threatening to our health as falling out of love. When one of us is "out of the system," the whole system feels the effect. In our eagerness to look for the psychological and social causes of illness, we have neglected these solid, tangible support systems.

The soft support systems are more difficult to measure than the solid supports. They include continued contact with other people, including family, friends, lovers, and colleagues. The research makes clear that placebo ability is measurably enhanced when the people around us are on our side, offering their own hope, concerns, and support.

A group of postsurgery patients was randomly selected as "targets" for prayer by persons outside the hospital. The people offering their prayers knew only the first names of the persons they were praying for. Another group of postsurgery patients was not included in the "prayer target" group. Both groups received exactly the same medical care. The group receiving the anonymous prayer had fewer postsurgical complications, more rapid recovery, and earlier dismissal from the hospital. The "soft" and less tangible support of anonymous healing prayer had enhanced the placebo ability, the self-healing, of the prayer target group.

When I presented this finding to a medical audience, the snickers of disbelief and skepticism were scattered through the room. "But why did every one of the target prayer receipt group do better than the nontarget group?" I asked the audience of doctors.

"Just pure chance," responded one doctor.

"But this work has been replicated at many hospitals. This is not a one-time finding. Patients' families often speak of sending positive prayers and energy to their loved ones. Don't you believe in such a process?" I asked.

"Well, sure I do," answered the doctor, "but it isn't science. This stuff is soft data."

The doctor is right. The issue of emotional and loving support is "soft" in that our usual measurement techniques do not deal with such issues very well. In maximizing our placebo ability, however, it is to our benefit to look to both soft and hard supports. If we don't water our plants, they will die of lack of solid support. A well-watered but lonely and ignored plant will never flower to its full potential. How are your soft and solid support systems today?

3. Catastrophizing, Awfulizing, and Talking to Yourself with Respect

Psychologist Albert Ellis referred to catastrophizing as an irrational pattern of thinking based on the anticipation of the worst scenario in daily living events. Catastrophizers sabotage their own healing powers and their potential for the joy that enhances such powers by cognitively altering their own brain chemistry to catastrophic rather than curing patterns.

My clinical experience indicates that those persons who expect the worst of this world may find themselves leaving it sooner than those who expect better of their life experiences. The pessimists tend toward a passive dependency, almost waiting for the inevitable disaster that they have precipitated by their own self-fulfilling prophecies. Their self-doubt becomes a lack of confidence on the part of the healer within, and their placebo ability is diminished. Even health care workers trying to help the awfulizer seem to succumb to their pessimistic outlook. If the nurses and physicians begin to share in your surrender, all hope of speedy recovery is lost.

The self-talk of the catastrophizer is a subliminal set of instructions to the pharmacist within, and exactly the wrong set of psychochemicals is released. I warn my patients that when they talk, out loud or to themselves, their internal healers are listening. It is important not to predict disaster, for your internal chemistry can comply with such a prediction. A realistic but affirmative and positive self-talk is a key part of all healing, not only on the part of the patient but on the part of the care takers. I posted a sign in the emergency room that reads, "Caution! Healing in progress. Please speak hopefully!"

4. The Value of Enlightened Self-deception

Live by the foma (harmless untruths) that make you brave and kind and healthy and happy.

KURT VONNEGUT

Another component of your placebo ability is appropriate cognitive and emotional avoidance of those issues over which you have no control. Ignoring real symptoms, intentionally deluding yourself away from awareness of something wrong with you, is as unhealthy as catastrophizing. Such denial is similar to placing a blindfold over the eyes of your internal healer. Fixation and hypervigilance for something that may go wrong is similar to assigning your internal healer to perpetual guard duty. When a real invader comes along, the guard may be too tired and overworked to deal with the intrusion.

I pointed out earlier that there is evidence that we can actually increase our own endorphins, the brain and body chemicals of elation and anesthesia. Endorphin release is accompanied by attention reduction. The opposite seems to be true as well. By selectively and responsibly *not* attending to challenges from our environment or from within, we can increase endorphin release. This fact demonstrates how we can directly influence our own placebo ability.

One of the leading researchers in the field of constructive denial and avoidance is Richard Lazarus. He writes, "Illusion can sometimes allow hope, which is healthy. The critical determinant is whether you're denying facts or the implications. Implications are ambiguous." If we allow our emotional lives to be constantly bothered by ambiguous threats, we lack the energy to cope well when real challenges occur.

"If I thought about this terrible medication and radiation, I'd get even sicker," reported one of my patients. "So I just ignore the whole thing. I go for treatment, but I just don't think about it. The psychiatrist calls it denial and thinks I must talk about it. I told him it is not denial. I know what's happening, but I can't do a damn thing about it, so I am intentionally avoiding thinking about or feeling about the issue, not denying it." This patient's statement is a perfect example of the constructive use of Vonnegut's "foma." We need such foma not only to survive day to day but to enhance our placebo ability. We do need to be alert for threats to our health and well-being, but if we are hypervigilant we spend all of our energy defensively instead of in joyful living. It is not only how we work and love but what we believe about our living that determines whether or not we experience super joy.

5. Autonomic Lability: Hyperreacting to the Past

There are two major emotions which lessen our placebo ability: fear and guilt. Both are emotions accompanied by an overmobilization of the neurohormonal system. In effect, we stew in our own stress juices when fear or guilt dominates our emotional lives, and the joy response is the only known antidote for these two stress emotions.

Fear is a form of maladaptive hyperarousal. Because of past associations, we overreact to daily events as if they were life threatening when in fact they are only psychosocially threatening. A hypersecretion of stress chemicals results, the same chemicals that are as addicting as they are damaging to the body system. We become overready, preparing a hormonal nuclear arsenal to deal with a minor skirmish of everyday life.

Guilt is a form of learned helplessness. Again our past experiences may have predisposed us to a form of psychological paralysis, with feelings of ineffectiveness, helplessness, and hopelessness in reaction to events which are actually natural transitional life challenges. Placebo ability is exactly the opposite of learned helplessness. Researchers are discovering more daily about learned helplessness and its relationship to depression. Martin Seligman, the leading researcher in this field of study, suggests that traumatic events result in fear. Either the individual learns that he or she can do something about the challenge and fear and the stress response is reduced, or the person feels that nothing can be done about the situation, and the learned helplessness turns to depression.

Aaron Antonovsky discusses the concept of a "sense of coherence" that reduces learned helplessness. When persons feel that they can make sense out of what is happening to them, have the resources available to deal with their problems, and have the energy from within to keep struggling against the injustices they encounter, learned helplessness diminishes.

Autonomic lability is the tendency of the neurohormonal system to overreact to our overinterpretation of events in our lives. We become psychophysiologically labile, running too hot or too cold in our reactions to situations that require warmth or coolness. You can get a good measure of your placebo ability if you try the following test:

The Autonomic Lability Test

1. Think of a time when you were very afraid and threatened as a child. Any event will do. Perhaps you saw a spider, were severely punished, or were pressured in school. Describe the incident to yourself mentally in some detail. Now check to see how your body reacts to this description of a past event.

2. Next, think of a time when you felt absolutely helpless. Perhaps your car had stalled on a lonely highway, you were lost in a strange and threatening place, or you were ashamed of something you did or failed to do. Check now to see how your body reacts to this "re-motion."

Many persons experience their bodies as reliving a past experience almost as if it were happening at this very moment. The more intense the body reaction to this "re-motion," the more autonomic and neurohormonal lability you tend to experience. In effect, the past is dictating their emotional present and future.

Most of my patients experience what I call "ALMs." These are autonomic lability markers, specific but long-past events that continue to elicit intense psychophysiological reactions. The more ALMs, the lower your placebo ability, because the healing system is overwhelmed by psychochemicals attempting to deal with mental ghosts. These markers act like poison emotional pellets. When you allow them to re-enter your system, you surrender control of your life to a shower of stress chemicals that are useless for present coping, addicting for the selfish brain, and interfere with the possibility of super joy.

6. Wait a Healing Moment

A sixth component of our placebo ability is a capacity to delay gratification, to give healing a chance. We live in a society where fast is seen as best. We have few slow food restaurants or camp-in theaters. Even our Broadway shows are becoming intense mini-circuses where the actors are allowed to play on stage as components of a computerized show. The audience seldom has to think or personalize to such productions, because the "show is the thing." Gratification is immediate and intense, with audiences leaving more drained than reflective.

We make a dangerous mistake when we assume that medicine or X rays do the curing. No matter what the treatment, all healing ultimately depends on individual faith and the resilience of the body system. We must do a little waiting if we are to do a little healing, and we must be able to delay gratification and fulfillment long enough to let natural processes take their natural course.

"I kept doing my relaxation and imagery exercises," reported one patient. "I stuck faithfully to the macrobiotic diet and everything else, but when I went to the doctor, she said there was no significant improvement in my condition, so I went back to the hamburger place." Sometimes the magic of healing from within depends upon our respect for the privacy and pacing of our natural placebo ability, not on impatience with the pace of our own internal processes. Like children staying up all night to watch for Santa Claus, the magic of placebo, the magic of internal healing, never happens if our impatience gets in the way.

7. Tilling the Terrain: Fertile Soil for the Seeds of Healing

The germ is nothing. The terrain all.

LOUIS PASTEUR

A seventh factor in the development of our placebo ability is a true holistic approach to wellness. A major threat to the health of our country is the split that is occurring between so-called traditional and holistic medicine. If we turn our backs on the wonders of modern medicine, we are not truly holistic at all.

Hindering our placebo ability by denying the relevance and importance of modern medicine, or counting on imagery and positive attitude while flooding our system with junk food and failing to exercise, is to add a needless and senseless block to the power of placebo. The meaning of the word "placebo" is "to please," and contaminating or neglecting our bodies in favor of "holistic cures" does not please the healer within. Such either/or thinking, holism vs. contemporary medicine, has resulted in a failure of needed research to learn more about healing and how our placebo ability really works.

"I'm on my way to my relaxation class," said one patient. "I'm running late, so I'm going to grab some health food quickly and run on up."

"Right," responded another patient. "I just gave up my blood pressure medications and the dumb diet my doctor gave me. He doesn't know anything about holistic medicine and imagery."

This brief conversation in the hospital cafeteria indicates the dangerous gap that is widening between considered and reasonable medical care and so-called "alternative approaches" to health care. All medical treatments are alternatives. We select our care in partnership with our physicians, choosing from all we can learn about what can help us heal. The first step in developing our placebo ability is the protection and enhancement of our general health. When the term was first used in 1926 by Jan Christiaan Smuts, "holism" referred to an innate force toward integration and connection in all living things. Believing and joy are parts of such a "whole," not replacements for sensible self-care of the very system we are attempting to heal.

Exercising regularly at least every other day, eating as naturally as possible in a "grazing" rather than "gorging" process, sleeping regularly, and avoiding toxic substances such as tobacco, caffeine, and alcohol are still the wisest steps for health anyone can take. Research shows that one health behavior that has nothing to do with exercise, eating, or emotions is one of the biggest predictors of longevity of all factors considered. It is one of the simplest acts you can do to live longer. Wear your seat belt when driving your car! Driving to your exercise class without your seat belt on is like trying to buy new stock in the Edsel. It's a good idea to invest in health, but you could lose everything on one very unwise mistake.

8. The Challenge of Wellness

One of the most important studies of hardiness ever done was by Suzanne Kobasa. As mentioned earlier, she described three "Cs" of a hardy and stress-resistant personality. All three of these factors constitute the eighth through the tenth factors of placebo ability.

A sense of **challenge** is a strong buffer against the impact of stress and disease. Challenge refers to the welcoming of change, the positive anticipation of the impact of events, and an optimism regarding one's ability to learn and cope when change occurs.

What would your reaction be if I were to tell you that, as you read this paragraph, your car has developed a flat tire? Would you become angry, swear, even use words that issue a threat to defecate? Or would you sense a challenge, a problem to be dealt with, even an opportunity for learning?

"Are you nuts?" said one of my patients early in treatment. "A flat tire is a flat tire. It is a plain and simple pain in the ass. Challenge, my ass." He slammed out the door to attack his rubber enemy, much of his health left behind him and succumbing once again to stress addiction.

9. Committed to Health

The second C from Kobasa's research, **commitment**, is the opposite of alienation. Our placebo ability depends on a sense of meaning, significance, and relevance to the world and persons around us. This is similar to Antonovsky's "sense of coherence" discussed earlier.

I always ask all the chronically ill patients I see the same question. "Why do you want to get well?" The patients are often surprised at this question, responding that everyone wants to be well. But why? A basic question related to the joy response is "What is life for?" Your healing ability is greatly enhanced when you have an answer to this question that somehow ties your existence to other people and the world and gives your living significance beyond mere survival.

"I want to get well for my children," answered one woman.

"Then what?" I asked.

"Then I can love them, help them grow, help them be happier," she answered. "Then I can enjoy and be a part of their growing up."

"So what?" I asked her.

"So what?" she said. "That's what makes a better world. Lots of happy, loving people make a better world. I want to help my three children be a part of that."

"I see," I said. "You want to get better for all of us."

"I never thought of it that way," she said. "I guess I have a world responsibility to get better, don't I?" she laughed. Even though she was joking, the issue of commitment to a higher purpose is a key part of placebo ability.

10. Being the Controlling Partner in Your Own Healing

Control is the opposite of powerlessness, and powerlessness is one of the major risks to survival for any ill person. Your placebo ability is a part of your control over your destiny, the retention of a sense of capability and effectiveness even when the challenge is severe.

"When I got to the hospital, the first thing they did was take my clothes," said one patient. "I guess they do that so you can't run away. I think they give you that robe with the back by the butt wide open so they can kick you in the ass easier."

If your doctor is treating you, you are in big trouble. If he or she is doing the treating, you have surrendered control. If your doctor is a partner with you in healing, with you being the senior and controlling partner, learning and taking active part in the recovery of your own wellness, then you are hardy even if you are sick.

You read earlier that super joy requires these three Cs of hardiness, and all three are particularly important at times of illness. When you combine challenge, commitment, and control with the factors of balanced suggestibility, solid and soft support systems, positive and rational self-talk, constructive avoidance, low autonomic lability, the ability to wait for healing to take place, and attention to your overall physical condition and fitness, you have given yourself one of the most valuable of all gifts—the gift of enhanced healing capacity through mobilization of the joy response as placebo.

When I first introduced the concept of placebo ability and the ten factors that allow this ability to develop, one doctor asked an important question. "You know, I really think this is an important idea, but it seems like all of this is based on Eastern religion. It seems like guru stuff. This seems like Eastern medicine to me. Do you think this really works in the West?"

This doctor had raised an important issue in understanding

more about healing and joy. It has seemed that the search for the unification of mind and body, the search for super joy beyond just being happy, has drawn people to India's Ayurvedic medicine, Chinese medicine, Buddhist principles, and more recently what has been called the "new age" movement. This phenomenon has alienated some people who are more comfortable with Western religious orientations and the Bible. This philosophical discomfort results in a turning away from some of the sound health practices that become associated with unfamiliar belief systems.

I suggest that Western religious tenets encompass clear and explicit recommendations for healing and increasing our placebo ability and that these tenets relate directly to Buddhist principles, Eastern religious principles, modern psychological principles, and provide a distinct framework for health, happiness, and learning the joy response without requiring persons to alter their complete religious system.

I first presented the following ideas in a lecture to the 79th National Governors' Association Summer Conference in Traverse City, Michigan. The governors and their families were surprised to see that within the Ten Commandments were all of the principles of the joy of faith that anyone could ever need, all the principles of sound health, and all of the factors that relate to the most modern psychological findings. I have presented here each of the Ten Commandments, the relationship of each commandment to Buddhist philosophy, a related modern psychological principle encompassed in each commandment, and a wellness and joy recommendation based on the combination of these guiding factors. I hope this review helps you and your family to rediscover the old and basic truths upon which all true joy rests: a consistent set of beliefs about the purpose of life that translate into strategies for daily living.

Psychiatry and the Ten Commandments

Modern psychology and psychiatry have been advertised as sciences designed to reduce mental illness and promote mental health. In fact, these fields have been concerned exclusively with the first part of their mission, focusing as their traditional medical model heritage did on curing disease. Both fields have ignored religion or, worse, have viewed mystical systems as pathological or delusional.

Therapists have not asked the question, "What are healthy people for?" The failure to search for answers to the question, "Why am I?" has resulted in what psychiatry calls "anomie," an illness of loneliness, purposelessness, and despair. While psychiatry and psychology have labeled the lack of an answer or even search for the answer to the meaning of life as disease, both fields offer little or no help in the search itself.

Psychiatrist Arthur Deikman writes, "It may be that the greatest problem confronting psychiatry is that it lacks a theoretical framework adequate to provide meaning for its patients, many of whom are badly handicapped in their struggle to overcome neurotic problems because the conceptual context within which they view themselves provides neither meaning, direction, nor hope." The health care field, more accurately the sickness care field, assumes that people impose meaning on life rather than discover it through introspection and the development of their sense of connection and direction with others.

In Sigmund Freud's later writings, he began a process all of us begin too late. When we start to feel at middle age that most of our time has run out, we begin to ask the question we should have been asking all along: "What is it all for anyway?" Freud wrote, "I may now add that civilizations progress in the service of Eros, whose purpose is to combine single human individuals, and after that families, then races, peoples, and nations, into one great unity, the unity of mankind." This sense of unity and purpose is super joy, the celebration that individual consciousness can never die because there is no such thing as a truly individual person. The selfish brain only thinks it is alone, and when it awakens to its connection with all of us, joy happens.

The Ten Commandments present a clear and concise view of the universal connection of all of us. I have found that a universal threat of responsible interaction of all persons is at the core of every religious system from Taoism to Sufism. We need not be frightened off by the literature of Eastern psychological disciplines. We have only to open the Bible to find guidelines for the joy response.

I have attempted to integrate some of the major concepts of the Ten Commandments, Buddhist philosophy, and modern Western psychology into some ideas toward a model of extreme psychological well-being. Fundamentalists may feel that I grossly oversimplified what they consider to be sacred concepts of their own faith. Others may feel that religion has no place in a model of psychological health. I hope my oversimplifications will not be offensive and that you will read through the following material and take from it your own concepts of how and by what principles an extremely healthy, super joyful person may lead his or her daily life.

The First Commandment and the Discovery of Self

THOU SHALT HAVE NO OTHER GODS BEFORE ME.

The word "doctor" or "physician" is never used in the Bible. The Greek word "physician" was used to describe a follower of Aesculapius. This was a medicine based on simple cause-and-effect ways of understanding sickness, and included belief in many gods, spirits, and the simplistic dualism of good/bad, healthy and sick. Illness was seen as caused by something "out there" that somehow got "in there" and had to be purged by a "physician" practicing at a temple of Aesculapian worship. Soon the physicians themselves became the gods, and the patients became the flock in need of treatment and purification. People were seen as sick or not sick. There was no discussion of joy, hardiness, and happiness.

Even today, this Greek mythology of our historical heritage plays itself out in massive temples of so-called health care where medical "priests" practice on appropriately clothed and deferring worshipers. The priests are assisted by deferring maidens, followed and idolized by student priests, sometimes funded by the cult of the blue cross without which these shrines of sickness could not exist. So separate are "worshipers" (patients) in these shrines that they are never allowed to see the magic "operating rooms" where the special services of cutting are conducted.

Psychiatrist Jerome Frank presented an amusing tongue-in-cheek detailed description of these "health healing places" in a commencement address to medical students. He writes, "All are expected to dedicate themselves to the service of the shrine, regardless of personal hardships or interference with connubial felicity and other satisfactions of life."

The Old and New Testaments spoke only of healers and emphasized the role of internal faith in one God, a God who is one and the same with the unified and connected "self." The Bible speaks of miracles, spiritual healing, and the power of prayer. Jesus of Nazareth was approached by a woman bleeding profusely from her uterus. As she touched the hem of his robe, she was instantly healed. Jesus explained to the woman that it was her faith that had made such healing possible. This self-faith is the focus of the first commandment. What we call the "new" medicine as opposed to traditional medicine actually has a history thousands of years in the making.

Determination on the part of the patient, not the physician, is what makes healing and joy possible. Buddhist philosophy stressed the importance of determination. The Buddha said, "It is you who must make the effort. The masters only point the way." Modern psychologists call this combination of faith and determination "a sense of trust," a trust in the spirit of God within each of us as the source of all joy, not a trust in artificial shrines.

The first commandment, then, encourages us not to place our faith in the authority of the doctor or in popular gurus who promise magic solutions to life's problems. This commandment also teaches us of the relative powerlessness of disease-causing organisms and agents in comparison to the power of a joyful and faithful spirit. The healer is within us, and inside is also where our joy is.

In Exodus 20:1–17, God tells the Hebrews that He has given them the prescription for a healthy life in His Ten Commandments. The first of the commandments is a prescription for faith in self and faith in God as a unified process for finding joy and health. More trips to ourselves and fewer trips to the doctor, psychologist, or self-help bookstore may be the best way to learn the joy response.

Researchers are now studying a group of people they call the "worried well." This group either has no organic problem at all or they have medical problems directly related to psychological causation. These are persons who travel from doctor to doctor, new program to new program, searching for a cure for their problems. It is a group that makes up almost eighty percent of the medical bill in the United States, yet it is a group that will never find a "cure" until its members find themselves, their faith, and their one all-powerful God to replace the mini-gods in whom they have misplaced their trust. As Mark Twain put it, "God cures, and the doctor sends the bill."

The Second Commandment and Moving Outside the Circle

THOU SHALT NOT MAKE UNTO THEE ANY GRAVEN IMAGE, OR ANY LIKENESS OF ANYTHING THAT IS IN HEAVEN ABOVE, OR THAT IS IN THE EARTH BENEATH, OR THAT IS IN THE WATER UNDER THE EARTH.

An extension of the prescription to trust in self and God is the warning that there are many distractions in our world, caused primarily by the selfish brain. "Graven images" are the brain bunk I mentioned, the distractions from the true meaning of life by dissatisfaction, selfishness, and intolerance of self-change and learning. The second commandment enjoins us to move beyond the immediate gratification of intense sensory images, "graven images," to the more profound and peaceful images from within, where God is.

To overcome the brain's perpetual boredom and addiction to intense stimulation, we have turned to artificial drugs and stress chemical addiction. As Arthur Deikman writes, we have attempted to ". . . substitute sensation for meaning." These "sensations" are the addiction of the always starving brain, the graven images that threaten our health.

Buddhist philosophy teaches the same lesson as the second commandment and refers to wisdom, the development of a control of the undisciplined mind that prefers the graven image over the meaningful and truly joyful images of love. The "three marks of existence" in Buddhist philosophy refer to the facts that nothing in human experience is permanent, that possessions and stimulation from outside will never calm an untrained selfish brain, and that "self" is always changing and developing, not static and trapped in a perpetuation of addictive behavior.

Modern psychology refers to the freedom from graven images or the Buddhist wisdom as "a sense of autonomy." This autonomy means transcending our too willing compliance with an accelerating world of intense external stimulation, finding instead a sense of self-worth and self-value. Autonomy refers to acquiring not only skills and mastery of developmental tasks but to the discovery that our real world is created from within.

The only true "nongraven" image is one that comes from a peaceful and disciplined mind free of the compulsive search for happiness through intensity of external stimulation. We can break the addictive circle of seeking more and more sensory pleasure, finding more and more discontentment, and chasing the illusion of the separate self if we learn the witness way I mentioned earlier. By learning to observe our brains, to control them and make them a part rather than a controller of our lives, we learn to recognize graven images when we see them and to thrill at the less tangible yet more joyful images of a connected self aware of the autonomy of humankind.

The following report from one of my patients illustrates what I mean by autonomy from graven images. "It was a funny way to learn this thing about wisdom, graven images, and the selfish brain. I watched my dog chasing his tail. He went in violent circles until he actually caught it. The stupid dog looked up at me with his own tail in his mouth. He was absolutely exhausted. He seemed to be asking, 'What did I want this for in the first place?' I hope I will never chase my tail again. I want to stay free of such a small and violent circle."

The Third Commandment and
a Return to Self-discipline

THOU SHALT NOT TAKE THE NAME OF THE LORD THY
GOD IN VAIN; FOR THE LORD WILL NOT HOLD HIM
GUILTLESS THAT TAKETH HIS NAME IN VAIN.

I have spoken about maladaptive hyperarousal and autonomic lability in this and earlier chapters. We have learned to become
hostile and impatient with ourselves, and when we do, we cuss
ourselves out. We may do this by swearing, using the Lord's name
in vain, or screaming at someone else, but the ultimate punishment promised by the third commandment is exacted upon ourselves through heart and other diseases. We are not "guiltless"
when we refuse to keep ourselves under control.

Our society has given us the wrong message. Pop psychology,
without research support, has told us to "get it out," to "let go"
and "express our anger freely." Listen to your anger vocabulary,
for the words you use narrate your own ultimate destruction. Sharing feelings openly and sensitively with someone is healthy. Blasting people with an anger tantrum accompanied by verbal instructions to "damn it" only results in a damning of your own health.
When you add God's name to the tantrum, you are jeopardizing
your last hope for wellness by damning the healer within.

I ask my patients to tape or write down their anger vocabularies.
When they listen or read back the diatribes, they are stunned.
Such vocabulary usually condemns their families, someone else's
family, parents, God, and in some perverse way confuses the intimacy of sex with violence and attack. "Don't you think your spirit
is taking you seriously when you say these things?" is my question
to the group. "Shouldn't you be busy calming the system, sharing
the fear and guilt that always are at the base of such an anger
tantrum, rather than cursing yourself and all that can make you
happy?"

The Fourth Commandment and
the Power of Stillness

REMEMBER THE SABBATH DAY, TO KEEP IT HOLY.

The fourth commandment prescribes rest. This is not a rest of collapse into the sloth and torpor that result from six days of overdoing it, of constant stress chemical addiction, followed by a coma of psychological fatigue. This can be a day of new beginnings, of recommitment to spirit and peace rather than rest for renewed pursuit of success, status, and money. This commandment asks us always to make room for a day of reinvigoration of the spirit.

In the movie *Chariots of Fire* the main character is confronted with extreme pressure to run a major race on the Sabbath. When he refuses to do so and says that he will not run "on God's day," he makes the hard choice all of us must make if we are to honor our higher purpose by taking time to worship that purpose.

Ask most people to name the first day of the week, and they will typically name Monday. Actually, the Bible teaches that the Sabbath is the first day of the week, a priority day. Unfortunately, we use any day "off" as a day to be either totally "on" by working on the house or recreating vigorously or perhaps just recuperating passively. Our health depends on a focus on a time for reverence and solemnity, not only on just one day, but every day of our lives. Setting aside one special day helps remind us to do so.

The Buddhist philosophy emphasizes the concept of energy. We tend to "spend" ourselves rather than pace ourselves, using up our energy rather than using our energy for personal and spiritual growth. We seem to have lost the art of stillness and quiet. T. S. Eliot said, "Teach us to sit still," but few of us can.

Psychologists refer to the concept of a sense of initiative, the initiative the runner showed in *Chariots of Fire*. We must learn to take the initiative not only in career but in resting. Most of my patients find it much easier to find something that needs doing than to make time for contemplation regarding why we need to do all that we do.

We forget that we can be the directors of the movies of our minds. We can call out, "Cut," when we want to. Imagine a day when everyone was resting, praying, and spending time helping others to be more at peace. Researchers know the importance of the relaxation response, and the fourth commandment is a reminder that our health depends as much on being still enough for health to find us as it does on being active enough to stay fit.

The Fifth Commandment and the Value of Family

HONOR THY FATHER AND THY MOTHER: THAT THY DAYS MAY BE LONG UPON THE LAND WHICH THE LORD THY GOD GIVETH THEM.

Of all the stressors I have seen in almost twenty years of doing psychotherapy, family stress seems to be the most intense, pervasive, and debilitating. Stressors that are ambiguous, chronic, and that elicit ambivalent and helpless feelings on the part of the stressed person have the most negative impact on our health. Family stressors typically have all three characteristics.

It is difficult to focus on exactly what is bothering us when a problem parent or problem child is upsetting us. At times it seems as if everything is fine, and then everything seems to be falling apart. We feel love and almost at the same time strong dislike, even hate, for the parent or child who seems so insensitive to our needs. The stress seems unrelenting, and nothing we do seems to be effective in reducing the pressure. I believe this happens so often in families because we have lost sight of the important health recommendation suggested by the fifth commandment.

To "honor" our parents and family is related to, but different than, "loving" them. When couples on the verge of divorce come to my clinic, it is usually not just because love has left the relationship. The problem is more often that neither partner is mature, responsible, or energetic enough to "honor" the other. To honor is to tolerate, to accept, to treat with dignity even when we are challenged by the behavior or perceived attitudes of someone else. To honor is to continue to hold our family members in high esteem even when their own behavior is demeaning to themselves. To honor is to give our loved ones credit, respect, and acceptance during times of conflict, or when feelings of love are pushed to their limits.

Buddhists refer to the importance of patience. The Buddha wrote, "At the end of the way is freedom. Till then, patience." Parenting and "childing" require the most patience of any human endeavor, and it is the lesson of the fifth commandment that such patience is reward by a healthier individual and family spirit.

Psychologists refer to our "sense of identity," our concept of who we are and how we fit with others. When we become impatient, we disconnect, we lose our identity in a storm of intolerance and projected blame and helplessness. Identity requires the ability to honor others as the ultimate form of honoring ourselves. As Rabbi Kahlil wrote, "If I am not for myself, who will be for me? If I am only for myself, what am I? And if not now . . . when?" His statement illustrates the balance between patience and honor for others and the maintenance of our dignity and self-responsibility. Such a balance may be the most difficult of the Ten Commandments to obey, for without the patience required to honor our families and all others we become impatient with ourselves and our ability to fulfill any of the other nine commandments. Most particularly in our own families, we must not lose sight of the honor bestowed upon us by those with whom we live and who gave us life and a place to live.

The Sixth Commandment and Love

THOU SHALT NOT KILL.

Buddhists refer to the concept of loving-kindness. In Chapter 8, I defined love as sympathetic joy, a delight in the well-being of others. The sixth commandment teaches us that to take the life of anyone, in fact or by indirect actions, is to rob ourselves of living. What we do to others we ultimately do to ourselves. All killing, whether intentional or unintentional murder or psychological slaughter, is ultimately an act of suicide.

Psychologists refer to the development of a "sense of intimacy." Chapter 8 discussed the joy of love and the several dimensions of loving behavior, thought, and feeling. When we develop a sense of intimacy, we discover ourselves in all others, and it becomes impossible to harm anyone else.

The sixth commandment has to do not only with the act of murder but with a "killing" of the spirit, hope, and human dignity in others. We "kill" when we separate and scorn the AIDS patient. We "kill" when we verbally abuse a child or aging parent. We "kill" when we disregard the starving people of the world. We "kill" when we abuse substances or drink alcohol and drive. We "kill" when we create a psychological environment for our young people that is corrupt and morally bankrupt. We "kill" when we pollute our environment. We "kill" when we are irresponsible world citizens, uninvolved in the struggle to hold back the moving hands on the clock of nuclear holocaust. A true sense of intimacy is the nurturing of the feeling that not just life but quality of living is sacred in all of us.

The sixth commandment is an instruction to protect our own wellness. Deuteronomy 4:15 advises, "Be exceedingly heedful of yourselves." In effect, this is a commandment to take responsibility for our own health, to make sure we do not end up slowly but surely killing ourselves through the practice of unhealthy living. We have a moral obligation to protect and enhance the health and well-being of ourselves and all others.

The Seventh Commandment and Responsible Sex

THOU SHALT NOT COMMIT ADULTERY.

Buddhists emphasize "ethicality" as one of the ten perfections. In modern business parlance, sexual morality always involves a "win-win" situation. Both partners and the world system in which they live should be enhanced by sexual intimacy. If one partner—or anyone—is hurt by a sexual act, the health of the entire system suffers.

The AIDS crisis has brought into focus the issue of promiscuity, but anonymous sex has always been one of the most significant health risks. The immune system, including both physiological and psychological immunity, is impaired by multiple, quick, anonymous sexual activity. The sexual response is just too complex to be handled in a casual way.

The seventh commandment was prophetic in its warning that continued failure to achieve intimacy would result in suffering. AIDS is a disease of civilization and not a gay or drug users' disease. AIDS is symptomatic of more than a virus. AIDS is a lesson in mutual responsibility for one another. The initial isolationist and accusational reaction to AIDS only slowed the final solution to the epidemic. Perhaps now we will treat AIDS as "our" problem and not as the nonexistent "theirs."

Psychologists refer to a "sense of generation," of creativity and growth of spirit that must take place as human development progresses. The key question for sexual ethics and morality is, "What has grown as a result of this sexual act?" Has there been an increase in closeness, enhancement of both partners' living, some strengthening within the system or subsystem? If not, the sex becomes an act of disconnection instead of merging, with the predictable outcome of physical and spiritual suffering. Our society has made sex a shared reflex and endless search for "fulfillment" by effective timing and skill. Sex can be the healthiest of human activities when we transcend the reflex and genital focus to an emphasis on merging, sharing, experiencing, and developing together over time.

Adultery is unhealthy because it always involves the deception of all parties. The deceived partner is robbed of a misplaced love they cannot reclaim. The adulterer deceives himself or herself by looking outside for what is missing within. I have never worked with a couple experiencing infidelity who did not fail to see that what they sought elsewhere was always available within their own relationship or through the resolution of the marital deficiency, either by constructively ending the marriage or by solving the problems that hampered its progress.

The seventh commandment is a commandment of responsibility to our primary adult relationship. The adultery is not only sexual but an unfaithfulness to the integrity of a relationship we promised to work for and within. Allowing our work or our play to rob our relationship time is another form of "adultery" that is threatening to our health. Violation of the seventh commandment violates all the first six, for trust, autonomy, discipline, initiative, identity, and intimacy are all destroyed. As a result, no generation, no creativity, is possible.

The Eighth Commandment and
Robbing Ourselves

THOU SHALT NOT STEAL.

Buddhist philosophy focuses on generosity. Psychologists describe the ability to share as an important trait of maturity. As pointed out earlier, giving and altruism are among the most joyful and healthy of all human acts. Stealing, either of goods, time, dignity, or the right to self-fulfillment, depletes the system of its energy. A balance is disrupted as someone takes from someone else instead of giving to that person.

Stealing is the ultimate form of selfishness and, as such, it isolates and separates the thief. Super joy always involves some form of giving of self. Stress addiction always involves our own stealing from our natural supply of resilience and healing.

The Ninth Commandment and the Lingering Lie

THOU SHALT NOT BEAR FALSE WITNESS AGAINST THY NEIGHBOR.

A dangerous threat to the joy response is the loss of integrity in America. Few of us trust the salesperson, and few salespersons trust us. Few of us put forth the effort, the preciseness and open vulnerability of speech required to maintain the "truthfulness" discussed by Buddhists.

Psychologists discuss the "sense of integrity" as one of the most high-level indicators of psychological health. There are two parts to such integrity: honesty with others and honesty with oneself. The concept of denial discussed earlier in this chapter is a form of self-deception that places our health at risk. We can never know joy if we cannot face the fact that life is always difficult. We can never know joy if we cannot give honestly of ourselves, for no one will be able to know whether our joy is real and therefore will not be able to affirm us and join us in our joy if we do not give honestly and openly of our feelings.

Scott Peck's *People of the Lie* describes the problem of deceit. He writes, "We can not hope to heal human evil until we are able to look at it directly." We cannot hope to fulfill our natural potential for joy until we are able to look at ourselves and others directly.

Medically, when doctors deceive their patients, they hamper the patients' healing. Doctors do not have to "tell" their patients anything. If doctors listen, their patients will tell them. The best health care is direct, honest, open, and always aware that nothing is certain. Diagnoses are never verdicts, but deception can result in a false imprisonment of the healer within.

The Tenth Commandment and the Simple Life

THOU SHALT NOT COVET THY NEIGHBOUR'S HOUSE, THOU SHALT NOT COVET THY NEIGHBOUR'S WIFE, NOR HIS MANSERVANT, NOR HIS MAIDSERVANT, NOR HIS OX, NOR HIS ASS, NOR ANYTHING THAT IS THY NEIGHBOUR'S.

By now you have noticed the overlap between the super joy program and the Ten Commandments. Simplicity, or what Buddhists call renunciation, is a key to all health and the joy response. Psychologists speak of maturity as related to the ability to be satisfied with less, not more. To covet is to waste energy that could be spent in learning joy. To covet is to "want" while ignoring what someone else may "need."

Most of my patients find the most comfort at those times when they are free from "wanting" things. It was difficult for them to break the "covet habit." I saw a bumper sticker that said, "Born to shop!" Once my patients free themselves of wanting, they have more time and energy for enjoying what they are experiencing.

A Simple Psychological Test of the Ten Commandments

Answer yes or no to each of the following questions. Discuss your answers with someone who knows you well. These ten simple questions may predict your joy potential and wellness better than any test you can take. I have included the major Buddhist principle and a Western psychology concept that relates to each commandment.

First Commandment: Would you trust you? _____
(Determination and a sense of trust in your own strength)

Second Commandment: Do you feel and act responsibly for all of your actions and feelings? _____
(Wisdom and a sense of autonomy)

Third Commandment: Are you moderate in your responses to challenges, running warm and cool instead of hot and cold?
(Equanimity and a sense of control) _____

Fourth Commandment: Do you take time daily to rest, contemplate, meditate, or pray? _____
(Controlled energy and a sense of initiative in the interest of self-peace.)

Fifth Commandment: Would you want you for a child or parent? _____
(Patience and a sense of identity)

Sixth Commandment: Could you fall and, more importantly, stay in love with you? _____
(Loving-kindness and a sense of intimacy)

Seventh Commandment: Could your behavior, thoughts, and feelings stand up to public scrutiny? _____
(Ethicality and a sense of generation and public contribution)

Eighth Commandment: Are you giving to people and to your world at least as much as you are taking? _____
(Generosity and a sense of sharing and connection with others)

Ninth Commandment: Do you believe in others and in what they say and would you believe you? _____
(Truthfulness and a sense of integrity)

Tenth Commandment: Are you content with what you have and free of wants and desires? _____
(Renunciation and a sense of stability and satisfaction)

The more unequivocal "yes" answers you have to the above questions, the more likely it is that super joy is and will be a major part of your life. Integrating work for the common good, a love of commitment, sympathy and altruism, and a dynamic but consistent belief system is the basic prescription for the psychochemicals of the super joy response.

CHAPTER TEN

Finding the Light of Joy

> After a time of decay comes the turning point. The powerful light that has been banished returns.
>
> I CHING

There is something very special about persons who have rediscovered their own super joy. There is something radiant about persons who have freed themselves from their own white whales and their addiction to the SAD cycle and its accompanying overdose of harmful psychochemicals. Such persons seem to sense a light, a glow from within, a "light light" that is not limited to the chest but glows from the spirit. People around joyful people can almost feel the light, and are somehow enhanced, awakened, by just being near the super joy response.

William Wordsworth, in his *Ode: Intimations of Immortality,* laments the dimming of this joy light, the loss of what he called a sense of the "celestial light" that seemed to give a glory and freshness to the simplest of daily life experiences. He writes, "The things which I have seen I now can see no more." Our daily vocabulary often refers to this lost light, with such phrases as "see the light," "dawn on me," and being "in the dark."

Super joy is the source of the light we seek. As I have pointed out in the first two sections of this book, we are naturally addictive. Our addiction has been too often to stress and depression, the states of immediate survival. We can redirect our addictive tendencies to concerns for the longer term, for the purpose of life, for the joy of living. We can see and experience the light of joy if we "deautomatize," if we break our habitual dependence on a cycle of interaction with life based exclusively on the whims of a selfish and survivalist brain.

Super joy is your God-given right, a human capacity for celebration of living that is accompanied by healthy and healing psychochemical changes deriving from the development of an enduring self-esteem, a feeling and daily behavior that represent competence, faith, and the belief that things will always work out because all of us are connected for and by a common higher purpose.

You have read in this book about a new psychology, a joyology that emphasizes not just health but extreme well-being and the conquering of our SAD or stress and addiction cycle. You have learned about the Captain Ahab complex that can result in our drowning with our own life fixations that become the persecutors to which we addictively tie ourselves in an attempt to survive instead of experience super joy. You have read about a new way of thinking about daily living, the psychochemistry of super joy, and a program to help you bring super joy into your own life. You examined the joy of working, loving, and believing and ways to cope with special challenges to super joy. In all of this material, I hope you have come to see the beginning of a conspiracy, a conspiracy for hope, happiness, and healing that is emerging as the scientists whose work is listed in the references to this book discover what we should have known all along: that we were made for far more than how we are living day to day.

Before you read about some very specific challenges to super joy and ways to conquer these challenges, here is a restatement of some points related to the joy response to keep in mind as you continue on your journey for joy, as you move further toward a universal realization that we must learn to celebrate together before our addiction to our other human responses ends up killing us all.

1. "Things" don't "just happen" to you. Physics now teaches us that the natural system "is," and we are a part of that system.

When we learn this fact, when we change our well-entrenched perception of ourselves as helpless travelers on a road to nowhere, stumbling upon crisis after crisis, we discover that we are not on a path at all. We are all moving along *with* the infinite system, and you are happening with the system, the system does not happen to you. You are no longer "victim" when you become the "event."

2. The body does not stop at the outside boundary of the skin. Science now teaches us that all divisions are delusions, artificial creations of our egocentric, lazy, shortsighted brains who "think" they are "us." Once you are able to experience the person sitting next to you as "you," you begin to relearn the unity dimension of the joy response.

3. Disease is *not* caused by viruses, modern medicine has not been the major influence on ending disease or improving health, and all major threats to our health ultimately are caused by a loss of the joy response and cured by its rediscovery. When self-esteem, self-efficacy, and connectedness with others are disrupted, we get sick. The virus is only a part of the process of illness, not a cause.

4. Dis-ease is healthy and deviance is normal. When we become aware of something being "wrong," our own internal health maintenance systems are working well. If we wait for doctors or other people to tell us when we are sick, if we turn our internal health resources over to the muddle of modern medicine, we ultimately lose our capacity for healing from within. The miracles of modern medicine are always the realization that something you do yourself can affect your destiny; doctors only serve as partners in the process of healing. Dis-ease forces us to "be," and to stop all of our "doing" to look at how we are living.

5. The healthy emotions are not just the positive emotions. The only negative emotions are the feelings that you will not allow yourself to acknowledge to yourself and to others. To laugh, to cry, to hope, and to worry are all processes of the joy response. The tears of discovery of the wonder of life are the tears of the joy response.

6. You are not your "brain." The brain has evolved for one purpose only: to keep us alive as individuals. It does not "know"
about the system other than as a source of the stimulation to which
it is addicted, about the system in and for which it lives. The brain
must be exposed in its selfishness and disciplined from its "mind-
less" quest for more and more external stimulation to verify its
existence. We can teach our brains to relax and enjoy their un-
tapped potential for joyful thought by teaching them that there is
really no "outside" of us, that all persons and things are part of us.
The saber-toothed tigers are gone; the threat now comes from
within. If the brain keeps "looking out," it will forever be blind to
the beauty of our spirit. "Looking in" is the view of the joy response.

7. Loving is synonymous with super joy, but our focus on the sex
response has smothered our capacity for the joy of loving sympathy for others. When we connect with others beyond physical connection, we lower our threshold for the joy response and see new
meaning to the phrase "coming together." At work, at home, and
on the subway, we will either learn how to join with one another
or we will spin off into our own worlds, alone, drifting, and sometimes colliding. Loving is volitional and requires effort, endurance, discipline, and the ultimate realization that being the right
lover is more important than finding the right person to love.

8. We do not have to settle for "coping" with stress. We are addicted to a stress and depression cycle that is accompanied by disease-causing psychochemicals, spiritless "adrenalinaholics" seduced by modern psychology and psychiatry into thinking that we
can somehow learn to live with our addiction instead of overcoming it. We will always be stress and depression addicts; it is in our
very genes and evolutionary destiny. But we do not have to allow
this propensity for trading survival for health to dictate how we
live. Super joy is the antidote for stress and depression addiction, a
replacement addiction to the healthy psychochemicals that have
always been there for our healing. A new psychology and medicine are needed to study why people stay healthy in our stressful
world, and to apply the findings of these studies, as I have tried to

do in this book, to the enhancement of the human condition, to hardiness instead of coping.

9. The dominance of the "yang" or male orientation to living has crowded out the healthy counterbalance of the "yin" or female approach to life. This yin/yang imbalance goes far beyond social roles of men and women in our society. No matter what our gender, our yin represents our intuition, wisdom, and impulse for synthesis and the psychology of the whole. Our yang side represents our rational, analytic, controlling, separatist life orientation. Without a rediscovery of a balance in these forces of life beyond the purchase of a yin/yang pendant to hang around our necks, our world will go even further off its axis, our national defense program will become the greatest threat to our national security, we will fail to find the joy of a balance between the feminine and masculine styles of life. A "woman's movement" is as dangerous as male dominance if we lose sight of the fact that our survival depends upon both the yin and the yang, a rhythmic dance within the healthy boundaries of integration and self-assertion.

10. Preventive medicine, holistic medicine, modern medicine, no medicine will ever bring us joy, for all of these movements are pathology oriented. We really do not have a health care system at all, but a sickness care system that is collapsing under its own inefficiency, insensitivity to world health, financial ineptitude, and failure to help us feel "hale and hearty." Our sickness care system has succeeded only in frightening us into preventive measures when it should have been busy helping us celebrate the natural cycle of sickness and health, the joy of living. We must learn to be health oriented, to take charge of the internal pharmacy capable of dispensing the most powerful drugs in the universe. Whether or not you write yourself a fatal or healing prescription from this pharmacy depends upon whether or not you intentionally add major doses of the joy response to your life, on whether or not you choose to make joy a priority in your life or only a hoped-for result of a perpetual effort to survive. There is a new healing emerging, a "thriving" being rediscovered, and the joy response is at the center of the revolution for wellness. Imagery, exercise,

meditation, health foods, and stress reduction courses will never bring us health if we fail to learn that the joy response is something we can learn and experience in everything we do, a prerequisite for, rather than a result of, healthy living.

Time is not running out. Time is not running at all. In fact, time "isn't." We create our experiences every day through our perceptions, our hopes, and how we choose to interpret our world. I hope, I pray, that some of the ideas in this book about super joy will contribute in some way to helping you to see your world more joyfully, to learn to have the time of your life.

Part Three of this book contains a discussion of six specific challenges to the super joy response. As you read each chapter and consider the impact of each of these challenges in your own life, remember William Wordsworth's search for "The glory and the freshness of a dream." It is the energy generated by this search, particularly at times of challenge and crisis, that results in the glow, the light of joy itself.

PART THREE

Six Special Joy Messages

All of us experience transitional life crises. Such crises are either signals for despair or challenges to change, adaptation, and spiritual growth. Instead of seeing times of challenge as times when things are going wrong, we must learn to see these times as periods in our lives when things are actually finally going "right." Crises are the times when life is being readjusted, when the overall process of the life system is affecting us directly.

If we approach crisis times in our lives without the super joy response, we are leaving behind the one tool we need to make sense of what is happening to us. If we attempt to survive instead of to grow and develop through crises, we are simply like deckhands rearranging the chairs on the sinking *Titanic.* Any crisis is a call for adapting, for adjustment of our system of living, and there is no growth or meaning to life without crisis, no beginnings without endings, no love without the experience of loneliness, and no health without the experience of illness.

The chapters that follow are in the form of messages about some of the ways in which the principles of super joy and joyology can be applied at times in our lives when we feel we need something more to make it, to go on living with happiness.

I have chosen the six most frequent "disrupters" of super joy that I have seen in my clinical work. Of course, there are many other human problems that make up the life cycle of growth, challenge, adaptation, and back to growth. The problems of sadness and depression, difficulty with our emotions, loss of a loved one, concerns for our health and serious illness, and feelings of being unloved were the most frequent reasons why patients seemed to lose sight of the light of super joy. As you read each chapter, try to remember the times in your life when you experienced these problems. If you are experiencing these problems now, try to remember that the principles of super joy are even more important when life seems to have lost its joyfulness.

CHAPTER ELEVEN

A Joy Message for Times When We're Sad

The world partly comes to be how it is imagined.
                                    GREGORY BATESON

Love says: "I am everything." Wisdom says: "I am nothing." Between the two my life flows.
                                    JAKE KORNFIELD

Every minute of every twenty-four-hour day, one child or young adult will try to kill themselves. Eighteen of these young persons will succeed in ending their own lives. More than one half million teenagers attempt suicide every year, and more than five thousand will kill themselves. Suicide is the second biggest killer of our children and teenagers and is responsible for emotional agony in thousands of families throughout the United States. This letter is to sad persons everywhere, and particularly to sad young people. When large numbers of our young people do not want to live, something has happened to the joy in all of our lives.

DEAR SAD PERSON:
Being very, very sad is very, very normal. It is a part of growing up. There could be no real happiness if there was no sadness because, just as day follows night, both feelings are a part of our humanness. If you are very sad and feeling hopeless right now,

you are just like millions of other people, and the fact that you can be so sad means you have the capacity to be very, very joyful. In fact, there is something inside you that is telling you that joy is missing. If you will take the time to read this special letter for you, you will learn a new way to be sad that doesn't take away all of your energy for living.

First, be sure you clearly understand your feelings. Don't hide from them and hope they will go away. Even though the people who love you—your parents, grandparents, and the rest of your family—will be afraid of your sad feelings, you must face them directly. Your family is only afraid of your sadness because they feel that they may have failed you in some way or that they cannot seem to do anything to help you be happier. They may even get mad at you for being sad, and that only makes you sadder. Remember, they are only mad because they feel helpless. When you were younger, they could make the hurt go away. Now that you are growing up or grown up, they just can't seem to take care of everything for you. You know that, but they are having trouble realizing this new limitation, and their helplessness may make them seem uncaring or unable to understand your sadness.

Here are the normal feelings of sadness that all of us, and particularly young people, will always have sometimes. Don't let them frighten you, because they are a sign that you are developing as a person. Just as a new plant is vulnerable and unsteady, still unsure of how or if it will flower, so are we all unsure. Your growth to happiness depends on some sadness as the fertilizer for your future flowering. No one likes the fertilizer itself, but there would be no growth without it.

The Fertilizer Feelings Test

1. Do you feel almost totally hopeless, as if nothing is going to work out for you or even for the whole world? _____

2. Do you feel as though no one seems to really talk to you or listen to you, really hear you? _____

3. Do you feel as if no one understands you and how you feel? Do you feel as though nobody feels the way you do? _____

4. Is it difficult for you to concentrate because you get so sad? Do you feel distracted and isolated? _____

5. Do you daydream a lot, sometimes about how bad or useless things are? Do you just seem to "drift away" sometimes? _____

6. Do you have worries that you just can't tell people about or can't seem to put into words? Are you afraid or ashamed to share some of your worries? _____

7. Do you feel tired a lot, and even after you sleep for hours, do you still feel like staying in bed? Even though you are tired, do you have trouble sleeping? _____

8. Do you feel like eating all the time or many times like not eating at all? _____

9. Do you just want to be left alone? _____

10. Have you thought about dying? Have you thought about your own death or your parents' deaths? _____

11. Do you feel frustrated and angry, even though you are not sure exactly what you are frustrated and angry about? _____

12. Do you feel moody, really up sometimes and then crashing at other times? _____

13. Are you concerned about your body and how you look, sometimes feeling very bad about your overall appearance? _____

14. Do you have some secret pact with a friend, telling that friend things you feel you could never tell your parents? _____

15. Are you worried about sex? Do you feel guilty about what you have done or haven't been able to do sexually? Are you worried or guilty about your fantasies?   _____

16. Have you been frightened by drugs, either because of a bad experience with drugs or because you only feel really good when you use drugs?   _____

17. Do you feel as though you have been trying to get your parents' or other family members' attention and everyone seems too busy to listen?   _____

18. Does everyone keep telling you how great you have it and how wonderful you are while you feel miserable?   _____

19. Do you have health worries that bother you much of the time?   _____

20. Do you wonder if the world will even survive long enough for you to enjoy adulthood? Do you think that the world is going to end anyway, so why go on?   _____

21. Do you have one big secret, something you did or something that happened to you that you feel you could just never share with anyone?   _____

How many "yes" answers did you have? Here is the good news. The more "yes" answers you have, the more potential you have for the joy response, the topic of this whole book. Persons who are deeply sensitive and deal directly and personally with the issues in the items above actually have the most ability not only to survive but to thrive. The trouble is that some people misunderstand and try to run from these normal feelings. They actually become depressed and frightened by their sadness because they have not been told the "facts of sadness." Take a deep breath and get ready to learn about the importance of being very sad in order to be very, very happy.

The Facts of Sadness

FACT 1: The sadder you can feel, the happier you will be able to feel. Intense people feel everything intensely. You can be sure that your favorite rock star and movie star have the same answers to the "fertilizer feelings" test that you do, because they are successful, sensitive artists. (Of course, your parents may not think that your favorite rock star is an artist, but anyone who succeeds at what he or she does has had to be a sensitive person who can be sad and happy in large doses.)

FACT 2: When you get so sad that you feel that you could end your own life, there is professional help available that "works." No matter what you have heard, real depression is curable! There are diet changes, medicines, and counseling that can successfully treat depression. If you think your sadness is getting out of control, ask your parents to take you for help. Help for depression works! Honest! I myself have worked with hundreds of people just like you, and I have seen them conquer their depression.

FACT 3: You may think that you have told other people a thousand times how sad you are, and you may think that they don't really understand. The sadness fact is that you must say the words out loud over and over again. You can't just "send signals" and sulk.

One young woman patient said, "When I was so depressed that I didn't care if I lived, I thought it was so obvious. I didn't realize that my parents were afraid to see how depressed I really was." Go past the fears of others and their apparent insensitivity and tell them out loud how you feel. "I am so sad I could kill myself." Say the words to them and add, "I'm not kidding, I am really sad. Help me." You know how hard it is to understand other people's feelings sometimes, and other people feel the same way about you. Send a sadness letter if you have to, but get the message to them. A tremendous amount of pain and senseless loss could be prevented and there would be fewer suicide notes if sad people sent more sadness notes.

FACT 4: If one of your friends tells you not to tell their parents that they are thinking about ending their life, tell their parents at once! It is not "finking" or "telling on" someone when you reach out to find them help. You are never breaking a confidence when you try to save someone's life. Even doctors and religious people must not keep secret the possibility that someone is thinking of ending a life. It may be difficult to understand at first, but your life is not just your life; it is a life that is shared by all of us. Suicide is really murder, hurting everyone and killing everyone to some degree.

FACT 5: All talk about suicide is serious. There is no such thing as a "fake" attempt or "just trying to get attention." When you yourself or a friend talk about ending life, it is always for real. Take action by telling someone now!

FACT 6: Suicide is not always related to depression. Sometimes a person seems to be "doing much better" just before they try to kill themselves. This happens because they mistakenly feel that they have finally made a decision and their unhappiness will soon be over. When you or a friend have been very sad and talking about ending life and then become suddenly and without explanation very happy, settled, or seem to be saying good-bye by being friendlier than usual, the problems that led to sadness still have to be dealt with.

FACT 7: Religious people can be of great help. Even if you haven't been to church or the temple for a long time, go to your priest, minister, rabbi, or any clergyperson. Some people forget about the fact that religious people are trained to talk and listen about very complicated things. They can keep your discussion confidential. And by the way, if you have sexual concerns, talk about them openly and directly with a professional person or family member. Professional people are now trained to talk about such issues. Even if they don't ask you about sex directly, you can go ahead and raise the topic. They will be able to talk about sex once you have let them know that you want to talk about sex. They are just waiting for your permission.

FACT 8:   The world is not going to end. The problems in our world are very serious, but the universal joy response you can read about in this book is very powerful. We need your help, not your surrender. Most of the sad people I help are surprised when I ask them to begin to read about world problems. I tell them to stop watching television for news about the world. Television makes its money from broadcasting crises. If you will read about what is happening, you will see that thousands of people are working to save the world. Since you can be very sad, you have the sensitivity to be a part of the peace race. The sadder you are, the more depression you can feel, the more our world needs you, because you are capable of the depth of feelings that can save the world.

FACT 9:   Some forms of depression are actually addicting. The chemicals in your brain work like a lock and key. Once the depression chemicals get flowing, they can take up much of the space in the locks. You can open the locks by actually changing how you think and behave. If you are very sad right now, try this little experiment. Put this book down, leave a bookmark on this page, and take a long brisk walk with a stereo cassette playing. Walk to the rhythm of the music. Pick some music that gives you a "high" and march along to it. Notice how you feel a little better. Your feelings changed a little because your behavior changed. You opened up some locks that were flooded with depression chemicals so that there was some room for the joy juices.

FACT 10:   Depression is not inherited, and neither is mental illness. If someone in your family has been very sick, this does not mean that you are destined for the same fate. The research in this book on super joy teaches us that we can take control of our own thoughts, feelings, and behaviors. We all have part of our families within us. How these parts are ultimately put together and what we do with the final product is not predetermined by heredity.

When you are very sad, things can seem inevitable. Your brain is just being lazy when it thinks this way.

A teenager who was born blind said, "I thought of ending it all. After all, I'm blind for life. Then I thought, 'Who's telling me to give up?' It was just brain bunk. I decided it was selling pencils on the street corner or Harvard Law School. See you in court."

These are the sadness facts. The world you are growing into has always been reluctant to talk about the "two Ss": sex and sadness, so sad people have been left alone with their problems in these two key and natural areas of life. Once you realize that your sadness is a natural step in learning to be joyful, once you tell people how you feel, once you reach out and connect, I promise you that the sadness you have been feeling will only be the spark for a celebration of living.

If you don't believe me, I dare you to prove me wrong. If you are still very sad after reading this letter, put this book down and go and tell someone how you feel. You will see that this first step is like peeking out from behind the curtain at a large and wonderful concert, the concert of life. It may be difficult to look, but before you know it, everyone will be singing with you.

Chapters Two, Three, and Four of this book are directly related to the issues raised in this letter. Two other books related to conquering sadness and depression are:

Jane Leder, *Dead Serious: A Book for Teenagers about Teenage Suicide* (New York: Atheneum Press, 1987).

David Burns, *Feeling Good: The New Mood Therapy* (New York: Signet Books, 1980).

CHAPTER TWELVE

A Joy Message for Times When Our Emotions Control Us

We can consider the process of healthy growth to be a never ending series of free choice situations, confronting each individual at every point throughout his life, in which he must choose between the delights of safety and growth, dependence and independence, regression and progression, immaturity and maturity.

ABRAHAM MASLOW

When you say "I feel tenseness," you're irresponsible . . . But when you say "I am tensing" you take responsibility.

FRITZ PERLS

The single most frequent mental error in our society is our tendency to ascribe our feelings to external events and the behavior of others. "He drives me nuts," said one wife. "He makes me feel so guilty whenever I go shopping." This wife's statement typifies the irrational process of making our own feelings someone else's responsibility. The following letter is for those persons who feel that their own emotions somehow "happen" to them and that they are helplessly reacting victims to the whims and wills of others. When we make this error, we turn any hope for super joy over to what we see as the occasional charity and kindness on the part of others.

DEAR EMOTIONALLY TROUBLED PERSON: Has your wife, husband, child, parent, or friend made you angry lately? Have you felt that you are the victim of others' thoughtlessness and lack of caring? Does it seem as if people are trying to make you feel guilty? Has someone at work made you behave childishly? If you can answer yes to any of these questions, you have turned your life and living over to people and events that you will never be able to control. You have lost your "self." True joy will depend on your learning to reclaim responsibility for how you feel.

Well-being, health, and joy depend on good "I sight." We have learned a very narrow definition of what is "I" or self and what is "It" or "out there." Freud wrote, "There is no inherent opposition between the 'I' and the 'It,' both belong together." Whenever we ascribe our emotional reactions to others or to what happens to us, we separate the "I" from the "It." Freud wrote, "In cases of normal health, it is practically impossible to distinguish between the two [the I and the It]." Wellness is the ultimate awareness and responsibility for self, the ability to unify what seems to be "out there" with what we experience "in here," and to maintain our feeling of effectiveness in our day-to-day world, to see self as a part of everything and everyone, not as a target for anyone or anything. The true art of being selfish is learning to be a part of and responsible for everyone and everything in our lives while maintaining a clear sense of who we are. We can know that we are a part of the system without becoming victimized by that system.

Researchers have shown that something they call "self-efficacy" is a key to health. It may not seem possible at first glance, but it is true that how you choose to perceive what is happening to you actually "determines" what happens to you and what you can do about it. Psychologist Albert Bandura demonstrated that body chemistry changes and that our capacity to deal with stressors is altered by how we perceive our capacity to cope.

Some people are afraid of spiders. "Spiders scare the hell out of me," said one woman. Bandura's studies showed that when he was able to strengthen a group of women's sense of general self-efficacy their fear responses and accompanying stress chemical secretions significantly diminished. What the woman afraid of spiders should have said to herself was, "I am allowing myself to be afraid of spiders. I have the feeling of fear, but I am not fear itself. I can do something about my feelings and what happens to me."

Another one of my patients said, "I have terrible arthritis. I have read about it and I know I won't improve." You can see by this man's statement that he himself has *become* his arthritis and shows very little self-efficacy. Psychologists at the Stanford Arthritis Center wanted to see if a comprehensive course about arthritis, related exercises, meditation, and relaxation would help reduce arthritis symptoms and pain. They found a twenty-eight percent reduction in pain experienced by the arthritis patients, as well as a twenty percent reduction in swollen joints and a fourteen percent decrease in overall disability. This means that almost one fifth of the illness experience of arthritis was measurably reduced. The research team discovered, however, that it was not the exercises or increased knowledge about arthritis that made the difference. Those patients who improved did so because of increases they themselves made in their view of their own abilities to cope with their disease. They took responsibility for their own wellness. They were aware of their illness, but they did not become their illness. They learned that they were "arthritising" and could do something about that process. Self-efficacy is a component of the joy response, a sense that "I can do it" and an integration of the "I" and the "It" in place of the "It" doing to or taking over the "I."

As you read this letter, ask yourself if your moodiness is not really more related to your perceptions and not to events. The ultimate goal of all psychotherapy is to teach self-responsibility and self-resilience, and you can be your own teacher of these qualities. Here is a list of efficacy and resilience affirmations used by the joy group. Take some time to look in the mirror and say these affirmations out loud to yourself. Say them with a joy partner. Take some time to sit quietly and say these affirmations to yourself slowly and with contemplation of what each statement means.

The Efficacy and Resilience Affirmations
for "I-sight" Improvement

Life is a process. Things always change.

I am life in process. I make life happen and give it meaning.

My body may get angry, but "I" am not anger. If I do not become anger, anger vanishes.

My body may get sick, but "I" am not sickness. If "I" do not become sick, illness vanishes.

The things I want are all temporary. I am not things.

My needs are not me. My body has needs, but "I" am always needless.

I experience emotions, but I am not my emotions. I can sense my feelings and change them if I want to.

I have thoughts, but my thoughts are not me. Thoughts come from me and I create and control them.

When I feel helpless, it is a signal that I am ready to help my "self." I am in control of me.

People happen to me, but they are not "me." I determine the effect people have on "me."

These ten affirmations are only a starting point. You can probably make a better affirmation list for yourself. Make sure to take your "affirmation vitamins" every day. Research shows that just saying these concepts to yourself actually alters your entire body and mental system. The key point is to focus on the idea that "self" is not controlled, attached, and determined by anything or anyone.

If you find yourself being moody and talking to yourself or others as if your "self" is out of your control, you are giving up your chance for joy. Some of my patients would argue about this issue of self-efficacy, insisting that a wife, husband, child, or boss had "upset them" or "made them angry." Some patients would say, "I have arthritis," even when I warned them that their language was the software directing the body's computer system. When these patients learned to say, "I am getting myself upset," or "I am arthritising," they noticed immediate improvement emotionally and physically.

Taking self-responsibility is not the same as blaming the self. Self-efficacy is the recognition of the power of our healing and healthy spirit, not the reassignment of blame from outside to inside. "I know I caused this cold I have," said one woman. "I am responsible for giving myself this cold." Instead of maintaining the power of self and her clear "I-sight," this woman was diminishing the power of the "I" by seeing the self as shopping around for outside problems to bring into the body.

The fact is that no one really knows completely why anybody gets sick. To get well again requires the maintenance of the idea that, whatever is happening, "we" are not consumed by events and always have control over our destiny and experience of events. This is what Freud meant when he said the "I" and the "It" are the same. Everything, including "us," is a part of the overall system, and when we disconnect from that system we lose our capacity for joy. We must always know what our "Is" are doing, remembering process and unity in place of problems and separateness. To "re-member" the self with the "It" while maintaining a clear view of self is to put ourselves back together again.

Here is an "I-sight" Test to help you recognize when you are not seeing these ideas about self-efficacy very well:

The I-sight Test

1. Do you spend time during the day talking about what people have done *to* you? _____

2. Do you talk about "they" and what "they" are doing rather than what you are experiencing? _____

3. Do you feel that "anybody" would be upset who had to put up with what you have to put up with? _____

4. Do you feel exasperated, frustrated, and angry at one particular person, turning over control of your emotions to that one person? _____

5. Are you so busy that you sometimes forget you even exist? _____

6. Does it seem that your moods swing without your giving them a shove? Are you very sad or very happy without taking self-responsibility for both of these feelings? _____

7. Do you lecture other people on what they do to you or what they make you do or feel? _____

8. Do you feel that you could be a much better person if it wasn't for the people around you? _____

9. Do you "should" on yourself? Do you feel a sense of perpetual obligation, as if your days are not your own? _____

10. In your private thinking moments, do you think about what happened to you or what people or a person did rather than what and how you experienced your day? _____

11. Are your phone conversations spent in review of the "out there" and "them" rather than the "I" and "us"?   _____

12. Are you clobbering yourself with self-criticism while pretending that someone else is holding the club?   _____

13. Do you relate to others as if they are "out there" and not really a part of you?   _____

14. Do you talk more in monologue than dialogue, more in the I-you than in what philosopher Martin Buber called the "I-thou"?   _____

15. Do you swear, cuss, and use an explosive, accusatory vocabulary, either to self or others?   _____

The more "yes" answers to these questions, the weaker your "I-sight." The corrective lenses you need are rose-colored in tint and ground for a clearer vision of self-responsibility. If you learn to replace "I-It" language with "I-me-us" system language, your self-talk will be a language of self-love that makes every day more worth living. It is much more important to learn to accept others and ourselves than to struggle to approve of people and self. Please reintroduce yourself to yourself today.

Chapters Two, Three, and Six would be particularly relevant chapters for persons interested in the above letter. Parts of these chapters deal with understanding what joy and self-responsibility are, a more complete discussion of self-efficacy, and the issue of the effect of perception on our health and daily living.

Two books related to the issue of self-responsibility for emotions are:

A. R. Assagioli, *Psychosynthesis* (New York: Viking/Compass, 1965).

Fritz Perls, *Gestalt Therapy Verbatim* (Los Angeles, California: Real People Press, 1969).

CHAPTER THIRTEEN

*A Joy Message for Times
When We Lose Someone*

The more absolute death seems, the more authentic life becomes. . . .

JOHN FOWLES

Knowing the reality and certainty of death reminds us that we do not have time to be casual or thoughtless with our lives. We only have time to live.

SARAH CIRESE

Two imperfect people can create a perfect process out of which everything can be dealt with and turned into growth. The process is not dependent on outcome. . . . I don't believe people put themselves through very painful situations unless that is the only way they can learn what they need to know.

SHIRLEY LUTHMAN

All relationships end. The only question to be resolved is how and when. Researchers estimate that children have seen more than eighteen thousand deaths on television before they are fourteen years old. Most of these deaths are violent or criminal, and the emotions seen are at best fleeting. As a result, we become numb to real loss until we experience it first hand. This letter is for those who have lost someone they loved, either by death, divorce, or other separation, for these people have experienced what playwright Richard Anderson writes about: "Death ends a life, but it does not end a relationship, which struggles on in the survivor's mind towards some resolution which it never finds."

DEAR PERSON WHO HAS LOST SOMEONE YOU LOVED:
None of us are ever ready for the full impact of the end of a loving relationship. We may have read about the stages of grieving, but we will not be fully ready when our turn comes to grieve. You have already found that out. Whether by divorce, death, or other process of ending, you have experienced the most painful of human experiences, the disruption of a human bond.

The process of "disbonding" is bereavement. The emotional reaction to bereavement is grief. This grief is as natural a human reflex as the joy response, and I have found that my patients who grieve the deepest are able to rejoice the most intensely. There can be no real joy without the true understanding and acceptance of loss and endings.

I have found that there are ten phases to this grieving process, and perhaps you will find some comfort in knowing that we all must follow these paths of adjustment to loss. Even though death is the most profound example of bereavement, our grief is real whenever we lose any relationship. Our health suffers when we fail to see that any loss results in grieving.

The Grief to Joy Cycle

DENIAL: At first we are protected from the sharp and severe shock of complete endings by an emotional and pyschochemical reaction that allows us to keep going, keep living while we confront and behaviorally cope with the details and sociocultural requirements imposed by our loss. Such denial is healthy if it allows us to get our socially required work done and then yields to the next natural phase of grieving.

PROTEST: Once denial weakens and outlives its usefulness, we begin to struggle against the inevitable realization that a relationship is forever over. Once again, such protest is natural if it yields to appropriate sharing of emotional reactions of anger and a sense of injustice and unfairness. A protest turned inward interferes with the natural flow of grieving, so letting people know how mad and hurt you are, even if such anger and pain seem unrealistic, is a key part of the protest phase of grieving.

RAGE: The sharing of emotional protest will give way to rage, a desire to be violent against an unknown enemy that has seemed to cause this ending. This temporary fury may be directed at innocent persons, sometimes those very people who are trying their best to comfort us. These persons can take only a little of this fury before they withdraw because of their own fear and anger, so awareness of this need to strike out and allowing yourself some physical outlet for such expression is important. Banging, hitting, and kicking some inanimate object or just screaming out can help. "I began to run," said one woman. "I mean I just ran and ran and ran. It was like my feet were stomping on someone or something."

SURRENDER: If you have allowed yourself a free but brief physical and emotional expression of your grief rage, you will begin to feel drained both emotionally and physically. You may become lethargic, even deny the impact of the loss. You may experience actual physical symptoms such as nausea, digestive upset, headaches, chest pains, or even the symptoms once experienced by the person you have lost. This is a particularly vulnerable time for illness, because our immune systems begin to be fatigued because of all of the physical and mental energy used in denial, protest, and rage.

FALSE AND HEALTHY HOPE: The fatigue of the surrender stage can cloud our judgment. We turn next to hope of return of the relationship. We may actually see the lost loved one as an apparition, convince ourselves that a lost marriage can really be saved after all, or turn to occult sources to understand our loss. What we need most here is an intact belief system, some explanation of the meaning of living and losing that fits our chosen life purpose. Without such a belief system, we flounder in a sea of false hope, gimmickry, and false prophets.

If we are able to manifest a strong belief system or rediscover such a system long ignored, we can actually find some joy and happiness at the acceptance of endings as being as natural as beginnings. As Carlos Castaneda writes, "There is a strange consuming happiness in acting with the full knowledge that whatever one is doing may very well be one's last act on earth."

DISILLUSIONMENT: Whether or not we pass through the fifth and pivotal hope and belief phase of grieving, we all become disillusioned. We begin to question the meaning and value of living, the existence of God, and even the purpose of being born at all. If we are ready for this natural phase of disillusionment, we can use it as a stimulus for learning and growing, for further developing and deepening our transcendent life philosophy. If we think that we are the only persons who become disillusioned or allow this disillusionment to make us regress to protest and rage, we may isolate ourselves from important support systems.

I have never worked with a grieving patient who did not feel this disillusionment. Those patients who saw such disillusionment as a stimulus for a new set of questions rather than a declaration of surrender were able to find renewed joy in living even as they grieved and were deeply sad. The joy response is a celebration of all of the natural processes of life, not a naive smiling in the dark of delusion and self-deception.

ACTING OUT: Whether or not we rediscover the joy of living through the pain of losing, we all "act out" when we lose someone. We may try to numb our pain by getting lost in our work, our parenting, or in a vigorous search for new love. We seem to try to be too busy to hurt. Once again, this is a natural and healing part of the grief process if it does not become a point of fixation in the life cycle. Workaholism, alcoholism, and promiscuity are typical overreactions to the acting-out stage. If we know that we will go through the acting-out phase, we can allow ourselves to overdo for just a little while even as we know that we must resume responsibility for ourselves, in effect acting out a role. Such play acting is healthier than acting out.

FINALITY: With true grief comes the realization that endings, particularly death, are final. "I can't tell you exactly how it felt," said one woman, "but I can tell you that the finality of my divorce hit me like a brick. I just sort of looked off into space and thought that this is for real." The finality of loss by death of a loved one is so intense that the mind cannot grasp the infinite complexities of the mystery of such an ending. The brain prefers despair to the struggle to find meaning.

"My son asked me where he was before he turned up in my uterus as a baby," said one mother. "I couldn't answer that any better than I could tell him where his grandfather went after he died." The presence of a strong belief system is the only buffer against emotional shock and regression when we confront our own mortality and the inevitable end of all relationships.

SETTLEMENT: During this phase the person who has negotiated the first eight phases of the grief process begins to talk freely about their loss and the person who has been lost. Memories of the relationship are prominent and solidifying, with relationship imprints present that are able to elicit the same emotional reaction as occurred when the lost person was actually present.

In a sense, the settlement period is a rediscovery of the infinite nature of the feelings for the person who has been lost, a rediscovery that our "self" will always be able to experience "re-emotion" in reaction to thoughts of the person who is gone. A rebirth of the lost relationship takes place on an imagery and emotional level if the grieving person has allowed himself or herself to pass naturally through all of the first eight phases.

RECOMMITMENT: As the grieving cycle continues and intertwines with the grieving cycles of other people and various other grieving cycles that we ourselves have started out upon, we are able to rejoice in the rediscovery of the fact that consciousness is infinite. As Ken Wilber writes, "Only the transpersonal self is immortal, timeless, or nonhistorical—not the individual ego. Your true glory, your greatest potential, lies just on the other side of you."

At this last phase of the grieving cycle, the joy response emerges again, a joy in the realization that the higher you is forever. Living with the intensity of the joy response in our daily living is the best way of being sure that we don't die before we die.

If you have recently lost someone, discuss this grieving cycle with a joy partner. Find the phase that best describes where you are, where you have been, and most importantly where you are going in this cycle. Remember, the joy response is a part of the cycle of loss if we can be patient enough, contemplative enough, and believe enough to let joy return.

Chapters Two, Three, Eight, and Nine would be the most important parts of this book to read if you are going through the grieving cycle. Chapter 9 discusses the power of faith and belief, the key components of turning the natural sadness of bereavement back into the natural beauty of human joy.

Two books that the joy group members found helpful when they experienced loss are:

E. Becker, *The Denial of Death* (New York: Free Press, 1973).

R. A. Moody, *Life after Life* (New York: Bantam, 1975).

CHAPTER FOURTEEN

A Joy Message About Our Immune Systems and the Threat of AIDS

There is a deep reciprocity at work, an unseverable linkage between the hideousness of illness and the splendor of health.

LARRY DOSSEY

But now it is important to calm the fears of those who are not at great risk and provide help and education to those who are.

RICHARD STENGEL

We really have not seen much evidence for the spread of the virus into people who are not in risk groups. . . . For most people the risk of AIDS is essentially zero.

DR. HAROLD JAFFE
CHIEF AIDS EPIDEMIOLOGIST
ATLANTA CENTERS FOR DISEASE CONTROL

The faces of 24 men, women, and children who died from AIDS stared out from the cover of *Newsweek* magazine. Three hundred and two additional pictures of persons dead from AIDS were included inside the magazine, representing only a fraction of the more than 4,000 persons killed by AIDS over a twelve-month period. From the first 31 cases of AIDS reported in 1981, the death toll now stands at more than 30,000. The *Newsweek* article uses such words as "pestilence," "plague," "epidemic," and "victim." It warns that the AIDS problem will only get worse, referring to a possible "body count" of 179,000 by 1991. The warning is clear. AIDS is out of control, spreading wildly into a helpless population who can only hope that monogamy, celibacy, or a miracle drug will save them.

If you have tested positive for exposure to HIV (also called the HTLV-III virus), such reports are damning. Even if you are afraid you might have been exposed to the virus or may be in the future, such dramatic presentations as the *Newsweek* article go beyond their intended education and warning to cause fear and hopelessness. The following letter is written for anyone personally concerned about AIDS. It is not a letter about symptoms and the serious threat of this complicated disease. It is a letter about hope, healing, and the joy and positive news that have been overshadowed by fear, exaggeration, and a plague mentality that has never been successful in stopping the spread of any major disease.

DEAR PERSON CONCERNED ABOUT AIDS:

No one "gets" AIDS. We are not completely sure what causes AIDS, but there is a virus that attacks the immune systems. AIDS *can* be treated. AIDS is not spreading widely into the heterosexual population in this country. AIDS is not a "gay" disease. AIDS is not a sexual disease, but it's a disease that can be passed on by certain sexual acts. There is much we can all do to help AIDS patients and to prevent the spread of AIDS. There are not "victims" of AIDS, innocent or guilty. We are not all doomed to die from an AIDS plague.

Most of what you have been hearing about AIDS may make the statements in the preceding paragraph seem surprising. The fear of AIDS ("FAIDS") is interfering with our greatest hope against AIDS: hope, faith, joy, and a joining together to strengthen ourselves against AIDS or to fight the disease in those who have it. Like the weather, everyone is talking about AIDS and talking as if no one can do anything about it. This is completely wrong! If you read through this letter, you will see that we are ultimately stronger than any disease process if we remember the principles of the joy response.

Let me explain to you the reasons why each statement in the first paragraph of this letter is correct by presenting some basic steps for the cure of our fear of AIDS.

The Cure for "FAIDS"

No one "gets" AIDS. AIDS stands for a deficiency of the immune system that is acquired. We also can suffer from "DIDS" or a developed immune deficiency syndrome caused by poor nutrition, lack of exercise, emotional stress, and other abuses of our immunity that we cause ourselves by our own poor health behavior, not by some virus. Current evidence suggests that one factor in the "acquisition" type of immune deficiency is a virus, the human immunodeficiency virus (HIV) or the Human T-Lymphocyte Virus III. We do not "get" the deficiency but are exposed to a virus which in turn weakens the immune system in twenty-five to fifty percent of the people exposed to it.

AIDS is related to many factors that are still unknown. We are not sure why some people do not become ill after exposure to the virus, why some people get less severe forms of AIDS (ARC or Aids Related Complex), or why AIDS takes the forms it does in different people. We have oversimplified a very complex and mysterious process when we say that we "get" AIDS. AIDS isn't out there waiting, it is a disease like all others, a disease that occurs in a complex system of people, environments, diets, general health, and feelings. It is the old pathology model with its focus on the "germ" theory that distracts us from understanding that the immune system under attack by AIDS and the HIV is a worldwide immune system, not just one person's struggle against illness.

The cause of AIDS has *not* been found. Just because we have learned that the HIV virus is related to AIDS does not mean that the virus itself is the one factor sufficient to "cause" AIDS. It is likely that there are many cofactors that determine infection and the course of that infection, and some of these factors may be psychological. There is no known disease that is caused exclusively by one factor. Even the common cold viruses interact with other causative factors of immunoefficiency in each individual, which in turn are influenced by general health, environmental health conditions, and personality factors. We must continue to look for multiple causes of AIDS and not just focus our attention on "the" virus. Avoiding sexual intimacy to avoid AIDS while engaging in other behaviors which compromise the immune system or the health of our world will never solve the AIDS problem.

There is no such thing as an AIDS virus. One virus (HIV) has been shown to be related to AIDS. There may be others. It is misleading to think that a single virus is the complete cause of any disease, for if we think in this way we are confronted with the bitter reality that no virus has ever been conquered. We have been able to prepare our immune systems by prior rehearsal (vaccination) to fight certain viruses, but viruses themselves are immortal. We must think about strengthening our immune systems, the targets of the one virus we are aware of as related to AIDS.

AIDS can be treated. Right now, there is no "cure" for an immune system deficiency related to HIV. There are, however, many treatments. The following recommendations are good practices to follow to enhance and protect the immune system.

Some Steps for IES
(Immune Efficiency Syndrome)

1. Maintain good overall physical health.

2. Learn the joy response! The joy response strengthens the immune system.

3. Get good nutrition, rest, and exercise. New research emphasizes the importance of dietary approaches to immune problems. Caloric requirements go up when your immune system is compro-

mised. A rule of thumb is to use 50 calories and 1.5 grams of protein per kilogram (2.2 pounds) of ideal body weight per day. Supplements such as Ensure, Nutrament, Sustacal, and Sustagen may be helpful. Check with your doctor.

4. Reduce immune system stressors such as smoking, drugs, and alcohol. These drugs can cause "DIDS" (developed immune deficiency related to our own behaviors which weaken our immunity).

5. Take precautions to prevent sexually transmitted diseases. There may be a link between HIV and other infections.

6. Keep your vaccinations current (pneumococcal, flu, hepatitis B) but avoid contraindicated vaccinations. If immune function is low, live viral vaccines should be avoided (oral polio, MMR, yellow fever). Talk to your doctor about these issues and immunoefficiency testing.

7. In the absence of certainty, there is nothing wrong with massive doses of hope. Remember that our selfish brains prefer the easier and quicker route of surrender and despair. As long as we keep telling persons infected with HIV that they will die, we add nothing to their living. The joy response can override this brain laziness. Remember, you are *not* an AIDS victim, you are an immune-challenged person preparing to fight back. If you have been exposed to the AIDS virus, your immune system has been challenged. Respond to the challenge and find a doctor who will fight with you. This is why we address the economics of AIDS to be sure that income level does not determine survival.

8. Inform others with whom you will interact intimately if you have been exposed to the HIV virus. All disease affects the entire human system. You need strong people to help you stay well, so keep as many people as well as possible by being responsible for your condition. Don't tell people what you "have," tell them what you are doing. What you are doing is "strengthening your immune system against the HIV challenge you are facing."

If your doctor offers no hope, fire your doctor! Find a healer who will work as a team member with you as you confront your immune system challenge. Your doctor is ethically and morally bound to offer comfort and treatment even though he or she cannot offer a cure. There is a big difference between curing and healing. Curing is getting rid of a disease. Healing is making and keeping a person whole even when the person is sick.

AIDS is not spreading widely into the heterosexual population in this country. In my more than twenty years of work in the field of sexuality, I have never been able to clearly identify what people call the "heterosexual population." I have never been able to tell how "hetero" or "sexual" or how much of a "population" this group really represents. Whom we choose to make love with is a highly intimate issue, and many people say one thing and do another. The high-risk groups for exposure to the HIV are still homosexual and bisexual men and intravenous drug users. Only four percent of reported cases of AIDS are classified as instances of heterosexual transmission, but many of these cases may actually be related to the high-risk behaviors of drug use or promiscuity. The overall incidence of AIDS is actually slowing, although infection in intravenous drug users and their sexual partners continues to increase. We simply are not refined enough in our designations of "heterosexual," "bisexual," and "homosexual" to ascribe any disease to a given sexual orientation.

AIDS is not a "gay" disease. Whom we make love with is not a "sexual preference." It is an orientation evolved through a complex interaction of psychological and biological variables that have not been clarified. The "who" of sex is not at all related to AIDS. It is the "what" and "with how many" and the health status of a given partner that relate to AIDS infection, not gender orientation. The ultimate conquering of AIDs depends on the "connection" and a systems approach to living. When we think that only "they get it or have it," we forget that there can be no "they" in a world that is ultimately "us." We finally began to make some progress in understanding AIDS when "we" became concerned about all of "us."

Aids is not a sexual disease. One of the ways we can be exposed to the HIV is by exchange of body fluids, particularly if such fluids can find their way into the blood. Some sexual acts involve the exchange of body fluids; however, it is not the sex that is the problem but the type of sex engaged in with an infected partner. Responsible sex has always been essential to health, and because of our "FAIDS," we are forgetting that other sexually transmitted diseases are spreading much more rapidly than AIDS.

Chlamydia, a bacterial infection transmitted through sexual intercourse, affects 4.5 million people per year, and one third of men and three quarters of women who carry the chlamydia bacteria show no symptoms but keep giving the gift that keeps on giving. Penicillin-resistant gonorrhea has increased ninety percent in the United States. This "super gonorrhea" can have damaging effects on health. A million new cases of genital warts are reported each year. Cautious, openly discussed, responsible sex is a basic good health practice. AIDS should not distract us or frighten us away from the fact that sexual choices are always first and foremost health choices.

My work with persons challenged by the HIV indicates that these persons often withdraw from sexual interaction. I suggest that they return immediately to touching, holding, rubbing, self and partner masturbation, whatever sexual behaviors they used to find pleasing. They should avoid any exchange of body fluids, use condoms, and avoid any exposure to open sores or wounds, but they should also avoid sacrificing their sex lives. Sexual fulfillment is an immune system builder and it should be a source of responsible response to the AIDS challenge, not a sacrifice to it. I have noticed that we tend to withdraw our touch from all seriously ill patients, and this is exactly the opposite of what healing is all about.

Hope and AIDS: There is no such thing as false hope if we are educated about disease threats and the behaviors that reduce these threats. Education and responsible sex combined with immune-enhancing health practices can do much to help stop the AIDS crisis. Our immune systems have been put at serious risk not only by HIV but by a world environment of conflict, pollution, and discrimination. If we can find more joy in our daily living and pay for this joy through behaviors which show respect for our world, if we show compassion for those who are personally struggling against the AIDS challenge, and if we allow AIDS to teach us instead of frighten us, we will be able to rediscover the joy of intimacy that we lost when we went chasing after the joy of sex.

Chapters Eight and Nine are directly related to the issues raised in this letter to persons concerned about AIDS. Accurate, detailed information about HIV infection, prevention of transmission to others, sound health habits, and relearning the joy response even at times of challenge to the immune system are crucial in dealing with AIDS.

Sources of information about AIDS are:

Toll-free AIDS Hotline 1-800-342-AIDS

A self-care manual entitled *Living with AIDS*. Write for free copies to AIDS Project, Los Angeles, Inc., 7362 Santa Monica Boulevard, West Hollywood, CA 90046

Facts About AIDS. Write to AIDS, Suite 700, 1555 Wilson Boulevard, Rosslyn, VA 22209.

CHAPTER FIFTEEN

A Joy Message for Times When We're Sick or Hurt

Instead of looking at illness as something wrong, think of it as something finally going right.

FRED WOLF

Deviance is normal.

AARON ANTONOVSKY

The ills from which we are suffering have had their seat in the very foundation of human thought.

PIERRE TEILHARD DE CHARDIN

Our society seems to be on the "disease of the year" plan. Influenza, gonorrhea, herpes, measles, polio, scarlet fever, AIDS, and most recently the concern for the Epstein-Barr virus end up on the covers of our weekly news magazines, pathology celebrities vying for our personal and financial attention. We cannot seem to learn that social and cultural changes are always behind these diseases, and that social and cultural changes are what are ultimately necessary to conquer them. But what of the individual person who is sick right now? What of the person ill with a form of cancer, heart disease, or some damage to the body that imposes severe challenges in daily living? This letter is for you.

DEAR SICK OR INJURED PERSON:

You have heard it all by now. "You can do it," they tell you. "Come on, you can beat this thing. It's just a matter of mind over body." You see books every day that tell you that the right amount of meditation, laughter, positive mood state, and magic imagery can conquer any disability. Has anyone told you that disease is healthy, a normal part of living that does not mean that you have failed in any way? Has anyone told you that most of the people in the world are sick right now? Has anyone told you that it is just as important to experience your problem and learn from it as it is to get better? Has anyone told you that illness is healthy?

If you are in a wheelchair as you read this, or if you are lying in a hospital bed, I hope you will think less about why you are ill and more about what you want to do with your life in spite of your illness or impairment. I hope you will be able to use your illness as a teacher, not about why you got sick or about healthy practices, but as a teacher about living. Sickness is a part of health.

It is difficult to do this with everyone running around trying to "attack your disease" and *"make"* you get better, but you can do more for your natural healing by accepting illness than by only trying to defeat it. You can do more for yourself when you are sick by accepting disease as a part of the natural growth, breakage, and repair system of life than by yielding to a "holistic" medicine that is just as consumed with pathology and its avoidance and cure as any form of modern medicine. Something is "right" when you get sick because your body is behaving naturally. It was designed to be sick just as it was designed to be well, and both parts of living are natural.

"Tuning in" to illness is not in vogue. We are supposed to be healing, not learning. Biofeedback, imagery techniques, nutritional approaches, and megadoses of vitamins are "in." We are supposed to be busy conquering or avoiding illness, not experiencing sickness as a learning process. If you are sick or physically impaired, you know that your illness has caused you to become "all ears." You are attending more than ever to "you" and the amazing relationship between how you feel and who you are, the physical representation of "you." Physical and health challenges command us to pay attention, to attend to the fact that there is more to life and living than just a healthy body and mind. We are more than brain and body, we are a spirit, and very sick people can become keenly aware of that spirit and its relationship to everything in the world.

If all of this sounds a little strange, think of how you were thinking before you experienced your present problem. You were probably to some degree just going through the motions. Even if you were having fun, you were not focusing on your relationship to life and living to the degree you do now that you are sick. Illness is another of life's lessons. It is not a punishment but an opportunity.

Our society thinks of stress as "bad." We must learn to "cope" with stress, somehow survive it. I suggest that all of us are stressed, all of us get sick, and that we all move along a line from super healthy to very, very sick during our lives. When we get sick, we become aware sometimes for the first time that we are walking along that life line and that we can make adjustments not just of the body but of the spirit that can move us a little more toward the health side of the line, even if our bodies cannot always come along with us. To be truly optimistic about life, you must be pessimistic enough to realize that everybody gets mentally and physically hurt and eventually dies, that we are all "on the line" all the time.

The new "health optimism" movement suggests that we can lengthen the life line, that we can live past a hundred years and enter a marathon on our hundredth birthday. This is just plain wrong. If you think of life as a line, the line is not likely to get much longer for any of us, and we will all have terrible breaks along that line. If we bend that line into an infinite circle, we may learn that there are many orbits in which this circle travels. Our bodies inevitably "get off" the ride, but we don't have to if we can realize our innermost sense of "self" when the body is challenged.

Unless seventy-five-year-olds race against seventy-five-year-olds, the seventy-five-year-old who wins the race will always be a fluke. Understanding your illness or impairment depends upon learning that illness and death are part of life, not failures to qualify for holistic awards of longer and livelier living. Even when things are happening to us which challenge us, we must remember that illness is not separate from health but part of wellness.

Once you face the fact that your illness is not a failure, really not something that has gone "wrong," you can begin to learn about the joy response as it relates to illness. Physicist Fred Allan Wolf describes what he calls the "do-be-do-be-do" phenomenon. He states, "Our bodies reflect the do-be-do-be-do of the Sinatra melody—the creation and rest from that creation. Illness, I propose, results from a disharmony produced when parallel universes [the different orbits I mentioned above] sing out of tune because they fail to listen to each other." Illness is the "be," daily living is the "do." There can be joy in being, even when we are sick, if we become more aware of "self" when we have the imposed time to extend the "be" of the melody of life. Illness is the minor chord of living, drawing our attention and anticipation to changes that can make the major chord all that more meaningful and satisfying. Varieties of music are created by minor chords. In fact, the finale is more intense when it is preceded by the enjoyment of well-placed and appreciated minor chords throughout the symphony.

One of my patients was told by his doctor that he "had the Epstein-Barr virus." His tests had actually shown that his blood contained antibodies to the Epstein-Barr virus, the agent which causes infectious mononucleosis and an array of weakening, debilitating symptoms. Millions of persons carry the antibodies to this virus, meaning only that they have been exposed to the virus. My patient said, "Now I have to go on a macrobiotic diet and start meditation. Can you help me?"

This patient's orientation to this new "pop" disease (which is not new at all and is really not one disease but a virus with many impacts) symbolizes what I mean by our sick view of sickness. By no means all of the people who test positive for the Epstein-Barr virus develop illness, and the type and degree of the illness vary from person to person. Each of us has our own "sickness style," and if we focus on "how" we are being sick instead of just looking for why, we can maintain the healing joy response at times of illness.

A study of the Epstein-Barr virus supports my point and illustrates what I call the "modern medicine muddle." We look for trouble, not joy, when we study disease. Stanislav Kasl studied cadets at the United States Military Academy. He found that about 432 of a new group of 1400 cadets were susceptible to mononucleosis because of the presence of antibodies for the Epstein-Barr virus. Of the susceptible cadets, 194 contracted mononucleosis during their four years at the Academy.

Kasl found that the cadets who became ill showed three characteristics. First, each intensely wanted a military career. Second, the fathers of these cadets were "overachievers" and very successful themselves. Third and finally, the ill cadets were doing poorly academically. The combination of all of these "Ps"—pressure, poor performance, and a powerful parent—seemed to be related to the susceptibles becoming sick. Is the lesson of this study to do well, avoid pressure, and find a father who is not too successful? I don't think so.

As with all viral illness—and, I suggest, all illness—we have forgotten to look at the joy factors of staying well because of our focus on the stress factors that can make us sick. What about the 238 susceptible cadets who did not succumb? Who studies them? Didn't the illness of the cadets who did succumb offer them the opportunity to pay attention to the stress factors related to their illness? Did they learn from their illness? Shouldn't my worried patient be focusing on life purpose, joy, direction, and celebration as much as he does on diet, exercise, and biofeedback? It is not surprising that pressure and disappointment should contribute to illness. I find it more surprising that anyone under the extreme pressure of a military academy should ever stay healthy at all, particularly when already exposed to the Epstein-Barr virus!

We really don't know why the cadets who didn't get sick escaped the illness, because we do not think joyfully about illness. Modern medicine is concerned with negatives, not joy. It may not be the opposite of the "Ps" of pressure for the cadets that can lead to health or that protected the cadets who did not get sick. What are the factors that Aaron Antonovsky calls "salutogenic"? We will never be well if we only worry about avoiding "pathogenesis."

Being well is also a process of finding the "salutogenesis" in our life.

I told my patient to take time to consider his goals and direction. I asked him if he was having fun. He answered, "Well, I don't know what you mean by fun. I am jogging, eating well, and I go out a lot. I'm happy enough. Now that you ask, I haven't paid much attention to fun lately. My job is a hassle, and my dad really wants me to do well this time. I screwed up at the last job he got me." This patient needed to look at his living, not just how he could avoid disease.

Patients are coming to me in higher numbers now regarding the Epstein-Barr virus issue. I see a pattern of pressure, failure, and lack of direction and strong, mutually pleasing relationships in most of their lives. I see very little consistent joy, only the "foreplay" and preparation for joy that they hope will come later. If you are sick now, look for where the joy can be for you in spite of the limitations that may be imposed by your impairment.

"You know what?" said one of my patients newly relegated to a wheelchair for life because of an auto accident. "I am not going to enter the wheelchair Olympics. I am going to sit and read, talk, watch, listen, and see if I can be more 'me' on two wheels than I was when I was driving too fast to nowhere on four wheels." She had learned from her challenge to "be" more her, not struggle to be "just like everyone else again."

There is no denying the suffering, pain, grief, and despair that can come with the illness or impairment you may have. You can, however, be free of the pressures to blame yourself or struggle to be a super patient. Illness is a chance to be you, even a new you, integrating whatever remnants of disease may remain. You don't have to smile, sing, and be strong. You can cry, swear, and reach out for help from those who are still singing the "do" part of the melody while you are trying to learn the rhythm of being.

Chapter Nine is the most relevant to the material in the letter above. Technical discussion and elaboration of the "salutogenic" orientation are presented in Aaron Antonovky, *Unraveling the Mystery of Health: How*

People Manage Stress and Stay Well. Other books that you might find helpful when you are forced to start "being" more than "doing" are:

Paul Pearsall, *Superimmunity* (New York: McGraw-Hill, 1987).

Joan Borysenko. *Minding the Body, Mending the Mind* (Reading, Mass.: Addison-Wesley, 1987).

CHAPTER SIXTEEN

A Joy Message for Times When We Can't Seem to Find Someone to Love

I'm giving up on men. The only ones I meet are married men wanting to cheat on their wives, single men who are completely nuts, super studs, and wimps.

32-YEAR-OLD WOMAN

I've been out with seven different women this month. I still don't know what they want from a man.

27-YEAR-OLD MAN

I'm on my second marriage. I mean I'm "on" it, not "in" it, like on a boat to nowhere.

42-YEAR-OLD WOMAN

As soon as I get close to a man, he runs like a frightened dog. If we have sex or talk about the future, everything seems to change.

36-YEAR-OLD WOMAN

I have spent the last twenty years in my clinical work talking with men and women about their search for someone to love. Although each person experiences his or her own private struggle in the search for loving, there seem to be patterns that repeat themselves

275

in their influence on persons who can't find a love partner. If you can't seem to find your lover, if you have been frustrated and disillusioned in your efforts to find someone with whom to share the joy of love, this letter is for you.

DEAR FRUSTRATED LOVE-SEEKER:

Most people in the world have not yet found someone to love and be loved by. As sad as this statement may seem, the status of American marriages and the perpetual courtship problems, affairs, breakups, and misunderstandings are testimony to the fact that the most important yet difficult development task in all of our living is the challenge of finding someone to love. You are certainly not alone in this search, and the fact that you are reading this letter indicates that you are more than ready to love. Here are some recommendations for finding what one of my patients called a "longtime lover," someone to love for a lifetime.

Lessons for Finding a Longtime Lover

LESSON ONE: You will never find a lover who is any more lovable than you are. Even though many of my patients don't want to face this fact, most of us get (or don't get) exactly what we deserve in a love match. Your first step is to make a serious assessment of your own "lovability quotient." Are you just as you wish your ideal lover would be? If not, this is where you must begin— not just focusing on loving yourself but on being the lover you would want to love you.

LESSON TWO: Most men have a serious "intimacy deficiency." Psychologist Carol Gilligan describes the fact that men have been raised to be independent and learn to see intimacy as a threat, something that may weaken them or rob them of autonomy. The hunt for love is fun for men, a test of their independent hunter skills. The "settlement"—giving in "with" someone and turning a part of self over to someone else—is like being called home too early for dinner while all of your buddies mock your sissyhood and lack of independence.

Men must be aware of their student status in the intimacy issue and women must be aware of their teacher status. Women have been raised to fear autonomy as a sign of failure rather than strength, an inability to be adequately marketable. One reason for love bonds is the counterbalancing of the independence/autonomy issue, and this same struggle extends particularly to homosexual relationships in which socially assigned roles may play themselves out in even more subtle and less socially dictated ways.

LESSON THREE: Sex is very dangerous for love. Sex can threaten any potential for the development of lasting love, because men may crave the conquest but fear the commitment and women may seek the commitment and feel that they have prematurely traded off sex as a negotiable item. As anachronistic as it may sound, my clinical experience teaches that sex should happen only after love has been affirmed and communicated. Delaying sex for love is placing the purpose of sexual intimacy in its proper perspective, not "using" it as reward or control.

LESSON FOUR: Beware of sexual "addicts." The terms "Don Juanism," "nymphomania," "satyriasis," "hypersexuality," "sexual compulsion," and most recently "sexual addiction" have been used to refer to someone for whom sex has become a mood-altering, almost trance-inducing "substance," an internal hormone high from using the bodies of others. P. Carnes's book, *Out of the Shadows,* discusses what he calls sexual addiction and proposes a twelve-step treatment program modified from the Alcoholics Anonymous program.

My clinical experience does not support the addiction model for sexuality, for there is no external substance involved and no physiological tolerance or withdrawal phenomenon in the case of a "sex addiction." I have found that what psychiatrists and psychologists call an "atypical impulse disorder" more accurately describes persons who "use" instead of "share" sex, a type of "impulsive intercourse syndrome." Unless you understand this syndrome, you will never find a longtime love.

Seven Symptoms of the Impulsive
Intercourse Syndrome

1. Persons with IIS (impulsive intercourse syndrome) experience a rapid and intense buildup of sexual impulse and interest. The intensity is of such magnitude that the "act" replaces the "person," and any need for closeness is rapidly translated to *genital need.*

2. Persons with IIS begin to *lose interest* in a sexual partner once the sexual impulse is discharged. They are entranced with the sexual encounter, feeling empty when the encounter ends.

3. IIS is what psychologists call *"ego-syntonic,"* which means that IIS persons feel comfortable with this syndrome and may report enjoying sex and intimacy. They may be "excellent lovers," with well-practiced techniques and broad experience, or they may be sexually impaired, acclimated to their own sexual inadequacy. In either case, very little dissonance is experienced, and sex seems "just great."

4. The IIS is accompanied by impulse problems in other areas of life. At work and at play, IIS persons are intensely involved, sometimes on the go constantly, almost *hyperactive.* Again, when the energy of the impulses is dissipated, there is generally a feeling of apathy and withdrawal. In relationships, such withdrawal is experienced as rejection by the sexual partner.

5. IIS is often accompanied by a "life theory of intimacy" that includes feelings of "not getting too close too soon," or "having been hurt before," or "being afraid that people will take advantage of me." The *intellectualization* by the IIS person extends to rationalization as to why "they didn't call" after a sexual encounter, when the real reason relates to immaturity and fear of self-disclosure and closeness.

6. IIS people have *trouble saying good-bye.* They more typically just disappear, sometimes making more and more feeble excuses as to why they are not coming around much anymore. Since the actual "hello" has been more conquest than invitation to intimacy, the good-bye seems almost irrelevant to IIS people, somehow "too serious" or "too uncomfortable to deal with."

7. Intercourse for IIS people is *"doing,"* not experiencing. Sexual fantasies are about "women" or "men," not a given woman or man with whom they have already been sexual.

I have never seen a patient in my office who is having sex with multiple partners or very early in a new relationship who seems to be able to find someone to love over time. Premature sexual relations can be a "quick fix" to the IIS person, who then desires to move on for the forever elusive higher high, never knowing that love is a volitional, effort-requiring behavior and is not measured by a "usury" of genital reflex to replace absent feelings of intimacy.

LESSON FIVE: Finding a longtime lover is *not* separate from finding a meaningful life. Patients on love hunts often ignore the importance of their careers, their parents, their spiritual beliefs, and the pursuit of some higher purpose in life. They have ignored the joy response in favor of looking for someone else to give joy to them. If you want to find someone to love, you can start by making sure you are loving your parents, career, and the meaning and purpose of your life.

The women who come to me for therapy come in search of love. The men who come to me come in search of "stress reduction," career help, or strategies to reduce what they call their type A behaviors. Ironically, it seems that the "cure," discovering the joy response, rests with each gender learning to look more intensely for exactly what the opposite gender is in search of. Men can't seem to see that it is not their "type A" behavior that will kill them but their "type L" or lonely behavior and feelings that will eventually catch up with them as what they will see later as a "midlife crisis" that has actually been an all-life crisis too long ignored. Women seem to believe that finding the right person will result in their discovery of the right life, realizing sometimes very late in life that persons, not genders, all need a balanced life free of dependence on any one set of factors.

I have also noticed that the search for a longtime lover has been hampered by social pressures on men and women to be free of "sexist" approaches to life. Some women have disavowed their need for love, mistaking it for a sign of capitulation to archaic roles for less than modern women. Too late, they begin to examine their need for love, for children, for family, as they sit behind the desk in their executive office tearfully congratulating the young secretary who is going on maternity leave. Some men, in their efforts to be "liberated males," have found themselves interacting with women only as "one of the guys." Their needs for a loving wife, children, a family, and strong support from a woman have been hidden for fear of being accused of being sexist. Both genders have the same need for the joy response, and social sanctions against free expressions of these needs only interfere with the chance for men and women to find longtime love together.

Now that you know about the IIS syndrome and some of the lessons of loving, here are some suggestions that might help you in your search for a longtime lover.

1. Don't have sex with someone until each of you is in love with the other and you both tell each other about your love.

2. Don't hold back any feelings during courtship. Don't say to yourself, "Well, it's too soon to be talking about that." If you are feeling something or thinking something in a relationship, that's the time to share what you are feeling and thinking.

3. Don't wait for phone calls. Call the person you are interested in when you feel like calling. Don't play games and try to manipulate the relationship. If how you are and how you feel are not acceptable to the person you are interested in, then the relationship will never last anyway.

4. Marriage will make any problems you are having in your courtship worse! Get professional help if you think you need it *before*

you get married. Time never healed anything; people heal themselves and their relationships. Get the problem out in the open and try to fix it now. There will never be a better time.

5. Stop talking about "men" and "women" and start focusing on "that man" and "that woman." Many couples spend time theorizing about relationships instead of experiencing and trying to improve them. Talk about you, him or her, and "us," not "relationships of men or women in today's society."

6. Even if you think you are feeling just a little love, tell him or her right away. Don't concern yourself with being hurt, because love always involves some pain. Just because you are feeling the stirrings of love doesn't mean you will cook the whole love meal. Telling someone you are feeling love is not "playing your cards too early." This is not love poker. You are searching for a love bond. If you wait until you are completely sure this is "really" love, you may miss your chance. Love is something that must be developed and worked on, so don't wait for it to grow and explode into some wonderful flower. You are the seed and you must nourish your own loving.

7. Avoid "love experts" and friends who will seek to advise you from "their own experience." Even if it seems that your friends have a great relationship, you just can never be sure. What they consider great may not be what you would want for a loving relationship at all. Share what you are feeling, but don't look for love advice. Only you know how to love your own way.

8. Diversify! Go out, date, go to concerts and classes. Get yourself "out there." Even if you think you are "really falling" for someone, until a statement of exclusivity is made by both of you, go out with other people and let your partner know you are going out. This is not a technique intended to manipulate your partner into jealousy, it is just good sound love-search practice to keep your options open. Most relationships don't work out, so until one does, keep your eggs available for many baskets.

9. Directly and openly discuss religion, parents, kids, career, and plans for the future. There is no timetable for dating, with one date for acquaintance, another for talking about career, and moving on until it is time to talk about "the biggies" of kids, religion, or the "M" word, marriage. Anybody you are courting who stammers and stutters and has hot flashes when the "M" word is mentioned is going to need a lot of help in developing their comfort with intimacy anyway, so start right away. Just because you are talking about marriage doesn't mean you have to, are going to, or even want to get married to this person.

10. Your long-love partner will probably come into your life by chance. If you keep going out, making yourself visible, doing things that enhance your general life and that you experience joy in doing, you are more likely to "run into" a person you can learn to love for a long time and who can learn to love you.

Chapters 7 and 8 are related to the material in this letter. Chapter 7 discusses the joy of working, which is a prerequisite to being able to love over time. Chapter 8 presents the love star concept that can be used to discuss loving with others.

Two helpful books about loving are:

G. R. Bach and R. M. Deutsch, *Pairing* (New York: Avon, 1970).

E. Fromm, *The Art of Loving. An Inquiry in the Nature of Love* (New York: Harper and Row, 1956).

CHAPTER SEVENTEEN

A Super Joy Contract

> Work as if everything depends on work.
> Pray as if everything depends on prayer.
>
> G. I. GURDJIEFF

The super joy journey begins with a commitment. This commitment is a type of spiritual contract, a "deal" with yourself that you will attempt to channel your natural addictive nature toward an addiction to joy. I suggest that you make a super joy contract with yourself as you finish this book. This contract must be uniquely yours, but it must take into account the principles of super joy you have read about in this book, including a new self-responsibility for your own time, working, loving, and believing. This new contract must be a statement of purpose, a decision to attempt to improve your "I-sight," a new awareness that you are capable of extreme health and happiness every day of your life if you realize that your perceptions of your world actually create your world.

The first question you must ask in forming this new joy contract is, "What is stopping me at this moment, on this day, from being remarkably joyful?" Whatever the answer and the related problems of daily living, your super joy contract is an agreement with yourself that you will now attend at least as much to being remarkably happy as you attend to getting through the day. Your super joy contract is a personal promise to yourself that you will take

283

renewed responsibility for the joy of living, a promise that you will try to fall in love with life again.

Clare, the woman who survived the concentration camp with her inner super joy, was talking in my office about her joy of living even in the hell of that prison camp. When I continued to wonder at how anyone could maintain such personal joyful strength in that terrible situation, Clare lifted her purse from beside her chair. As she sorted through the contents of her purse, she said, "I want to show you something I think will help you understand."

She took out her wallet and quietly removed a small piece of yellowed paper that had been filed behind a picture of her grandchildren. She began to hand the paper to me but hesitated. "Now be very careful," she warned. "This paper is almost falling apart." She unfolded the paper as if holding a fragile bird in her hand. She handed the paper to me and smiled. "Here's my contract with me. I read it when I lose my happiness."

As I read the brief message I asked Clare where she had found it. "I don't know where it comes from or who said it," she answered. "The man in the camp gave it to me. He was the man I told you about. I held his hand when the guards came in. Remember him? He gave me that paper days before the camp was liberated. I never saw him again, but I remember him waving to me from the back of one of the trucks leaving the camp. I will always remember him smiling and waving on that liberation day."

I have since learned that Clare's message can be found in a book entitled *A Course in Miracles.* The authorship of this book is attributed to "a higher consciousness." Clare's joy contract may help you find the light for your own path to super joy. Her message read:

> Perception can make whatever picture
> the mind desires to see.
> Remember this.
> In this lies either heaven or hell,
> as you elect.

Glossary of Joyology

ACTH. This hormone, called adrenocorticotropin, is released by the pituitary gland and affects the adrenal glands, which in turn release stress chemicals called corticosteroids.

ADRENALINAHOLISM. Addiction to the stress chemicals of the human body, resulting in more and more "need" for these neurohormones to get a "stress high" and the experience of physical and emotional withdrawal when we are not on a "stress high" (such as on vacation or just sitting and attempting to relax). This addiction is a major block to the joy response.

ADRENALINE. The British name for epinephrine, a catecholamine made by and released from the inside of the adrenal glands (the medulla). This is a potent neurohormone to which we can become "addicted."

ALEXITHYMIA. The inability to express emotions or feelings in words, this condition is likely the result of disrupted brain and/or personality development and may also be related to learning disability. The joy response is severely impaired when alexithymia is present.

ALTRUISM. One of the healthiest of human capacities, this is

285

the ability to put others' needs before our own. Altruism is a major step toward the joy response and represents one way to "connect" with the world system by prioritizing this system even over the "self."

ANALGESICS.   Painkilling substances such as morphine that also seem to alter attention. The joy response is accompanied by the secretion of our own natural analgesics called endorphins.

AUTOMATIZATION.   A type of "automatic" thinking that allows us to function daily without "attending" to every detail in our lives. Too much automatization and we become slaves to our brains' selfish starvation for intense and regular stimulation, missing out on less intense and more meaningful sources of learning and joy. To experience the joy response, we must learn to "deautomatize," to pay attention to what and how we are thinking.

AUTONOMIC LABILITY.   The neurohormonal system contains a SAM system (sympathoadrenomedullary) and a PAC system (parasympathocortical), both of which can be overactivated in response to perceived stressors in our environment. This type of neurohormonal hyperreaction can result in adrenalinaholism and stress-related disease.

CAPTAIN AHAB COMPLEX.   The fixation on one or a few life issues at the expense of a more general and meaningful approach to life. In effect, the person is consumed by his or her own Moby Dick and may eventually be drowned while tied to this persecuting life fixation.

CATASTROPHIZING.   This term was coined by psychologist Albert Ellis to denote a style of overreactive, negative, and pessimistic thinking. I suggest that "joyistic" thinking can emphasize the positive in daily living and the fact that our world comes to be as we perceive it.

COMPETENCE.   Awareness of self and a sense of personal strength and resilience that is another prerequisite for the joy response.

CONNECTION. The joy response depends upon establishing and maintaining emotional, intellectual, and physical relationship with the world system, including all living things. When we "disconnect," we can become sick.

COPING. One's individual style of emotional, physical, and intellectual dealing with the challenges of daily living. The joy response is a "coping style," not the result of coping, a way of "being," not just doing. Coping means not just "surviving" but also "thriving."

DIS-EASE. When we disconnect from the world system and our coping strategies and sense of competence fail, we are no longer "at ease." When we are not at ease, we can become sick. Dis-ease is healthy in that our body systems were designed to deal with illness and we can learn about our living and the meaning and manageability of our lives when we are challenged by illness.

DIVERGENT THINKING. We can learn to "break out" of our automatic style of thinking, to see new and creative ways to solve problems and to lead our lives. Discovery of the joy response requires divergence of thought and action, an unorthoxy in our daily living.

EGOCENTRISM. The development of a narrow and limiting view of "self" equated with the brain's selfish view of the world and emphasis on self-preservation and self-enhancement at the potential expense of our health and the survival of our world. Psychologist Jean Piaget suggested the term "decentration" for the development of increasing awareness of other people and the world around us. Such decentration is a key component of the joy response.

ENDORPHINS. A combination of the words *endo*genous and *morph*ine, endorphins are produced and released from the brain. These are the key psychochemicals (sometimes called neuropeptides) that can alter awareness as well as reduce pain. Stress can influence endorphin secretion.

FRAMING. A person's style of perceiving and understanding his or her world. We are more likely to be joyful if we can learn to "reframe" events and see them in more creative and happier ways.

GELONTOLOGY.   The new field of study of laughter and the impact of laughing and humor on health and healing.

HARDINESS.   Psychologist Suzanne Kobasa's term for the development of a sense of commitment, control, and challenge in our daily living. Hardiness and a sense of coherence are essential for the joy response.

HOLISM.   A philosphy of life that emphasizes the fact that the connection between all people and things results in more than just the total of the parts of the whole. The joy response occurs when persons sense the holism that affects their lives.

HYPNOPOMPIC and HYPNOGOGIC.   Two examples of altered states of consciousness. Hypnopompic states occur just before awakening and hypnogogic states occur just before we go to sleep. These are good times to learn the joy response, because we are highly receptive, with sometimes vivid, original, and independent "reframing" possible.

IN-PRESSION.   Contrary to popular belief, our "expressions" are not just ways we automatically express our emotions. Instead, we "in-press" ourselves through muscle contractions in the face and body that result in emotional reactions and changes in flow of blood to the brain. Learning the joy response depends upon understanding that the emotions "follow" behaviors and do not "cause" our behaviors. We come to feel as we behave.

JOYOLOGY.   The history of medicine, psychology, and psychiatry is the study of sickness, not really a health care system but a sickness care system. I propose a new orientation to health that studies the well, those persons who are thriving even in a world that can kill us. The joy response is a neglected part of our human heritage, and its rediscovery can save not only the individual but the world.

LEARNED HELPLESSNESS.   Addiction to the psychochemicals of depression related to the repeated experience of ineffectiveness in dealing with stress. Learned helplessness is the counterpar of adrenalinaholism; instead of getting high, the person experienc ing learned helplessness gets used to 'getting and staying low."

LIMBIC SYSTEM. A hundred-and-fifty-million-year-old part of the brain between the brain stem and the cortex that is responsible for maintaining homeostasis or balance in critical life processes ˉuch as body temperature, heartbeat, and blood pressure. When we learn the joy response, we affect the brain, which can in turn have positive effects on our general health and body functions.

LOCK AND KEY CONCEPT. The way in which the neurotransmitters affect the brain is similar to a key fitting into a lock. If the psychochemicals of depression are "locked in," there is no room for the keys of elation to unlock the joy response. We can, however, make our own keys and remove the keys that are locking up the system by altering our thoughts, perceptions, and "self-programming" about our world.

MALADAPTIVE HYPERAROUSAL. Extreme and unnecessary hyperreactivity of the SAM system and stress hormones in response to relatively insignificant stressors. In effect, we prepare to defend ourselves to the death when there is really nothing threatening us except our own misinterpretation of life events.

NEUROTRANSMITTERS. Psychochemicals released from nerve endings, these chemical messengers are discharged in a fraction of a second. When we learn the joy response, we send psychochemical messengers with a code of health and hardiness instead of survival and struggle.

NOESIS A heightened sense of clarity and understanding, the experience of a new way of knowing about the world that accompanies the joy response. When we think differently and more creatively about our daily living, we also increase our chances for experiencing the joy response.

PARADIGM. A theory of living containing many small and sometimes automatic assumptions about life. Regular joy depends upon forming new paradigms about the meaning and purpose of living.

PARANORMAL. Events that are not presently explainable within our current paradigms or science. Awareness of such events increases with the joy response.

PATHOGENESIS. The traditional orientation of medicine, psychiatry, and psychology, this approach to understanding the human experience emphasizes illness and disease and the understanding of why people get sick. The opposite of pathogenesis is "salutogenesis."

PLACEBO ABILITY. A cluster of psychological and behavioral characteristics that predict a positive physical and mental reaction to suggestion. Persons with a high degree of placebo ability are more likely to experience the joy response.

PSYCHOGENIC. Conditions of the body, positive or negative, that are caused by or strongly related to emotional or psychological states. All disease and health is psychosomatic (due to mind/body interaction) but only some physical conditions have been shown to be psychogenic.

PSYCHONEUROIMMUNOLOGY (PNI). The new field of study that examines the interrelationship between the brain, emotions, behavior, and the immune system. The joy response is a healthy psychoneuroimmunological response.

PSYCHOSOMATIC. The mind *(psyche)* and the body *(soma)* interact in all aspects of human experience. Although the word "psychosomatic" is usually used to refer to diseases that have their origin in emotional problems (psychogenic), the joy response is one example of a positive psychosomatic state.

RENUNCIATION. The intentional surrendering of tangible goods and intense external stimulation in favor of a simpler life style and an emphasis on meaning instead of intensity in daily living.

SAD CYCLE. The pattern of stress addiction followed by the counterreaction of depression addiction, resulting in an emotional reverberating circuit accompanied by disease-producing psychochemicals.

SALUTOGENESIS. A word coined by researcher Aaron Antonovsky to refer to the study of why people stay healthy and even thrive in a generally unhealthy psychological and physical environment. This approach to wellness attempts to understand or explain behavioral and emotional relationships from a positive, healthy orientation as opposed to pathogenesis, which focuses on the etiology of disease.

SENSE OF COHERENCE. Another term coined by Aaron Antonovsky which refers to a sense of comprehensibility, manageability, and meaningfulness in daily living that protects us to varying degrees from the negative effects of prolonged stress. The joy response depends upon the factors that make up this sense of coherence.

SET THEORY. The concept that our perceptions are strongly influenced by looking for similarities and patterns rather than divergence and asymmetry. To learn super joy, we must sometimes "break out" of our "life set," our automatic patterns of reaction and interpretations of life events.

SOTERIOLOGICAL EXPERIENCE. A sense of reinvigoration and newness that occurs spontaneously. When we learn the joy response, we feel "born again," renewed and energized.

STATE DEPENDENCY. Our experience of our world is at least in part determined by the particular level of consciousness on which we are functioning at a given time. This phrase refers to the fact that there are many levels of awareness and several levels of experience, resulting in differing "rules" for these different realities. The joy response depends upon acceptance of the existence of multiple levels of consciousness and multiple and equally impactful levels of reality.

STRESS. Any event, from within or without, that requires psychological and/or behavioral adaptation. When we feel a deficiency in our capacity to adjust to the challenge (sometimes called a stressor) we may feel "strain" or a sense of mental, emotional, or physical tension that can result in disease.

SUFISM. Islamic mysticism which stresses communion with a higher purpose or deity. This approach has been used by some psychiatrists and psychologists to emphasize the importance of going beyond coping to a search for meaning in life. The joy response depends upon this search for significance, not just survival.

TAOISM. The Chinese philosophy/religion that focuses on unassertiveness and peacefulness in order to discover one's "fit" with all life energy. Learning to "be" instead of always "doing" is one aspect of Taoism and the joy response.

TRANSCENDENCE. Going beyond the usual limits we consciously and unconsciously impose upon ourselves by becoming aware of purpose, connection, and meaning in all of life.

TRANSPERSONAL. Going beyond the "personal," the self, to awareness of unity with all of life. Transpersonal psychology is a field that studies this approach to life and attempts to help people "transcend" their self-imposed limitations.

WITNESS WAY. A technique for learning the joy response involving observing the brain in action, taking time to sit quietly and focus on what the brain is thinking. Typically, people who do this exercise experience a sense of calm, almost a trance, as their brains settle down, as if embarrassed by being caught in the act of selfish, redundant patterns of cortical chatter that only result in chronic stress and a sense of obligation.

ZEN BUDDHISM. Zen is a Japanese system for learning self-discipline, meditation, and enlightenment. Some of the principles of Buddhist psychology can be combined with traditional Christian teachings and contemporary psychology to result in guidelines for learning the joy response.

Notes

CHAPTER ONE
BEYOND THE WALLS OF NORMALCY

p. 3 All addiction, including what I call the stress and depression cycle of psychochemical addiction (SAD cycle), follows a "feedback" process. More and more of our own internal and potentially toxic psychochemicals that temporarily relieve the anxiety of daily living are required for the same effect, meaning that a tolerance builds up for the SAD psychochemicals. Without these chemicals, we go into withdrawal, emotionally drained, overagitated, and eventually physically weakened. Sooner or later we seek the stress chemicals of our own agitated behavior or depression not because our anxiety is lessened by these chemicals but in order to get relief from the unpleasant state that develops during our abstinence from the SAD chemicals.

p. 3 For information on our naturally addictive nature, see E. M. Brecher and *Consumer Reports,* eds., *Licit and Illicit Drugs.* The damage that our stress and depression addiction can do to our health is documented in I. Wickramasekera, "Risk Factors Leading to Chronic Stress-Related Symptoms."

p. 10 The first description of the theory that emotions follow facial expressions is in I. Waynbaum, *La Physionomie humaine: son mécanisme et son rôle social.* His work and an updating of research supporting this view

293

of behavior affecting emotion are described in R. B. Zajonc, "Emotion and Facial Efference: A Theory Reclaimed."

p. 12 Many psychologists have been interested in our potential for experiencing multiple levels of consciousness. Fritz Perls wrote, "I would say the majority of modern man lives in a verbal trance." Philosopher Huston Smith discussed the "fully realized human being whose doors of perception have been cleansed." Spiritual teacher Ram Dass wrote, "We are all prisoners of our minds. This realization is the first step on the journey to freedom."

p. 13 The concept of the selfish brain is described by A. M. de la Pena in *The Psychobiology of Cancer.*

p. 13 A mythology about the human brain has evolved. The brain's primary purpose is not thought but health maintenance and keeping us alive. It is the body's largest secreting gland, and not at all like a computer or telephone switchboard, to which it is often compared. M. Hutchison points out in his book, *Megabrain,* that, contrary to popular belief, some part of the brain can be stimulated to growth, can regenerate, actually improve instead of decline with aging, and that a "synchrony" of the left and right hemispheres can occur, resulting in a joyful holistic cerebral rhythm of joy. It is up to us to control this rhythm and to teach our brains a synchrony of super joy.

Researchers now know that when the left side of the brain is damaged the person becomes depressed. Injury to the right hemisphere results in indifference or euphoria. This may happen because the left and right hemispheres mutually control each other, and when one side is damaged, the intact hemisphere is left to exert its emotional bias. For more information on the brain and emotion, see L. Miller, "The Emotional Brain."

pp. 14–15 The human brain is capable of joy only when it is synchronized. The brain is not "two-sided" but three-dimensional. Divisions in the brain are left and right, front to back, and top to bottom. Understanding the presence of complex multiple connections on these several levels is more accurate than the simplistic "left and right side" orientation of brain function so often written about.

p. 16 The "hidden observer" phenomenon and the existence of a "self" beyond the physical brain and body are described in E. R. Hilgard, "Hypnosis and Consciousness."

p. 18 The complex interactions between the brain, behavior, our emotions, and our immune systems are described in P. Pearsall, *Superim-*

munity: Master Your Emotions, Improve Your Health. See also R. Ornstein and D. Sobel, *The Healing Brain,* and S. E. Locke and D. Colligan, *The Healer Within.* For a more popularized discussion of the brain and healing, see J. A. Borysenko, *Minding the Body, Mending the Mind.*

CHAPTER TWO
CURING THE CAPTAIN AHAB COMPLEX

p. 27 G. S. Gelber and H. Schatz reported that patients experiencing central serous chorioretinopathy, a detachment of the retina at the area of most acute vision, resulting in blindness in one and sometimes both eyes, experienced very disturbing psychological experiences preceding their vision loss. Patients who could not heal the eye injury, according to Dr. Gelber, ". . . stayed tied to the traumatic event . . . and have what I call a Captain Ahab complex." These patients remained attached to their own psychological "white whale," the source of their self-created misery that blinded them to the joy of living and eventually resulted in their own ruin. See G. S. Gelber and H. Schatz, "Central Serous Chorioretinopathy and Stress Factors."

p. 29 What I call Ahab's diseases have also been called the "psychosomatic seven," or the "holy seven," and have been discussed in medicine for decades. The seven factors and related issues of psychosomatic disease are discussed in S. E. Locke and D. Colligan, op. cit.

p. 29 The relationship between the absence of joy and the presence of disease is discussed in F. A. Wolf's *The Body Quantum.* In his foreword to this book, physician Larry Dossey writes, "Why do the majority of patients who have their first heart attack in this country display none of the major risk factors of heart disease?" p. vii.

p. 34 For a discussion of ESP factors and the concept that all of us have a capacity for sensing beyond the see/touch world, see R. Targ and K. Harary, *The Mind Race,* p. 4.

CHAPTER THREE
JOYFUL THINKING FOR STRESSFUL TIMES

p. 45 Harvard psychologist Edwin Boring wrote, "Intelligence is what intelligence tests measure." His frustration with the elusive nature of the concept of intelligence was shared by psychologist Elric Neisser, who said, "Intelligence is what intelligent people do." The complexities and failings of testing are described in J. S. Ahmann and M. D. Glock, *Evaluating Pupil Growth*. The "D" formula for test discrimination is also described in this work.

p. 45   Insight into the simple genius of Einstein is found in N. Calder, *Einstein's Universe*.

p. 54   Discussions of the concept of time are in F. Capra, *The Turning Point*, and in L. LeShan, "Time Orientation and Social Class."

p. 62   A report on the positive effects of the internal joy chemicals on health and the immune system is in Y. Shavit et al., "Endogenous Opioids May Mediate the Effects of Stress on Tumor Growth and Immune Function." The relationship between stress and our natural internal opiates is described in S. C. Risch et al., "Co-Release of ACTH and Beta-Endorphin Immunoreactivity in Human Subjects in Response to Central Cholinergic Stimulation." See also K. M. Dillon et al., "Positive Emotional States and Enhancement of the Immune System."

p. 71   The cardiophysiology of "hot reaction" is described in T. M. Dembroski et al., "Moving Beyond Type A." See also R. S. Eliot and D. Breo, *Is It Worth Dying For?*

p. 72   Sociobiology, a field that attempts to explain social behavior in biological terms, views altruism as a means of protecting our chances of passing on our own genes by taking care of someone carrying our genes. This concept is discussed in W. D. Hamilton, "The Genetical Evolution of Social Behavior." The relationship of altruism, or what Hans Selye called "altruistic egoism," is described in his book, *The Stress of Life*.

p. 72   There is a health-inducing effect from simply watching caring behavior. See J. A. Borysenko, "Healing Motives: An Interview with David McClelland." See also D. C. McClelland et al., "Stressed Power Motivation, Sympathetic Activation, Immune Function, and Illness."

p. 73   A description of the concept of a paradigm and "paradigm shifts" is found in M. Ferguson, *The Aquarian Conspiracy*.

CHAPTER FOUR
YOUR SUPER JOY QUOTIENT

pp. 81–82   Two types of "tiredness," physical and mental fatigue, are described by E. Hartman in *The Functions of Sleep*. Physical tiredness is often accompanied by a calm feeling related to relaxed muscles. Mental tiredness is often accompanied by unpleasant feelings of being "drained." We seem to experience both a joyful and an unpleasant type of fatigue. The types of sleep and the repair function of sleep are described by K. Adam and I. Oswald, "Sleep Is for Tissue Restoration."

p. 82 The hypnopompic and hypnogogic states are described in T. Budzynski, "Biofeedback and the Twilight States of Awareness." See also H. Magoun, "Advances in Brain Research with Implications for Learning."

pp. 83–84 K. Ring studied 102 men and women who reported "near-death experiences." He found that these people experienced intense sensations of peacefulness and joy. See his work, *Life at Death: A Scientific Investigation of the Near-Death Experience.* Perhaps we have failed to learn to celebrate the full life cycle, endings as well as beginnings, in a society that attends more to the "now" than the "later."

p. 86 For a discussion of blood pressure changes as related to relaxation and attitude toward relaxation, see W. S. Agras et al., "Expectation and the Blood-Pressure Lowering Effect of Relaxation."

pp. 87–88 An accurate summary of nutritional issues as related to wellness and longevity can be found in K. Pelletier, *Longevity: Fulfilling Our Biological Potential.*

pp. 89–90 The impact of religion on our concepts of working, happiness, and daily living is discussed in D. J. Bronstein and H. M. Schulweis, *Approaches to the Philosophy of Religion.*

pp. 90–91 The concept of multiple realities and levels of attunement to these realities is discussed by L. LeShan in *The Medium, the Mystic, and the Physicist.* See also L. LeShan and H. Margenau, *Einstein's Space and Van Gogh's Sky.*

p. 91 The quote from R. Targ and K. Harary, *The Mind Race,* is on p. 4.

p. 99 See L. LeShan, *The Medium, the Mystic, and the Physicist.*

p. 100 Norman Cousins has become a spokesperson for the issue of self-responsibility for healing and the role of humor, optimism, and positive mood state in coping with disease. See his works, *Anatomy of an Illness, The Healing Heart,* and *Human Options.*

p. 103 William James discussed the power of "mystical experience" in his book, *The Varieties of Religious Experience.* He described what he called a "cosmic" or universal consciousness. To understand such experiences, it is necessary to experience a "deautomatization" or freeing of ourselves from the everyday consciousness that dictates the functioning of our selfish and stimulus-hungry brains. A description of this process, which is fundamental to learning super joy, is found in A. Deikman, "Deautomatization and the Mystic Experience."

pp. 103–4   The Saul Bellow and Arthur Rubinstein comments are discussed in M. Ferguson, op. cit., p. 366.

p. 104   R. B. Fuller's views of God are discussed in his *Critical Path*.

pp. 106–7   For a full description of differing views of time and the impact of these views on our perceptions of life events, see M. Ferguson, op. cit., pp. 104–5.

CHAPTER FIVE
THE PSYCHOCHEMISTRY OF SUPER JOY

pp. 110–11   For more information on the endorphins, see S. H. Snyder, "Brain Peptides and Neurotransmitters." See also R. F. Beers, *Mechanisms of Pain and Analgesic Compounds*.

p. 112   A hypothesis regarding the endorphins and issues of attention and denial is presented by D. Goleman in *Vital Lies: Simple Truths*.

p. 116   The process of becoming addicted to exercise is described by E. Grant in "The Exercise Fix."

p. 118   The relaxation response was first discussed by H. Benson in *The Relaxation Response*. See also his "Systemic Hypertension and the Relaxation Response" and *Beyond the Relaxation Response*.

p. 123   The P. Weenolsen research is described in T. DeAngelis, "What's It All Mean? We Never Stop Asking."

CHAPTER SIX
THE SUPER JOY PROGRAM

p. 128   For a complete review of the concept of small steps to learning and the idea of "successive approximations" or moving gradually toward our learning goals, see E. R. Hilgard and G. Bower, *Theories of Learning*, 3rd ed.

pp. 131–32   The McDougall Plan is a popular healthy diet program. The relationship of Dr. John McDougall's work to general health and the treatment of disease is described by Gary Null, "Eat to Live." This article also contains Null's discussion of the red meat and osteoporosis connection described on these pages.

p. 134 The physical and spiritual value of leading an uncomplicated life is explained in D. Elgin, *Voluntary Simplicity.*

p. 145 For a review of the research on stress in the workplace, see K. Pelletier, *Healthy People in Unhealthy Places: Stress and Fitness at Work.*

CHAPTER SEVEN
THE JOY OF MEANINGFUL WORK

p. 153 A description of the shift in work values from money, status, and security to issues of self-fulfillment is presented in D. Yankelovich, *New Rules.* He suggests that the issue at work now is becoming one of "why" more than "how."

p. 155 Psychologist Douglas LaBier describes the plight of the modern executive who pursues success only to feel alienated and unfulfilled when such success is achieved. He proposes a cycle of struggle, some satisfaction, inner turmoil because of lack of match between work task and life goals, followed by realignment of life purpose with work purpose. See his book, *Modern Madness: The Emotional Fallout of Success.* A discussion of combining dreams and aspirations about life in general with work goals is in D. Jaffe and C. Scott, *Take This Job and Love It!*

p. 156 For a complete discussion of the concept of metanoic organizations (organizations that show vision and the capacity to involve all workers in a common constructive mission), see J. D. Adams, ed., *Transforming Work: A Collection of Organizational Transformation Readings.* Such organizations are described as having clear and deep purpose, alignment of all workers behind this purpose, power distributed to all workers to achieve the purpose, and an interconnectedness between all workers that allows for spontaneity and intuition in balance with rational thought. A related book by psychologist A. Maslow is entitled *Eupsychian Management.*

p. 168 The first discussion and description of a "hardy" and stress-resistant personality in the workplace was done by S. C. Kobasa et al., "Hardiness and Health: A Prospective Study." See also ibid., "Personality and Constitution as Mediators in the Stress-Illness Relationship," and "Personality and Social Resources in Stress-Resistance."

CHAPTER EIGHT
THE JOY OF SYMPATHETIC LOVING

p. 170   Many of my patients find Scott Peck's book *The Road Less Traveled* to be of great help in their understanding of love as volitional and not emotional.

p. 173   To learn more about the true and limited role of medicine in the conquering of disease and suffering, see W. H. McNeill, *Plagues and Peoples.* See also T. McKeown, *The Role of Medicine: Dream, Mirage or Nemesis?* See also his "Man's Health: The Past and the Future." See also J. B. McKinlay and S. M. McKinlay, "The Questionable Contribution of Medical Measures to the Decline of Mortality in the United States in the Twentieth Century."

p. 184   For a scientific discussion of love and loving, see J. Money, *Love and Love Sickness: The Science of Sex, Gender Difference, and Pair-Bonding.*

pp. 191–92   For a discussion of sexuality and loving, see W. Masters and V. Johnson, *The Pleasure Bond.* See also my own *Super Marital Sex: Loving for Life.*

CHAPTER NINE
THE JOY OF FAITH: HOW TO DEVELOP YOUR PLACEBO ABILITY

p. 196   For a thorough discussion of the placebo issue, see L. White et al., *Placebo: Theory, Research, and Mechanisms.* See also A. K. Shapiro, "A Contribution to the History of the Placebo Effect." Researchers also discuss the "nocebo effect," or placebo-induced side effects similar to those related to active drugs. See A. K. Shapiro and L. A. Morris, "The Placebo Effect in Medical and Psychological Therapies."

pp. 197–98   For a discussion of hypnotic ability, see E. R. Hilgard, *Hypnotic Susceptibility,* and T. X. Barber, *Hypnosis: A Scientific Approach.* See also I. Wickramasekera, op. cit.

p. 200   For documentation of the differing impact of medications as related to belief and emotion, see S. Wolf, "Effects of Suggestion and Conditioning on the Action of Chemical Agents in Human Subjects." See also H. Benson and M. D. Epstein, "The Placebo Effect: A Neglected Asset in the Care of Patients."

p. 200   High and low hypnotic ability and related personality factors are discussed in E. R. Hilgard, "Hypnotic Susceptibility: Implications for Measurement."

p. 202 For a discussion of the relationship of support systems to health, see S. Cohen and S. L. Syme, eds., *Social Support and Health.* See also L. F. Berkman, "Assessing the Physical Health Effects of Social Networks and Social Support."

p. 203 For more about "catastrophizing," see A. Ellis, *A New Guide to Rational Living.*

pp. 204–5 For a review of the issues of denial and avoidance, see S. Bresnitz, ed., *The Denial of Stress.* See also D. Goleman, "Denial and Hope," and R. Lazarus, "Positive Denial: The Case for Not Facing Reality."

pp. 205–6 The concept of "autonomic lability" is discussed in H. J. Eysenck, *The Structure of Human Personality.* See also M. A. Wenger, "Studies of Autonomic Balance: A Summary." For more about learned helplessness, see M. Seligman, "Fall into Helplessness", *Helplessness: On Depression, Development, and Death,* and *Learned Helplessness.*

p. 206 The "sense of coherence" concept is discussed in A. Antonovsky, *Health, Stress, and Coping.* See also his *Unraveling the Mystery of Health: How People Manage Stress and Stay Well.* Antonovsky is the pioneer in research on the "salutogenic" approach to understanding health, and first coined the terms "salutogenic" and "sense of coherence." His work relates to the work of S. C. Kobasa et al. cited earlier regarding the "hardy and stress-resistant personality."

p. 208 For a review of the concept of "holistic medicine," see R. Grossman, *The Other Medicines.* See also his "Ecumenical Medicine: Notes on the History of a Possibility."

p. 209 See S. C. Kobasa et al., op. cit.

p. 213 The Deikman quote is in "Sufism and the Mental Health Sciences," p. 274.

p. 213 For discussions of the overlap between religion and healing, see B. L. Gordon, *Medicine Throughout Antiquity;* G. Dawson, *Healing: Pagan and Christian;* and J. Rush, *Notes Toward a Theory of Healing.* See also G. Epstein, "Hebraic Medicine."

p. 215 For a tongue-in-cheek description of hospitals, see J. Frank, "The Faith That Heals." See also his *Persuasion and Healing.*

p. 216 The concept of the "worried well" is described by C. Turkington in "Help for the Worried Well."

p. 216   The Deikman quote is in "Sufism and the Menial Health Sciences," p. 75.

p. 217   For a clear discussion of Buddhist philosophy as it relates to contemporary psychology, see R. Walsh, "The Ten Perfections: Qualities of the Fully Enlightened Individual as Described in Buddhist Psychology."

p. 225   For a discussion of the health impact of deceit, see M. S. Peck, *People of the Lie.*

CHAPTER ELEVEN
A JOY MESSAGE FOR TIMES WHEN WE'RE SAD

p. 239   Statistics on the prevalence of depression and suicide are not always reflective of the severity of the depression crisis. Researchers suspect that some type of "agent blue" is related to the depression issue, some environmental, neurochemical, and cultural combination of factors. See C. Leerhsen et al., "Depression," and R. P. Coughlin, "This Is a Book We Must Read . . . Honest."

p. 239   A newly understood source of depression is called SAD (seasonal affective disorder). See N. E. Rosenthal et al., "Seasonal Affective Disorder: A Description of the Syndrome and Preliminary Findings with Light Therapy." The environment in which our young people live day to day, the poorly and artificially lit schools and bombardment from strobe lights and other distractions may play a role in the depression of young people. See J. N. Ott, *Health and Light.* The mass exodus of our youth to beaches during spring break may reflect in part a starvation for cleaner air, healthier light, and freedom to merge beyond the lines and regimen of the educational setting.

pp. 240–42   For a discussion of depression as "the common cold of psychological disorders," and the symptoms of serious depression, see M. E. P. Seligman, "Fall into Hopelessness."

p. 243   Information on cognitive strategies for overcoming depression is in A. T. Beck, *Cognitive Therapy and Emotional Disorders* and *Depression: Causes and Treatment.*

p. 245   Data on the heritability of bipolar disorder (depression with both depressive and manic periods) and other data supporting the points made in this letter are in G. Winokur, *Depression: The Facts.* See also Winokur et al., *Manic-Depressive Illness.*

CHAPTER TWELVE
A JOY MESSAGE FOR TIMES WHEN OUR EMOTIONS CONTROL US

p. 248 Freud discusses his view of the unity of self with all persons, things, and events in *The Problems of Lay Analyses,* p. 71.

p. 248 The concept of self-efficacy is presented in A. Bandura, "Self-efficacy Mechanisms in Human Agency." For a review of the issue of self-efficacy as related to physical health, see A. O'Leary, "Self-efficacy and Health." The research on stress chemicals reducing in response to enhanced self-efficacy is in A. Bandura et al., "Catecholamine Secretion as a Function of Perceived Self-efficacy."

p. 249 The data supporting the relationship between enhanced self-efficacy and arthritis symptom reduction are in K. Gravelle, "Can a Feeling of Capability Reduce Arthritis Pain?" See also K. Lorig et al., "Arthritis Self-management: A Study of the Effectiveness of Patient Education for the Elderly."

p. 249 Yoga and other meditational approaches have suggested the effectiveness of "affirmation exercises" to bring to awareness the unity of self with all things. See R. Assagioli, *Psychosynthesis.* A more popular version of these concepts is found in T. A. Harris, *I'm O.K.—You're O.K.,* and E. Berne, *What Do You Say After You Say Hello?*

p. 253 "I-thou" language and conceptualization of relationships is in M. Buber, *I and Thou.*

CHAPTER THIRTEEN
A JOY MESSAGE FOR TIMES WHEN WE LOSE SOMEONE

p. 255 The Anderson quote is in his play, *I Never Sang for My Father.*

p. 256 The relationship between the immune system and stress factors is described in S. E. Locke et al., "Life Change Stress, Psychiatric Symptoms, and Natural Killer Cell Activity." See also R. B. Krueger et al., "Lymphocyte Subsets in Patients with Major Depression: Preliminary Findings," and J. B. Stoddard and J. P. Henry, "Affectional Bonding and the Impact of Bereavement." See also R. W. Bartrop et al., "Depressed Lymphocyte Function After Bereavement," and S. J. Schliefer et al., "Suppression of Lymphocyte Stimulation Following Bereavement."

p. 257 The Castaneda quote is in *Journey to Ixtlan,* p. 83.

pp. 258–59 The Ken Wilber quote is in his "Human Potential and the Boundaries of the Soul," p. 111.

CHAPTER FOURTEEN
A JOY MESSAGE ABOUT OUR IMMUNE SYSTEM AND THE THREAT OF AIDS

p. 260 The R. Stengel quote is in "Testing Dilemma: Washington Prepares a Controversial New Policy to Fight AIDS," p. 22. The Jaffe quote is in this same reference, p. 20. The pictures mentioned are in P. Goldman, "The Face of AIDS."

p. 260 The quote by Larry Dossey is in his *Space, Time, and Medicine,* p. 10.

p. 262 Information on HIV infection is from "Highlights of the Third International Conference on AIDS" (Washington, D.C., June 1–5, 1987).

p. 263 Nutritional recommendations for persons with HIV infections are in D. T. Magallon, "Counseling Patients with HIV Infections."

p. 265 The data on incidence of HIV infection in the United States heterosexual population are in R. Stengel et al., op. cit.

p. 266 Data on the spread of sexually transmitted diseases are in P. Adelmann, "Ignored Strains of VD Infection."

CHAPTER FIFTEEN
A JOY MESSAGE FOR TIMES WHEN WE'RE SICK OR HURT

p. 269 One of the most thorough discussions of the relationship between illness and health is in L. Dossey, *Beyond Illness: Discovering the Experience of Health.*

p. 271 The Fred Wolf quote is in his book, *The Body Quantum,* p. 262.

p. 272 The study on the cadets was done by S. V. Kasl et al., "Psychosocial Risk Factors in the Development of Infectious Mononucleosis." A discussion of the relationship between immunity, infection, and psychological factors is in J. B. Jemmott and S. E. Locke, "Psychosocial Factors, Immunologic Mediation, and Human Susceptibility to Infection: How Much Do We Know?"

p. 273 See A. Antonovsky, "A Call for a New Question—Salutogenesis—and a Proposed Answer—the Sense of Coherence."

CHAPTER SIXTEEN
A JOY MESSAGE FOR TIMES WHEN WE CAN'T SEEM TO FIND SOMEONE TO LOVE

pp. 276–77 One of the best discussions of male and female gender role and related psychological theories is by C. Gilligan, *In a Different Voice.*

p. 277 The first clear discussion of the concept of sexual addiction is in P. Carnes, *Out of the Shadows: Understanding Sexual Addiction.* See also C. Kasl, *Women and Sexual Addiction.* The Carnes treatment program for sexual addiction is presented in the CompCare Organization guidebook for support and treatment groups for "sexual addiction" entitled *Hope and Recovery: A 12 Step Guide for Healing from Compulsive Sexual Behavior.*

p. 277 For a review of the research related to the controversy concerning "sexual addiction," see R. J. Barth and B. N. Kinder, "The Mislabeling of Sexual Impulsivity."

Bibliography

Adam, K., and I. Oswald. "Sleep Is for Tissue Restoration," *Journal of the Royal College of Physicians,* 11 (1977), 376–88.

Adams, J. D., ed. *Transforming Work: A Collection of Organizational Transformation Readings.* Alexandria, Va.: Miles River Press, 1984.

Adelmann, P. "Ignored Strains of VD Infection," Detroit *News,* August 4, 1987.

Agras, W. S., et al. "Expectation and the Blood-Pressure Lowering Effect of Relaxation," *Psychosomatic Medicine,* 44 (1982), 389–95.

Ahmann, J. S., and M. D. Glock. *Evaluating Pupil Growth.* 2nd ed. Boston: Allyn & Bacon, 1964.

Anderson, R. "I Never Sang for My Father," in O. L. Guernsey, Jr., ed., *The Best Plays of 1967–1968.* New York: Dodd, Mead, 1968, 277–98.

Antonovsky, A. "A Call for a New Question—Salutogenesis—and a Proposed Answer—the Sense of Coherence," *Journal of Preventive Psychiatry,* 2 (1984b), 1–155.

————. *Health, Stress, and Coping.* San Francisco: Jossey-Bass, 1979.

————. *Unravelling the Mystery of Health: How People Manage Stress and Stay Well.* San Francisco: Jossey-Bass, 1987.

Assagioli, R. *Psychosynthesis.* New York: Viking/Compass, 1965.

Bandura, A. "Self-efficacy Mechanisms in Human Agency," *American Psychologist,* 37 (1982), 122–47.

———, et al. "Catecholamine Secretion as a Function of Perceived Self-efficacy," *Journal of Consulting and Clinical Psychology,* 53 (1985), 406–14.

Barber, T. V. *Hypnosis: A Scientific Approach.* New York: Van Nostrand Reinhold, 1969.

Barber, Theodore X., "Changing Unchangeable Bodily Processes by Hypnotic Suggestions: A New Look at Hypnosis, Cognitions, Imaging, and the Mind-Body Problem," *Advances I,* Spring 1984, pages 7–40.

Bartrop, R. W., et al. "Depressed Lymphocyte Function After Bereavement," *Lancet,* 1 (1977), 834–39.

Barth, R. J., and B. N. Kinder. "The Mislabeling of Sexual Impulsivity," *Journal of Sexual and Marital Therapy,* 15 (1987), 15–27.

Beck, A. T. *Cognitive Therapy and Emotional Disorders.* New York: New American Library, 1979.

———. *Depression: Causes and Treatment.* Philadelphia: University of Pennsylvania Press, 1972.

Beers, R. F. *Mechanisms of Pain and Analgesic Compounds.* New York: Raven Press, 1979.

Beisel, W. R. "Single Nutriments and Immunity," *American Journal of Clinical Nutrition,* 35 (1982 supplement), 417.

Benson, H. *Beyond the Relaxation Response.* New York: Times Books, 1983.

———. *The Relaxation Response.* New York: Morrow, 1975.

———. "Systemic Hypertension and the Relaxation Response," *New England Journal of Medicine,* 296 (1977), 1152–56.

———, and M. D. Epstein. "The Placebo Effect: A Neglected Asset in the Care of Patients," *Journal of the American Medical Association,* 232 (1975), 1225–26.

Berkman, L. F. "Assessing the Physical Health Effects of Social Networks and Social Support," *Annual Review of Public Health,* 5 (1984), 413–32.

Berne, E. *What Do You Say After You Say Hello?* New York: Bantam, 1974.

Borysenko, J. A. "Healing Motives: An Interview with David McClelland," *Advances,* 2 (1985), 29–41.

———. *Minding the Body, Mending the Mind.* Reading, Mass.: Addison-Wesley, 1987.

Boyce, W. T. "Influence of Life Events and Family Routines on Childhood Repiratory Tract Illness," *Pediatrics,* 60 (1977), 609–15.

———. "Social Support, Family Relations, and Children," in S. Cohen and S. L. Syme, eds., *Social Support and Health.* Orlando, Fla.: Academic Press, 1985.

———, et al. "The Family Routines Inventory: Theoretical Origins," *Social Science and Medicine,* 17 (1983), 193–200.

Brecher, E. M., and *Consumer Reports,* eds. *Licit and Illicit Drugs.* Boston: Little, Brown, 1974.

Bresnitz, S., ed. *The Denial of Stress.* New York: International Universities Press, 1983.

Bronstein, D. J., and H. M. Schulweis. *Approaches to the Philosophy of Religion.* Englewood Cliffs, N.J.: Prentice-Hall, 1960.

Buber, M. *I and Thou.* New York: Charles Scribner's Sons, 1958.

Budzynski, T. "Biofeedback and the Twilight States of Awareness," in G. Schwartz and D. Shapiro, eds., *Consciousness and Self-Regulation.* New York: Plenum, 1977.

Burns, D. *Feeling Good: The New Mood Therapy.* New York: Signet, 1980.

Calder, N. *Einstein's Universe.* New York: Penguin, 1979.

Capra, F. *The Tao of Physics,* 2nd ed. Boulder, Colorado: Shambhala, 1983.

———. *The Turning Point.* Toronto and New York: Bantam, 1983.

Carnes, P. *Out of the Shadows: Understanding Sexual Addiction.* Minneapolis, Minn.: CompCare, 1983.

Castaneda, C. *Journey to Ixtlan.* New York: Simon & Schuster, 1973.

Cohen, S., and S. L. Syme, eds. *Social Support and Health.* New York: Academic Press, 1985.

CompCare Organization. *Hope and Recovery: A 12 Step Guide for Healing from Compulsive Sexual Behavior.* Minneapolis, Minn.: CompCare, 1987.

Coughlin, R. P. "This Is a Book We Must Read . . . Honest," *Detroit News,* July 12, 1987.

Cousins, N. *Anatomy of an Illness.* Toronto and New York: Bantam, 1981.

———. *The Healing Heart.* New York: W. W. Norton, 1983.

———. *Human Options.* New York: Berkley, 1983.

Cunningham-Rudles, S. "Effects of Nutritional Status on Immunological Function," *American Journal of Clinical Nutrition,* 35 (1982), 1202.

Dawson, G. *Healing: Pagan and Christian.* Philadelphia: Lippincott, 1949.

DeAngelis, T. "What's It All Mean? We Never Stop Asking," American Psychological Association *Monitor,* 17 (1986), 40.

Deikman, A. "Deautomatization and the Mystic Experience," *Psychiatry,* 29 (1966), 329–43.

———. "Sufism and the Mental Health Sciences," in R. Walsh and D. Shapiro, eds., *Beyond Health and Normality: Explorations of Exceptional Well-being.* New York: Van Nostrand Reinhold, 1983.

de la Pena, A. M. *The Psychobiology of Cancer.* South Hadley, Mass.: Praeger, 1983.

Dembroski, T. M., et al. "Moving Beyond Type A," *Advances,* 1 (1984), 16–26.

Dillon, K. M., et al. "Positive Emotional States and Enhancement of the Immune System," *International Journal of Psychiatry in Medicine,* 15 (1985–86), 13–17.

Dossey, L. *Beyond Illness: Discovering the Experience of Health.* Boulder and London: Shambhala, 1984.

———. *Space, Time, and Medicine.* Boulder and London: Shambhala, 1982.

Elgin, D. *Voluntary Simplicity.* New York: Morrow, 1981.

Eliot, R. S., and D. Breo. *Is It Worth Dying For?* Toronto and New York: Bantam, 1984.

Ellis, A., and R. A. Harper. *A New Guide to Rational Living.* Hollywood, Cal.: Wilshire, 1977.

Epstein, G. "Hebraic Medicine," *Advances,* 4 (1987), 56–66.

Eysenck, H. J. *The Structure of Human Personality.* 2nd ed. London: Methuen, 1960.

Ferguson, M. *The Aquarian Conspiracy.* Los Angeles: J. P. Tarcher, 1980.

Frank, J. "The Faith That Heals," *Johns Hopkins University Medical Journal,* 137 (1975), 127–31.

―――. *Persuasion and Healing.* Baltimore: Johns Hopkins University Press, 1973.

Frankenhauser, M. "Coping with Stress at Work," *International Journal of Health Services,* 34 (1981), 217–20.

Freud, S. *The Problems of Lay Analyses.* New York: Brentano, 1927.

Fuller, R. B. *Critical Path.* New York: St. Martin's Press, 1981.

Gelber, G. S., and H. Schatz. "Central Serous Chorioretinopathy and Stress Factors," *American Journal of Psychiatry,* 144 (1987), 46–50.

Gilligan, C. *In a Different Voice.* Cambridge, Mass.: Harvard University Press, 1982.

Goldman, P. "The Face of AIDS," *Newsweek* (August 10, 1987), 22–39.

Goleman, D. "Denial and Hope," *American Health,* 3 (1984), 54–61.

―――. *Vital Lies: Simple Truths.* New York: Simon & Schuster, 1985.

Gordon, B. L. *Medicine Throughout Antiquity.* New York: Macmillan, 1935.

Grant, E. "The Exercise Fix," *Psychology Today,* 22 (February 1988), 24–28.

Gravelle, K. "Can a Feeling of Capability Reduce Arthritis Pain?" *Advances,* 2 (1985), 8–13.

Grossman, R. "Ecumenical Medicine. Notes on the History of a Possibility," *Advances,* 2 (1985), 39–50.

―――. *The Other Medicines.* New York: Doubleday, 1985.

Hamilton, W. D. "The Genetical Evolution of Social Behavior," *Journal of Theoretical Biology,* 7 (1964), 1–52.

Harris, T. A. *I'm O.K. —You're O.K.* New York: Avon, 1969.

Hartman, E. *The Functions of Sleep.* New Haven: Yale University Press, 1973.

Hilgard, E. R. *Divided Consciousness: Multiple Controls in Human Thoughts and Actions.* New York: Wiley-Interscience, 1977.

―――. "Hypnosis and Consciousness," *Human Nature,* 1 (1978), 42–51.

————. *Hypnotic Susceptibility.* New York: Harcourt, Brace and World, 1965.

————. "Hypnotic Susceptibility: Implications for Measurement," *International Journal of Experimental and Clinical Hypnosis,* 30 (1982), 394–403.

———— and G. Bower. *Theories of Learning,* 3rd ed. New York: Appleton-Century-Crofts, 1966.

Hutchison, M. *Megabrain. New Tools and Techniques for Brain Growth and Mind Expansion.* New York: Ballantine, 1986.

Jaffe, D., and C. Scott. *Take This Job and Love It!* New York: Fireside, 1987.

James, W. *The Varieties of Religious Experience.* New York: Longmans Green, 1980 (originally published 1917).

Jemmott, J. B., and S. E. Locke. "Psychosocial Factors, Immunologic Mediation, and Human Susceptibility to Infection: How Much Do We Know?" *Psychological Bulletin,* 95 (1984), 78–108.

Jensen, E. W. "The Family Routine Inventory: Development and Validation," *Social Science and Medicine,* 17 (1983), 201–11.

Jung, C. *Collected Works.* H. Read, M. Fordham, and G. Adler, eds. New York: Bollinger Series/Pantheon, 1953.

Kaplan, G. A., and T. Camacho. "Perceived Health and Mortality: A Nine Year Follow-up of the Human Population Laboratory Cohort," *American Journal of Epidemiology,* 117 (1983), 292–304.

Kasl, C. *Women and Sexual Addiction.* Minneapolis, Minn.: CompCare, 1984.

Kasl, S. V., et al. "Psychosocial Risk Factors in the Development of Infectious Mononucleosis," *Psychosomatic Medicine,* 41 (1979), 445–66.

Kobasa, S. C., et al. "Hardiness and Health: A Prospective Study," *Journal of Personality and Social Psychology,* 42 (1982), 168–77.

————, et al. "Personality and Constitution as Mediators in the Stress-Illness Relationship," *Journal of Health and Social Behavior,* 22 (1981), 368–78.

————, et al. "Personality and Social Resources in Stress-resistance," *Journal of Personality and Social Psychology,* 45 (1983), 839–50.

Krueger, R. B., et al. "Lymphocyte Subsets in Patients with Major Depression: Preliminary Findings," *Advances*, 1 (1984), 441–53.

LaBier, D. *Modern Madness: The Emotional Fallout of Success.* Reading, Mass.: Addison-Wesley, 1986.

Lazarus, R. "Positive Denial: The Case for Not Facing Reality," *Psychology Today* (November 1979), 44–60.

Leder, J. *Dead Serious: A Book for Teenagers About Teenage Suicide.* New York: Atheneum, 1987.

Leerhsen, C., et al. "Depression," *Newsweek* (March 4, 1987), 48–55.

LeShan, L. *The Medium, the Mystic, and the Physicist.* New York: Holt, Rinehart & Winston, 1976.

———. "Time Orientation and Social Class," *Journal of Abnormal and Social Psychology,* 47 (1942), 582–89.

———, and H. Margenau. *Einstein's Space and Van Gogh's Sky.* New York: Macmillan, 1983.

Locke, S. E., et al. "Life Change Stress, Psychiatric Symptoms, and Natural Killer Cell Activity," *Psychosomatic Medicine,* 46 (1984), 441–53.

Locke, S. E., and D. Colligan. *The Healer Within.* New York: Dutton, 1986.

Lorig, K., et al. "Arthritis Self-management: A Study of the Effectiveness of Patient Education for the Elderly," *Gerontologist,* 24 (1984), 455–57.

McClelland, D., et al. "Stressed Power Motivation, Sympathetic Activation, Immune Function, and Illness," *Journal of Human Stress,* 6 (1980), 6–15.

McKeown, T. "Man's Health: The Past and the Future," *Western Journal of Medicine,* 132 (1980), 49–57.

———. *The Role of Medicine: Dream, Mirage, or Nemesis.* Princeton, N.J.: Princeton University Press, 1979.

McKinlay, J. B., and S. M. McKinlay. "The Questionable Contribution of Medical Measures to the Decline of Mortality in the United States in the Twentieth Century," *Milbank Memorial Fund Quarterly,* 55 (1977), 405–28.

McNeill, W. H. *Plagues and Peoples.* New York: Doubleday, 1976.

Magallon, D. T. "Counseling Patients with HIV Infections." *Medical Aspects of Human Sexuality,* 21 (1987), 417 supplement.

Magoun, H. "Advances in Brain Research with Implications for Learning," in J. Kagan, ed., *On the Biology of Learning.* New York: Harcourt Brace Jovanovich, 1969.

Maslow, A. *Eupsychian Management.* Homewood, Ill.: Richard D. Irwin and Dorsey Press, 1965.

———. *Religions, Values, and Peak Experiences.* New York: Penguin, 1976.

Masters, W., and V. Johnson. *The Pleasure Bond.* New York: Bantam, 1976.

Miller, L. "The Emotional Brain," *Psychology Today,* 22 (February 1988), 34–42.

Money, J. *Love and Love Sickness: The Science of Sex, Gender Difference, and Pair-Bonding.* Baltimore: Johns Hopkins University Press, 1980.

Morrison, A. M., et al. "Executive Women: Substance Plus Style," *Psychology Today,* 21 (1986), 18–26.

Null, G. "Eat to Live," *Penthouse,* (July 1987), 109–14.

O'Leary, A. "Self-efficacy and Health," *Behavioral Research and Therapy,* 23 (1985), 437–51.

Ornstein, R. *Multimind.* Boston: Houghton Mifflin, 1986.

———, and D. Sobel. *The Healing Brain.* New York: Simon & Schuster, 1987.

Ott, J. N. *Health and Light.* New York: Pocket Books, 1976.

Pearsall, P. *Superimmunity: Master Your Emotions, Improve Your Health.* New York: McGraw-Hill, 1987.

———. *Super Marital Sex: Loving for Life.* New York: Doubleday, 1987.

Peck, M. S. *People of the Lie.* New York: Simon & Schuster, 1983.

Peck, M. S. *The Road Less Traveled.* New York: Simon & Schuster, 1978.

Pelletier, K. *Healthy People in Unhealthy Places: Stress and Fitness at Work.* New York: Delacorte Press/Seymour Lawrence, 1984.

———. *Longevity: Fulfilling Our Biological Potential.* New York: Delacorte Press/Seymour Lawrence. 1981.

Perls, F. *Gestalt Therapy Verbatim.* Los Angeles, California: Real People Press, 1969.

Ring, K. *Life at Death: A Scientific Investigation of the Near-Death Experience.* New York: Coward-McCann, 1980.

Risch, S. C., et al. "Co-Release of ACTH and Beta-Endorphin Immunoreactivity in Human Subjects in Response to Central Cholinergic Simulation," *Science*, 222 (1983), 77.

Rosenthal, N. E., et al. "Seasonal Affective Disorder: A Description of the Syndrome and Preliminary Findings with Light Therapy," *Archives of General Psychiatry*, 41 (1984).

Roszak, T. *Person/Planet*. New York: Doubleday/Anchor, 1978.

Rush, J. *Notes Toward a Theory of Healing*. Little Rock: Little Rock Press, 1985.

Schliefer, S. J., et al. "Suppression of Lymphocyte Stimulation Following Bereavement," *Journal of the American Medical Association*, 250 (1983), 374–77.

Seligman, M. E. P. "Fall into Hopelessness," *Psychology Today*, (1973), 43–48.

———. *Helplessness: On Depression, Development, and Death*. San Francisco: W. H. Freeman, 1975.

———. *Learned Helplessness*. San Francisco: W. H. Freeman, 1975.

Selye, H. *The Stress of Life*. New York: McGraw-Hill, 1978.

———. "They All Looked Sick to Me," *Human Nature*, 2 (1978), 1.

Shapiro, A. K. "A Contribution to the History of the Placebo Effect," *Behavioral Science*, 5 (1960), 109–35.

———, and L. A. Morris. "The Placebo Effect in Medical and Psychology Therapies," in S. L. Garfield and A. E. Bergin, eds., *The Handbook of Psychotherapy and Behavior Change*. 2nd ed. New York: John Wiley, 1978.

Shavit, Y., et al. "Endogenous Opioids May Mediate the Effects of Stress on Tumor Growth and Immune Function," *Proceedings of the Western Pharmacology Society*. 26 (1983), 53–56.

Slim, J. "Highlights of the Third International Conference on AIDS" (Washington, D.C., June 1–5, 1987), *Medical Aspects of Human Sexuality*, 21 (1987), 8–13.

Snyder, S. H. "Brain Peptides and Neurotransmitters," *Science*, 209 (1980b), 976–83.

Sorokin, P. A. *Social and Cultural Mobility*. New York: Free Press, 1959 (originally published 1927).

Stark, E. "The Making of a Manager," *Psychology Today.* 21 (1986), 28–32.

Stengel, R., et al. "Testing Dilemma: Washington Prepares a Controversial New Policy to Fight AIDS," *Time* (June 8, 1987), 20–22.

Stoddard, J. B., and J. P. Henry. "Affectional Bonding and the Impact of Bereavement," *Advances,* 2 (1985), 19–28.

Targ, R., and K. Harary. *The Mind Race: Understanding and Using Psychic Abilities.* New York: Ballantine, 1984.

Toynbee, A. *A Study of History.* New York: Oxford University Press, 1972.

Turkington, C. "Help for the Worried Well," *Psychology Today,* 21 (1987), 44–48.

Walsh, R. "The Ten Perfections: Qualities of the Fully Enlightened Individual as Described in Buddhist Psychology," in R. Walsh and D. Shapiro, eds., *Beyond Health and Normality.* New York: Van Nostrand Reinhold, 1983.

Waynbaum, I. *La Physionomie humaine: son mécanisme et son rôle social.* Paris: Alcon, 1907.

Wenger, M. A. "Studies of Autonomic Balance: A Summary," *Psychophysiology,* 2 (1966), 173–86.

White, L., et al. *Placebo: Theory, Research, and Mechanisms.* New York: Guilford Press, 1985.

Wickramasekera, I. "Risk Factors Leading to Chronic Stress-Related Symptoms," *Advances,* 4 (1987), 9–35.

Wilber, Ken, *The Spectrum of Consciousness,* Wheaton, Illinois: Theophysical Publishing House, 1977.

Wilson, C. *Mysteries.* London: Hodder and Stoughton, 1978.

———. *New Pathways in Psychology.* New York: Taplinger, 1972.

———. *The Philospher's Stone.* New York: Warner Paperback Library, 1974.

———. *Poetry and Mysticism.* San Francisco: City Lights Books, 1969.

Winokur, G. *Depression: The Facts.* New York: Oxford University Press, 1981.

———, et al. *Manic-Depressive Illness.* St. Louis: C. V. Mosby, 1969.

Wolf, F. A. *The Body Quantum: The New Physics of Body, Mind and Health.* New York: Macmillan, 1986.

Wolf, S. "Effects of Suggestion and Conditioning on the Action of Chemical Agents in Human Subjects: The Pharmacology of Placebos," *Journal of Clinical Investigation,* 29 (1950), 100–9.

Yankelovich, D. *New Rules.* New York: Random House, 1981.

Zajonc, R. B. "Emotion and Facial Efference: A Theory Reclaimed," *Science,* 228 (1985), 15–21.

Zilbergeld, B., and A. Lazarus. *Mind Power.* Boston: Little, Brown, 1987.

Index

Acceptance: death and, 64, 67, 83–84, 270–71; illness and, 18, 61–63, 231, 269–74; of the present moment, 188. *See also* Self-acceptance; Surrender
Achievement, 42; "Mad Juggler" syndrome and, 57–58; play vs., 49–51; over- and under- , 47–49, 272; "potential" concept and, 44–47. *See also* Productivity; Success; Winning
ACTH, 113, 285
Acting out, loss and, 257–58
Adaptability, 77, 94–95, 237–38
ADD (attention deficit disorder), 90–91, 112
Addiction (addictiveness), 2–4, 19, 27, 44, 70–71, 73, 216–17; achievement and, 48–49; altered states of consciousness and, 108–9; Captain Ahab complex and, 27–39; channeling to new ways, 3–4; to depression and stress, 3, 4, 5–6, 48–49, 50–51, 70–71, 245 (*see also* Depression; SAD cycle; Stress); detoxification and freedom from, 129–33, 229–34; joy response and curing of, 2–4, 14, 20–21, 34, 70–71, 126–28, 229–34; lying and, 142–44; to neurochemicals, 3, 4, 5–6, 14, 20–21, 216; "normalcy" and,

2–4, 5–6; psychochemistry of joy and, 4, 14, 20–21, 34, 110–25, 229–34; sex and, 277; simplicity and, 133–37; sleep and, 81; time and, 107; work and, 145–46
Adrenalizations, 132, 133, 285
Adult development, 94; aging and, 64–66, 67, 73, 147–48; death and loss and, 64, 67, 83–84, 254–59; joy and, 64–66, 67, 73, 147–48; mid-life crisis and, 64, 147–48, 279; work and, 155. *See also* specific aspects, concepts, problems
Adultery, 224
Aesculapius, 214
Aging, 64–66, 73, 147–48; early retirement and, 66–67; IN A JOY formula and, 38; youth (rebirth) and, 38–39, 127, 291
Ahab's diseases, 29–30, 71. *See also* Captain Ahab complex
AIDS, 92, 173–74, 222, 260–67; causes, 262–63; death rate, 173, 260–61; fear of (FAIDS), 261–67; high-risk groups for, 265; hope and, 264, 266–67; IES for, 263–65; myths and facts on, 261, 267; not a sexual or "gay" disease, 265–66; responsible sex and, 223–24, 264, 266; sources of information on, 267

319

joy and, 44–73 (*see also* Super joy); youth (rebirth) and, 38–39. *See also* Joy; specific aspects, concepts

Joy Quotient Test, 76–109

Joy reflex, 21–22; described, 21–22. *See also* Joy response

Joy response, 2, 21–22, 231, 233; AIDS and, 263; and loss, 254–59; as placebo, healing and, 211, 271–74 (*see also* Healing; Placebo ability); Ten Commandments and, 212–28; unity dimension of, 231, 245, 258–59. *See also* Joy reflex; specific aspects, kinds

Juggling, learning and, 144

Kasl, Stanislau, 272
Kennedy, Florence, 146
"Killing," 221–22
Kindness, 221–22, 227
Kobasa, Suzanne, 168, 209, 210
Krech, David, 93

LaBier, Douglas, 156
LaPatner, Barry, 93
Laughter (smiling), 10–11, 59, 70, 77, 99–100, 101, 112, 116, 161, 191–92, 231
Lazarus, Richard, 204–5
Lazy brain principle, 17
Learning, 143–44; "aha" phenomenon and, 143; attention and (*see* Attention); challenges and crises and, 209 (*see also* Challenges; Crises); interest levels and, 77, 93–94; joy of, 128, 143–44; noesis and, 34–35, 126; sickness and, 269; workplace and, 170. *See*

also Adult development; Growth; specific aspect, kinds

Life-styles. *See* Daily living styles

Listening skills, 179

Lombardi, Vince, 55

Loneliness, search for love and, 275–82. *See also* Alienation; Isolation

Longevity, 270–71; seat belt use and, 209. *See also* Death; Youth

Loss, 254–59

Love (loving), 68, 171–94, 221–22; communication and, 175–76, 178–81, 186, 188, 191, 194; Cupid complex and, 174, 176–81; family, 68, 171, 172, 220–21; "heart hours" and, 182–83; IIS and, 278–79; intimacy deficiency and, 276–77, 278, 279; "killing," 222; lapses, 176–79; loss of, 255–59; "lovability quotient" and, 276; meaning of, 171–74, 191, 279–80; rationality, talking, sensibility and, 176–81, 184; reliable, sexuality and touch and, 191–94, 277 (*see also* Sex; Touching; respectful, spirituality and tolerance and, 188–91; responsible, sensuality and trust and, 184–88; responsive, sensitivity and time and, 181–84; romance vs., 171–72, 177–78; search for, 275–82; star concept of, 163, 174–94; support-system nature of, health and, 201–3; sympathetic, joy of, 171–94; Tolerance Test and, 189–91; work and, 153, 154, 155, 172

Lying, 142–43, 177, 225;

In 1971, PAUL PEARSALL, PH.D., founded and continues to direct the Problems of Daily Living Clinic in the Department of Psychiatry at Sinai Hospital of Detroit. There he has worked with thousands of patients from whom he selected the exceptionally joyful people described in this book. Dr. Pearsall is also Director of Professional Education at the Kinsey Institute for Research in Sex, Gender and Reproduction, as well as Adjunct Assistant Professor in the Department of Psychiatry at Wayne State University Medical School and Professor of Psychology at Henry Ford College. An experienced clinician, educator, and lecturer, Dr. Pearsall lives in Franklin, Michigan, with his family.